SOFTWARE DESIGN:
METHODS & TECHNIQUES

LAWRENCE J. PETERS

FOREWORD BY
L.A. BELADY

SOFTWARE DESIGN:
METHODS & TECHNIQUES

Yourdon Press
1133 Avenue of the Americas
New York, New York 10036

Library of Congress Cataloging in Publication Data

Peters, Lawrence J.
    Software design.

    Bibliography: p.
    Includes index.
        1. Electronic digital computers--Programming.
I. Title.
QA76.6.P473   001.64'25   80-50609
ISBN 0-917072-19-7

Copyright © 1981 by YOURDON inc., New York, N.Y.

Printed in the United States of America

Library of Congress Catalog Number 80-50609

ISBN: 0-917072-19-7

This book was set in Times Roman by YOURDON Press, 1133
Avenue of the Americas, New York, N.Y., using a PDP-11/45
running under the UNIX[†] operating system.

[†]UNIX is a registered trademark of Bell Laboratories.

To those special people in my life
whose love, friendship, patience, and understanding
have made this book possible:

Bunky, Beans, and Smilin' Jack

Contents

Acknowledgments

I wish to express my appreciation to my reviewers, whose patience and determination greatly improved this work. Specifically, I wish to thank

Kyu Lee, Seattle University
Harry Walker, Weyerhaeuser Company
Paul DuBose, Weyerhaeuser Company
Phil Milliman, Weyerhaeuser Company
Laszlo Belady, *IEEE Transactions on Software Engineering*

I would also like to thank all my colleagues whose comments, ideas, and complaints have been woven into the collage that is this book. My thanks to Seattle University's Software Engineering Graduate Program for letting me use a draft of this text in the Software Design class, and to the students whose suggestions greatly enhanced the resulting book.

Rick Eiber and Alice Wherrette, who produced the graphics, are also to be commended. Lorie Mayorga, Janice Wormington, and all of the people at YOURDON Press are extended sincerest appreciation for their suggestions and wisdom in knowing when and where to kick an author and when to leave him alone.

Finally, since we live in a world that is largely the result of our own work and not that of nature, I want to thank the world's designers, whose efforts have greatly contributed to our physical surroundings, our lives, and the way in which we perceive reality.

Preface

Our advances in software design are a direct result of our increased capacity to deal with systems as abstractions.

—L.P.

The field of software development has undergone some of its most profound changes in the last ten years. Much of this change has been in response to ever-increasing demands on software systems in terms of their complexity, reliability, and resiliency. Symptomatic of such rapid evolution is the proliferation of methods and techniques intended to solve "the" software problem. However, real-world software design problems often exhibit characteristics that make them unique. This forces the software engineer to seek alternative ways of composing and documenting a design.

Software development challenges the software engineer in several ways. Unlike many other fields, software systems will not be mass produced. This divorces the software engineer from many problems associated with manufacturing. However, since he is dealing with logic — the abstract — the results of his labor are difficult to identify with. Software operates on a time scale and reference frame that are incomprehensible by human standards. These factors, and the lack (for the most part) of an engineering background on the part of software developers, have led to the naive view that software design is unique and that its problems are exclusively those of software. The software engineer also has less guidance than technicians in other fields regarding the scope of his problem or the acceptability of his solution.

Software Design: Methods & Techniques is intended to meet the need for software design guidance, by describing both methods (strategies, recommendations, or guidelines based on a philosophical view) and techniques (tactics or well-advised "tricks of the trade"). It is directed at the professional software designer, novice, student, software manager, and customer. The software manager and customer can both use the book to get a concise description of the issues, benefits, and liabilities associated with using certain techniques or approaching certain software design problems in a given way, and they may also use it to increase communication. The others can utilize it as a resource guide providing several alternative methods and techniques; to aid experimentation with existing technology; and possibly to spark some new ideas, complement limited experience, and provide further insight regarding what software design is and the pros and cons of currently available techniques. The objective here is simply to cut through the mystique surrounding software design and its accompanying methodologies, leaving only the basics.

Software Design: Methods & Techniques is divided into four parts:

- Part I describes what design is, per se; what software engineering is; and how design manifests itself when its intended product is software.

- Part II surveys different schemes for representing various software design characteristics and discusses their effectiveness and compatibility.

- Part III surveys different methods for composing software designs and examines their effectiveness in specific design situations.

- Part IV describes an approach for composing software design methodologies tailored to specific project issues, and discusses some of the fundamental issues facing the software designer today.

Software Design: Methods & Techniques treats the subject of software design from several standpoints: its commonality with the problem of design in general, schemes for formulating and documenting designs, and case study guidelines. It presents several dozen techniques and demonstrates the use of each in sufficient detail to effectively use each technique. Appropriate references are provided should the reader require more detailed information. This book, with its guidance and examples, will prove an asset to the software designer, both for composing a software design methodology to accomplish a given task and for selecting a single technique to solve a specific problem.

Foreword

There are only two ways open to man for attaining a certain knowledge of truth: clear intuition and necessary deduction.

— René Descartes

Software Design: Methods & Techniques is on the *process* of mapping real-world phenomena onto computer programs. Since it has been written by an engineer with extensive experience in software design, this book reflects both the breadth of the process in question and the practical leaning of the book's author.

The notion of software design, and the perception of its importance, are relatively new. One used to talk simply about programming when a model, usually mathematical and already well prepared for a desk calculator, was transformed into a machine-executable procedure. This was a relatively small step as compared, for example, to the computerization of an entire banking operation, which is a set of activities never before formalized, whose functioning relies on well-trained personnel to coordinate routine tasks and solve unforeseen exception cases.

By the mid-1970s, the view that programming is but a fraction of the software development problem became well accepted. Since then, focus has turned to design, a complex process covering a variety of activities that must precede the act of writing a compilable program. At the same time, software people also discovered that designing *anything* — a car, a washing machine, furniture — is rarely a well-documented activity, is difficult to teach, and must often be based on apprenticeship at the master's knee, complemented later by hard-won experience.

Nevertheless, as Peters points out, design theorists agree that there are two major phases of any design process: diversification and convergence. Diversification is the *acquisition* of a repertoire of alternatives, the raw material for design: components, component solutions, and knowledge, all contained in catalogs, textbooks, and the mind. During convergence, the designer chooses and combines appropriate elements from this repertoire to meet the design objectives, as stated in the requirements document and as agreed to by the customer. This second phase is the gradual *elimination* of all but one particular configuration of components, and thus the creation of the final product.

Since this end product, by definition, is something that never before existed, it may contain inconsistencies. These are often impossible to predict at the time the design choice is made, but become manifest rather later in a larger context. This problem has two implications: First, that a design decision, when elaborated upon, could lead to an insight, which in turn may alter the original decision; in other words, design is inherently iterative. The second implication is that design methods are needed in order to recognize the occasionally unavoidable inconsistencies easily and early, so that no time is wasted pursuing a decision chain that will have to be scrapped later.

During his work, two distinct productivity issues occupy the designer's mind a great deal: the productivity of the system he designs, and his own productivity in creating it. The chosen design alternative could turn into a wasteful product, but optimizing it beyond a point may be too costly, drastically reducing design — or programming — productivity. One definitely needs methods facilitating the rapid discovery of product inefficiency at early stages of the design.

The need to discover inefficiency early makes it important to *externalize* (that is, make visible) an evolving design at each stage. Engineering blueprints, for instance, serve this purpose and are useful not only for a designer by calling his attention to trouble spots and potential inconsistencies, but also for a team or an entire organization developing a product: Blueprints are the major medium of communication, criticism, and collective refinement. Moreover, representation methods must be relatively simple and direct in bridging the gap between reality and the program; and they must be efficient during the multiple iterative steps.

Many of the methods in this book are recommendations as to which way, and in which order, the designer should proceed to model real-life data and their manipulation in his program. The methods are essentially different ways of representing software as its design evolves, guiding the decomposition of the whole into independently manageable pieces, enhancing communication within the design community, and helping to uncover inconsistencies early. *Software Design: Methods & Techniques* is comprehensive, offering an almost frightening variety of approaches. This proliferation is partly due to the nature of software: namely, that it is not a physical, tangible entity, and representing it is not as obvious as showing a piece of machinery by its orthogonal geometric projections. It is also partly due to the fact that software engineering is too young a discipline to have formulated its best methods.

Software products have been observed to evolve through a virtually never-ending series of modifications. Therefore, the accompanying design documents must be updated to reflect changes in the code. This is not equally easy with all of the many methods of representation, since some of them exist today only in hard-copy form, which requires an extra reproduction budget for each modified version. With progress in display technology, this problem may be alleviated in the future; yet today this leaves us with an unduly large variety of potentially useful, but economically not yet feasible, methods.

Finally, before I let the reader go ahead and enjoy the substance of the book, I would like to say a few words on the role of mathematics in the design process, which is defined differently by each of the cited approaches: I think its role should be mainly to aid the process of selecting from alternate arrangements and parameters, whenever key attributes — functional correctness, performance, resource demand — can be formally stated. For instance, in mechanical engineering, a tentative design must be completed as a basis for a formal verification of the integrity of the proposed structure. The result of the mathematical analysis may thus lead either to the acceptance of the designed alternative or to the study of another one. This appears to be the case in conventional engineering, and will likely remain valid in software engineering for a while, until breakthroughs in artificial intelligence may relieve us (or deprive us?) of the chore of designing software.

L.A. Belady
Senior Editor
IEEE Transactions on Software Engineering

January 1981

PART I

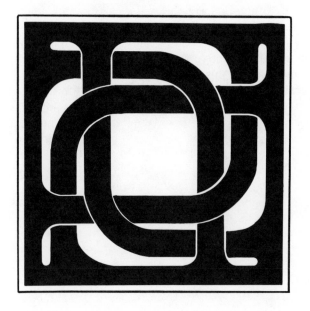

Software: Engineering and Design

PART I
Software: Engineering and Design

*Software design technology is
a system — not a secret.*

—L.P.

   People have been writing computer programs for less than two generations. Compared to other engineering fields, the development of software is a newcomer to technology. But fledgling as it may be, it has probably had the greatest impact on industrial society since the invention of the steam engine. Devices such as the steam engine were labor savers for certain types of physical activities, and as such they had an effect on how we viewed problems of logistics, as well as on the types of problems we would choose to address. The computer's far broader scope of application makes it a unique asset in solving problems and evolving our view of the world.

   Intuition might lead us to the conclusion that any field so important to other disciplines is, itself, a model discipline. Quite the contrary is true. Neither the subject of software engineering nor that of software design is a widely recognized discipline. The first graduate program in software engineering at an American university was launched only recently, with only a few other universities considering such action.* Worst of all, software engineers do not even know who they are! At the Third International Conference on Software Engineering, I asked an audience of more than 700 attendees how they had filled in the box marked "Occupation" on their income tax forms. By a show of hands, less than 10 percent indicated "software engineer" or, simply, "engineer." Clearly, the discipline still lacks recognition even within its own ranks. This situation is improving. At the Fifth International Conference on Software Engineering, I put the same query to an audience of about 500, and approximately 25 percent responded affirmatively — still not a majority, but a hopeful sign.

   There are probably many contributing factors to the identity crisis suffered by software engineers. The two most prominent ones are the training of the people who are doing software engineering; and, second, the nature of the products they build. To-

*Seattle University in Seattle, Washington began offering a Master of Science in software engineering in the fall of 1979.

3

day, people who produce software come from many academic disciplines — not just science, mathematics, and engineering. Many software developers who lack an engineering background think of engineering as an exact discipline that produces formulated, precise, closed-form solutions to problems. The inexactitude associated with software design seems intolerable to many designers, who feel that if there were a true engineering discipline for software, all estimating and scheduling problems would go away. Actually, nothing could be further from the truth: Engineering depends as much or more on common practice and empirical knowledge as it does on scientific fact. Hence, one reason for the identity crisis is that many software engineers do not recognize what they are doing as engineering.

The second factor contributing to the identity crisis — the product — affects much more than the self-image of software engineers. In most other engineering fields, the product is something that can be experienced by the engineer: Its time frame and physical properties can be seen, touched, and measured by humans.

But software engineering deals in another realm. This fact has had a profound effect on our view of the activities of software development. Even today, there are many software designers who support the need for refinements and reviews in the design of physical systems, but who openly resist the use of these common engineering practices in software systems development, viewing such practices as contractual nuisances. The difference in reference frame can affect our perception of engineering. Before we can attempt a meaningful discussion of software design, we must establish a working understanding of software engineering and design.

In Part I, we will put software engineering and software design into perspective. First, we will identify the scope, content, and structure of software engineering. Then, we will examine software design from two standpoints: as it relates to the larger discipline of software engineering, and as a discipline in itself.

CHAPTER 1
The Role of Software Design in Software Engineering

*Software engineering
is at the interface
between theory and practice.*
—L.P.

Before we can begin to describe meaningfully what software design is, we need to understand how it relates to the other activities associated with the development (engineering) of software. Many problems connected with software development, particularly software design, are related to ignorance of the nature of the subject area and of its issues. A psychologist might call this phenomenon an identity crisis. Whatever you choose to call it, a crisis it very definitely is.

Today, more than ever, society relies on software, not computers. How secure would society be about the future if it were generally known that this key element of progress was being developed by people who had little formal training in the software crafts, had no accepted standards for practicing this science/art form, and did not even recognize the field in which they were operating?

One of the earliest uses of the term "software engineering" was in the naming of the first NATO Conference on Software Engineering in 1968 [1]. This conference and the introduction of the term grew out of concerns on the part of customers and software professionals alike about the cost and quality of the software being produced. These concerns prompted the adoption of many methods and techniques, such as top-down design, each promising to remedy some symptoms of the perceived problem. These techniques, however, were not based on the application of an engineering discipline to the production of software.

Although we have come a long way toward remedying these cost and quality problems, the tough part of the journey is still ahead. No longer are we faced with technical problems that can be quickly remedied with reasonably obvious solutions (using design and code reviews or restricting the use of GOTOs, for example). Today's solutions are much more subtle, oriented toward remedying problems associated with the production of systems, not individual programs.

The term software engineering is used today to describe a loosely coupled collection of practices, techniques, and methods. More diverse than most other engineering fields, it includes activities ranging from the conceptualization of software systems

5

through their implementation and delivery. Mechanical engineers, for example, may design an aircraft component, but they are not responsible for producing the component. Manufacturing engineers and industrial engineers work on the latter task. In software, by contrast, the same engineers often design and produce a component.

We cannot hope to cure all of the ills of the industry in this book, but we can develop a framework and perspective with which to treat more effectively the subject of the remainder of this text. Specifically, the components of software engineering are organized into a model of the subject area in Section 1.3. A working model of the software development life cycle is presented, which describes the role and nature of software design within the context of software engineering. This model sets the stage for the more detailed sections on particular methods and techniques.

1.1 Scope

Software engineering literally encompasses all activities associated with producing software. The vastness of the topic and the fact that complex problems are being addressed by the practitioners of this art form have stifled attempts at describing its boundaries. But for the purposes of this treatment, the subject will include the spectrum of activities from analysis of requirements to installation. Although our emphasis will be on activities related to design, the role that design plays in the overall effort can be understood best if its relationship to software engineering is recognized.

1.2 A modeling approach

Subject areas as diverse as software engineering have been organized in different ways. For example, what mechanical engineering was thousands of years ago has evolved into a collection of specialty areas such as civil engineering, hydraulics, and heat transfer. Software engineering has had less time to mature. Hence, a natural structure has not evolved. Even worse, the complexity of problems being addressed is continually increasing, and consequently the state of the art is not yet well defined.

We could organize software engineering in various ways. For instance, we could identify a specialization of skills for each phase of software development. Another alternative would be to describe the functions performed by software engineers. We could also describe their activities, the tools they use, and what they build. But do these represent the basic or inherent properties that characterize the field?

One subject area that has had to deal with a similar sort of problem is biology, which makes sense out of (organizes) the immense volume of knowledge about living things. Take the case of plants: The great number of their characteristics — such as life span, method of reproduction, leaf size, shape, and preferred growing conditions — could give the person responsible for classifying them a nervous twitch. Fortunately, biologists have successfully developed a scheme with which to organize plants and other living things. Not a formal (mathematical) scheme, the approach is called morphological analysis [2].

Morphological analysis is extremely flexible in that it allows many different organizational schemes to be tried until one that provides some worthwhile insight or discovery is found. For example, the search for the so-called missing link was prompted, in part, by the use of an organizational scheme (or morphology) that characterized the developmental stages of man. The morphology revealed that the changes between stages seemed inordinately radical between two stages in particular. Hence, it was hypothesized that there may well have been another, as yet undiscovered, stage between these two. The search for the missing stage was aided by the fact that many of the characteristics of this creature could be surmised from the morphology. In this case, morphological analysis aided in both the understanding and the advancement of a subject area.

A morphology can be based on one or more characteristic axes that form a one or more dimensional space. The easiest morphologies to visualize are those with three or fewer dimensions, but we need not restrict ourselves to this limit. The steps involved in forming a morphological space are as follows:

1. Identify the distinct variables and parameters associated with the subject area under consideration.

2. Identify the variations in the parameter set, changes in value, or quantum levels associated with each of the results of step 1.

3. Propose classes into which the parameters may be organized, such that a parameter belongs in only one class. Try to limit the number of classes to three or fewer.

4. Using each class as an axis, make sufficient gradations for the results of step 2 to form categories or slots within each class. The relative position of each category or step on an axis should not be interpreted as having metric, hierarchic, or sequential connotations; these steps are merely for organizational purposes.

5. Form one or more two-dimensional boxes using axes and steps to form rows and columns.

6. Map the parameters and variables into the row-column combinations.

7. Inspect the results. If some variable or parameter does not map clearly into one row-column intersection, refine the morphology repeating steps 2 and 3.

Sets of these two-dimensional charts may be combined to form the complete morphological model. Not all of the possible combinations arrived at in modeling in this manner will be of interest, nor will they all make sense. For example, if the objects being organized are always circular or four-sided polygons, the other hypothetical possibilities may be ignored.

1.3 A model of software engineering

In spite of the resistance to many of the concepts encompassed by software engineering, much has been written about it, conferences have been held on the subject, curricula have been proposed [3, 4], and a morphological model of the subject has been published [5]. Let us examine that model briefly to gain further insight into the subject and its relationship to software design.

1.3.1 The Peters-Tripp model

The Peters-Tripp model was developed using morphological analysis. The resulting morphological box consists of three mutually orthogonal axes, which together comprise the various software engineering topics expressed in a three-dimensional space. Each axis describes a different class of concept: time, logic, and formalism. These three dimensions are described on the following pages.

Time dimension: As with all engineering fields, software engineering is concerned with time. The software development cycle is an excellent example of how this concern manifests itself in the performance of software engineering tasks. However, the concern with time is not to be construed as the same as the concern with other temporal aspects such as execution time or seek time, which involve the performance of the final product, not the conduct of software engineering tasks.

Many different authors have proposed models or sets of phases to describe the software development life cycle. Three such models proposed by Freeman [6], by Metzger [7], and by Boehm [8] are shown in Table 1.1.

Table 1.1
Three Software Life Cycle Models

SOFTWARE LIFE CYCLE PHASES	MODEL AUTHORS		
	FREEMAN	METZGER	BOEHM
	NEEDS ANALYSIS	(SYSTEM) DEFINITION	SYSTEM REQUIREMENTS
	SPECIFICATION		SOFTWARE REQUIREMENTS
	ARCHITECTURAL DESIGN	DESIGN	PRELIMINARY DESIGN
	DETAIL DESIGN		DETAILED DESIGN
	IMPLEMENTATION	PROGRAMMING	CODE AND DEBUG
		SYSTEM TEST	
		ACCEPTANCE	TEST AND PRE-OPERATIONS
		INSTALLATION AND OPERATION	
	MAINTENANCE		OPERATION AND MAINTENANCE

The model life cycle selected for this discussion is a consolidation of those in Table 1.1 and consists of four phases:

1. *System analysis* − The objective of the analysis phase is to demonstrate that the customer's problem is understood and to document it in a manner that will aid the design phase. Use of this phase is growing in popularity, as evidenced in published materials [9, 10], in training, and in recognition of its importance to the success of the software development effort. It is during this phase that the customer's problem is externalized, organized, and played back to him to ensure that the problem is understood.

2. *System design* — During this phase, the statement of the problem is addressed through the use of software design methods and techniques to obtain a logical or abstract model of the system solution. Implementation issues are not considered, as the goal is a clear perception of a solution concept.

3. *System implementation* — This phase begins with packaging of the logical design, followed by implementation of the packaged design in the target programming language and operating system environment, testing of the result, and installation.

4. *System operation* — This phase includes maintenance of the system's performance of original tasks, and enhancement to meet changing requirements; the phase leads to the eventual phase-out and replacement of the system.

These four phases or steps in our first axis may be viewed as having sequential characteristics. However, they still meet our need for categories of activities during the software development life cycle.

Logic dimension: The second axis contained in our model is used to categorize the activities that take place within each of the phases contained in the time dimension. Several different sets of categories or steps have been suggested for this dimension [11, 12, 13]. These have been modified to accommodate software engineering needs, and are described below:

1. *Problem definition and value system design* includes the study of the potential operating environment, the derivation of the system's objectives, and the definition of a set of decision criteria with which to evaluate alternatives [12].

2. *System synthesis* is the approach to collecting the various alternatives or, more simply, design.

3. *Systems analysis* is the identification of the implications of each of the alternatives collected during system synthesis.

4. *Optimization* is the evaluation of each alternative system through the application of the system objectives.

5. *Decision making* is the selection of the best of the alternative systems on the basis of the value system.

6. *Planning for action* is the formulation of a plan, including budgeting of resources, scheduling, and a feedback system to direct and control activities.

As in the case of the time dimension, the steps composing the logic dimension have a sequential ordering.

Formalism dimension: Also referred to as the model dimension [5], the formalism dimension takes into account that the process of software engineering is one of a continual construction and refinement of a succession of models. These models vary in detail and sophistication but do fall into three well-defined categories:

1. *Mental model*— Consists of hazy notions about a delivered system. It contains little, if any, detail and dwells primarily on gross system characteristics.

2. *Structural model*— Builds upon the mental model and consists of two subclasses of models: interpretive structural and basic structural.

> An *interpretive structural model* is a scheme for organizing and understanding complex systems and concepts by organizing empirical knowledge of the system. Examples of these models include PERT charts, DELTA charts, interaction matrices, and tree-like hierarchical displays. Although these have certain empirical rules, they do not have a mathematical (formal) basis.

> A *basic structural model* is based primarily on mathematics and transmits no empirical information. Formal mathematical operations can be carried out on a basic structural model. Graphs and digraphs are examples of this type of model.

3. *Linguistic model*— Takes the form of syntactic textual statements and comprises two subclasses: pragmatic linguistic and correctness linguistic models.

> A *pragmatic linguistic model* is directed primarily at accomplishing a task and secondarily at correctness issues. It includes all programming languages currently in use (for example, COBOL, PL/I, and FORTRAN).

> A *correctness linguistic model* has program correctness as its primary target. It may employ an existing programming language that has been enhanced to include an assertion capability, for example, or it may be a special-purpose programming language. Models in this class are provable, verifiable, and correct.

The time, logic, and formalism axes are assembled to form our morphological box (Fig. 1.1). The morphological model just described should not be viewed as the last word on software engineering. On the contrary, it should be considered a first cut, a working tool with which to further examine the practice of software engineering and the training of software engineers.

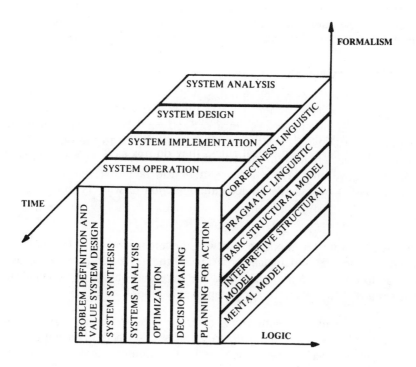

Figure 1.1. A morphological model for software engineering.

1.3.2 Implications for industry and education

The model developed in the preceding section does not distinguish between needs (problems) and means of filling needs (solutions). Clearly, the software industry, including software as an end product, as well as software supporting other types of production, needs skilled workers; but what skills are most important? Let's look at Fig. 1.1 again, but this time focus our attention on the morphological space or volumes currently emphasized in computer science and information science programs: implementation, the linguistic models, and the basic structural models. Do these volumes contain the issues (language and automata theory, for example) that are of *most* concern to the software engineering community? The issues emphasized in current education are deterministic in nature. That is, for purposes of this discussion, those issues are related to well-defined problems for which a solution can always be found. Some will require more time than others, but they can all be solved using known, mathematical methods.

Not so, in the case of software design. This is unfortunate, for the design errors in a system are the most persistent and costly ones with which to contend. For example, systems such as automobiles have always had bugs. But the bugs that cause the most embarrassment to engineers, and often cannot be remedied, are design flaws such as having to move a car's engine in order to gain access to all of the spark plugs. In software design, then, we have a paradoxical situation: Some of the most important skills — those needed to solve unstructured, poorly defined problems — must be provided through on-the-job training rather than formal education. As this on-the-job training varies considerably in quality, there is a need for textbook surveys of available software design techniques, and for the introduction of courses in this area by universities and professional training firms.

1.4 The software development life cycle

A common mechanism for planning, scheduling, and controlling engineering projects is to subdivide the development process into several steps or phases. Each step fits into the overall development process in a defined way, both by what it is supposed to accomplish and by its relative position in time with respect to the other steps. This approach provides project management with milestones and positive feedback during the project. However, we should not lose sight of the fact that this is just a controlling mechanism and is not necessarily an accurate depiction of what is going on.

1.4.1 The waterfall model

The so-called waterfall model of software development (Fig. 1.2) is marked by the apparently neat, concise, and logical ordering of the series of obvious steps that must occur in order to obtain a deliverable. But are they that obvious? Let us briefly examine what is supposed to happen in each step in this model:

- Systems analysis is sometimes referred to as the data collection phase, because it is here that the problem is described, data gathered with which to gauge its magnitude, and a fundamental understanding of the problem obtained.

- Requirements definition is sometimes referred to as system specification; it involves the formalization of the data gathered during analysis into a concise, clear, and consistent statement of what the system is to do.

- Preliminary design results in a high-level design or system model showing how the system will accomplish its task, but without sufficient detail to implement it.

- Detailed design is refinement of the preliminary design to the point at which implementation can begin.

- Coding is the implementation of the refined design, with the idiosyncracies of the programming language, operating system environment, and external (human and hardware) interfaces taken into account.

- Testing is ensuring that certain classes of errors do not exist within the system and that some predefined level of confidence in the system has been attained.

- Installation is the actual introduction of the finished system into its intended environment.

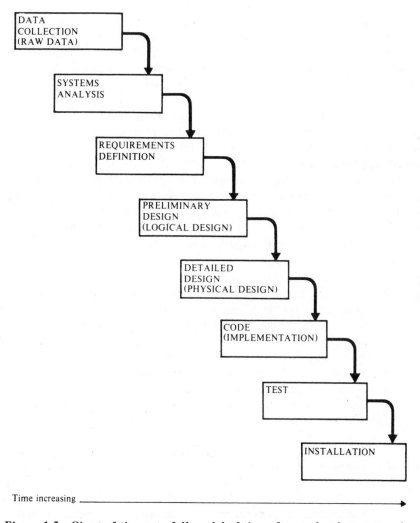

Figure 1.2. Chart of the waterfall model of the software development cycle.

The above descriptions are overly simple but they capture the basic thrust of the development life cycle, which presents software development as a set of sequential, interdependent steps resulting in a product. This would not be a particularly hazardous view if we were dealing with a tangible product, operating time frame, stimuli, and environment; but in software development we are dealing with logic. Things just do not work in this simple, sequential way. Problems crop up in later steps that affect the results of earlier ones, and so on. One contention is that the development process *could* work this way if we diligently completed each phase before going on to the next. Although this idealism sounds reasonable enough, it does not reflect what happens in any engineering and scientific fields. According to Rittel [14] and Freeman [15], we may never be able to stop discovering some new subtlety about the problem or its solution in the requirements definition and design phases.

1.4.2 The logicalized software development cycle

Experiences, not all of them positive, with the waterfall model of software development have indicated that considerable time and much money have been spent in the coding and testing phases to correct errors that were created during the requirements definition and design phases. This point was made quantitatively clear by Thayer and Boehm et al. [16, 17], who indicated that design errors not only outnumbered other errors three to two but were more persistent as well [17]. By 1975, attention was turning toward clarifying the problem definition end of the cycle. With the use of top-down decomposition and of abstract (or logical) software design models, alternate views of the software life cycle began to reflect a clear dichotomy between logical design and physical or packaged design [18].

Logical design is analogous to an artist's conception of a building: There is enough information to allow the customer and designer to communicate and to establish the building's pluses and minuses, but not enough detail to begin construction. A series of reviews, refinements, and the imposition of local building ordinances, for example, are necessary before that construction can start. So this logicalized model of the software life cycle views the process as one of establishing a logical model and then, as a separate task, addressing implementation issues. The complexity for the designer is greatly reduced, because the problems of conceptualizing a solution and implementing it often require conflicting points of view. Considered all at once, they can put the software designer into a quandary, in that each attempt at visualizing an abstract solution conjures up some implementation problem, so a complete solution (abstract or otherwise) may never be attained. Considering the solution strictly from an abstract view, then separately addressing physical design, establishes a baseline design: It clearly externalizes the decision making related to eventual implementation, and squarely addresses the tradeoffs involved in realizing the design in code. A view of information flow in this model appears in Table 1.2.

Table 1.2
Relationship of Stages, Tasks, and Inputs/Outputs in the Design Process

PHASE	INPUT	TASK	OUTPUT
ANALYSIS	Interviews, random data, and so on	Model problem and implied solution	Abstract model of implied solution
DESIGN	Abstract model of implied solution and environmental constraints	Model an implementable solution	Abstract model of an implementable solution
CODE	Abstract model of an implementable solution	Implement solution	Executable solution

The development of this model clarified matters greatly, but some nagging problems still needed attention. One problem, that of bridging the gap between requirements and logical design, became the main thrust of the structured life cycle model.

1.4.3 The structured life cycle model

Separating conceptual from practical issues has apparent advantages over earlier models, but the problem of assuring that the design addresses the stated requirements remains. Since requirements are stated as what the system will do, and design as how it will do it, how can these two be compared? The task has been accomplished since the early 1970s by using the life cycle model of structured analysis [9]. Requirements definition and logical design are linked or integrated into a single phase called structured analysis (or, more simply, analysis). Closer customer or user participation is also employed to ensure that the results of analysis do reflect the customer's needs based on the present situation (current physical model), its abstract equivalent (current logical model), and the new system or solution model (new logical model). Hence, the life cycle can be modified to reflect these changes and the integration of coding and testing. Although the exact mechanism by which this life cycle model is employed ranges from structured analysis/structured design to any of dozens of variations developed by various firms, the advantages are significant and include

- *enhanced customer/contractor communication:* Since the customer and contractor communities are working together as a team, using written and graphic tools that they both understand, the communication-inhibiting "guru" attitude is avoided.*

- *enhanced analyst/designer communication:* Following DeMarco [9], use the same notation in analysis as in design. This reduces information loss between the two camps of developers. The situation is aided even more when one group does analysis and design, particularly if group members maintain the mental discipline needed between phases.

- *better overall quality in both analysis and design phases:* The goals in each phase are limited, realistic, and objectively measurable. Although analysis or design could be refined ad infinitum [14], there is at least a minimum set of goals that must be present [10]. Since the objective is defined and realistic, people work in a much more productive manner than when they have no way of knowing when they are done.†

But some difficulties still remain. For example, it is difficult for customers to visualize what the software system will be like.

1.4.4 The prototype life cycle model

The prototype life cycle model combines the concepts of the structured life cycle model with some principles established in engineering [19, 20]. The basic notion is to provide the user with some feedback early in the development cycle on what the final system will be like. This approach adopts the philosophy that as long as we will have to build the system twice, we might as well plan it that way [21]. The term prototype refers to a skeleton system that contains only those essential elements of the system needed by the user to get an idea of what the final system will be like.

---

*This is an attitude in which the contractor implies that he knows the customer's problem best and that the problem will be stated in a foreign tongue spoken only by the data processing staff; this puts the customer on the defensive.
†DeMarco [9] also provides subphases to aid management in measuring progress.

For example, if we were developing an interactive graphics system, the prototype might include only those elements needed to log-on, display the menu of options, and allow the invocation of one or two simple functions. This affords the user and development team experience with the system's idiosyncracies. Feedback can be obtained before the final system is delivered. The advantages of using prototypes include: early feedback on whether the development group is on the right track; identification and solution of system interface problems in a low-pressure situation (early in the project); demonstration of the impact of design decisions and customer requests; psychological identification by the user with the system — when it is delivered, it is more likely to be viewed as his system rather than the contractor's, since some features are in it solely because of customer feedback; and an opportunity to give at least a part of the development team experience with coding together in a relatively low-pressure situation, which aids in getting rid of personality, managerial, and procedural bugs, and also builds the team confidence so valuable to newly assembled teams.

The prototype life cycle model is shown in a simplified form in Fig. 1.3. The greatest danger involved in employing this life cycle model lies in the temptation to view software development as the old-fashioned unstructured process of "code first and design later." The development team must be disciplined to avoid this. In situations in which the user has only rudimentary ideas regarding what he wants, this life cycle approach is well advised.

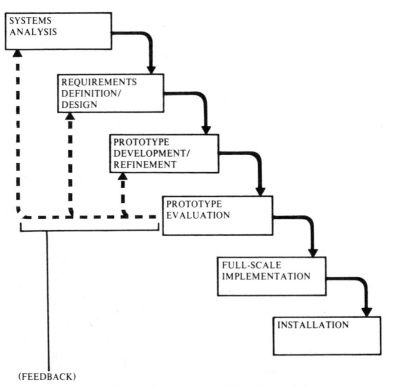

Figure 1.3. The prototype life cycle model.

1.4.5 Hybridized life cycle models

Use of modifications of the standard or waterfall life cycle model is becoming more and more common. These hybrids are developed in response to a particular set of circumstances [20]. Each is directed at addressing the pitfalls that the development team foresees in the ensuing project, and is not intended as a generic model. These hybrids do not represent a departure from prudent engineering practice, but are a natural outgrowth of it. Each custom-tailored life cycle actually falls within the general bounds of the waterfall model, but places emphasis on a different set of issues. For example, in the prototype life cycle shown in Fig. 1.3, the prototype acts as an aid to specification and design. Hence, the differences among these life cycle models may appear to be only cosmetic, but their impact on project management and user involvement varies significantly. A key role in the life cycle is software design, which lies at the interface between problem and solution.

1.5 Introducing software design

The art of programming may date back to prehistory, the first instance being one individual's effort to communicate to another instructions on how to build a fire or set up camp. Or, it might have started more recognizably around the twelfth century, when water-wheel-driven drums with moveable cams were designed to ring church bells in various significant patterns.

Still more recently, the use of the Jacquard loom made the weaving of a particular cloth pattern a matter of programming the right combination of holes and cards. The point of all this is that, prior to high-speed electronic computing devices, programming and the design of programs was very different. The monk who programmed church bells knew what he wanted and knew whether he had attained it. The same is true of Jacquard. They were dealing with physical stimuli, time frames, concepts, and natural phenomena with which they had first-hand experiences. A dry-run or manual check of a suspicious result could usually be done.

Today, things are different. The volume of data and the blinding speed at which they can be gobbled up and digested by the latest electronic marvel defy comprehension. Computer programming deals with a time frame, stimuli, and activities that are unfamiliar. Even the language for programs is not native to people. We are dealing with logic — the abstract — not the physical. Whereas we can examine and comprehend a house design, for example, by relating it to our physical experiences with houses, we cannot experience the design of program logic in and of itself. In fact, even after the design has been implemented into an executable program, we can only experience the results of the actions of the program, *not* the program itself. This forces us to conjecture or model what a program is going to do before it is built. This practice permits wide latitude in experimentation with different program arrangements and interpretations in the syntax, semantics, and control language required by the target computer. The construction of such models is the act of software design.

Designing software requires both patience and bravery: Patience is needed to keep from rushing toward a solution that may, due to haste, be incomplete, and bravery is required because many discoveries will be made as we proceed from problem to solution [15]. It is much like attacking the mythological Hydra: Each time one of its many heads is cut off, two grow in its place. In software design, each time some aspect of the problem is understood and solved, others appear. Although this situation is not hopeless, it has been characterized as wicked [22].

But even more than patience and bravery, software design requires self-discipline. As pointed out earlier, the very nature of software short-circuits much of everyday, accepted engineering practice. Electrical engineers do not wind the transformers they design, but software engineers deal with both design and "manufacture" of their product. It is seemingly easy to identify a local or sub-problem within a large software effort and envision how to code it. At times, reviews and standards appear to stand in the way of getting the job done. This temptation to switch from abstract design concerns to concrete coding problems is almost unique to software. Granted, discoveries are being made during design; but often it is difficult to remember that startup, support, and maintenance costs are very small for design as compared with code.

1.6 Issues in software design

The remainder of this text is devoted to the description and analysis of many of the available software design methods and techniques. By far, the majority of them were developed in response to a need or problem encountered by their originators. Some of these are markedly different though intended to solve the same problem, while others are noticeably similar though directed at different problems. But these problems are only symptoms of the following higher-level issues with which the software designer must contend:

- *Can software systems truly be designed top-down?* Much has been written about the positive effects of using top-down design, and there is widespread agreement that it is a good thing. But on what is one to base this decomposition? Experience, world view, what? Many of the methods discussed in Part III provide both the what and the how.

- *How should a design be documented?* A wide variety of schemes exist to portray a software design graphically. Each scheme highlights certain features of the design, while ignoring or only implying others. Is there a "best" way to depict a software design? The authors of the design representation schemes described in Part II might each propose an approach, but when would one approach be more appropriate than another? Part II provides some guidance along these lines.

- *Can the requirements of a non-trivial system be stated in a useful, functional way with no design information?* Based on experience in other fields, this does not seem likely.

- *What is the relationship between database design and program design?* Part II will examine the possibility of considering both subordinate to system design.

1.7 Conclusion

In the remaining chapters, several techniques and methods will be discussed, each potentially helpful to the software designer. None of them is universally applicable or complete; each leaves some issues unaddressed. The key to utilizing this plethora of tools is to be constantly aware of the intrinsic character of a given software design problem with the issues it presents, and of the issues addressed by each technique. In this way, the designer can make a conscious effort to view software design as a system and not a secret.

EXERCISES: Chapter 1

1. Do you consider yourself a software engineer? Why or why not?

2. The morphology of software engineering presented in Fig. 1.1 is only one view. Develop a morphology of software engineering utilizing your own viewpoint.

3. Examine the roles played by engineers in other fields. Compare and contrast these with that of the software engineer.

4. Is software development an engineering endeavor? Provide research or evidence to support or refute this position.

5. Given the position that software development is *not* an engineering field, what is it? Use a morphology or taxonomy as an aid.

6. When we design a product such as a car, we can obtain feedback on our design from a direct user. When we design a software system, who or what is the direct user? the indirect user? Does this present any special problems? Elaborate.

7. Have you ever worked on a project in which the standard waterfall life cycle was used? How did it work out? Could changes have been made in the life cycle that would have improved matters? If so, what changes, and in what way would they have affected the outcome?

8. What approaches do you now use to define system architecture — that is, come up with the initial system architecture? Why do you use these and not some others?

9. What approaches do you now use to document or represent a software design once you have defined it? Why use these and not some others?

REFERENCES: Chapter 1

1. P. Naur and B. Randell, eds., *Proceedings of the NATO Conference on Software Engineering* (Brussels, Belgium: NATO, 1968). [Reprinted in *Software Engineering, Concepts and Techniques, Proceedings of the NATO Conferences,* eds. P. Naur, B. Randell, and J.N. Buxton (New York: Petrocelli/Charter, 1976).]

2. F. Zwicky, "The Morphological Approach to Discovery, Invention, Research, and Construction," *New Methods of Thought and Procedure,* eds. F. Zwicky and A.G. Wilson (New York: Springer-Verlag, 1967).

3. P. Freeman and A.J. Wasserman, "A Proposed Curriculum for Software Engineering Education," *Proceedings of the Third International Conference on Software Engineering* (New York: IEEE Computer Society, 1978), pp. 56-62.

4. L.J. Peters and L.G. Stucki, "A Software Engineering Graduate Curriculum," *Proceedings of the ACM '78* (New York: Association for Computing Machinery, December 1978), pp. 63-67.

5. L.J. Peters and L.L. Tripp, "A Model of Software Engineering," *Proceedings of the Third International Conference on Software Engineering* (New York: IEEE Computer Society, 1978), pp. 63-70.

6. P. Freeman, *Tutorial on Software Design Techniques* (New York: IEEE Computer Society, 1976).

7. P.W. Metzger, *Managing a Programming Project* (Englewood Cliffs, N.J.: Prentice-Hall, 1973).

8. B.W. Boehm, "Software Engineering," *IEEE Transactions on Computers,* Vol. C-25, No. 12 (December 1976), pp. 1226-41. [Reprinted in *Classics in Software Engineering,* ed. E.N. Yourdon (New York: YOURDON Press, 1979), pp. 325-61.]

9. T. DeMarco, *Structured Analysis and System Specification* (New York: YOURDON Press, 1978).

10. V. Weinberg, *Structured Analysis* (New York: YOURDON Press, 1978).

11. A.D. Hall, III, "Three Dimensional Morphology of Systems Engineering," *IEEE Transactions on Systems, Science, and Cybernetics,* Vol. SSC-5, No. 2 (April 1969), pp. 156-60.

12. J.D. Hill and J.N. Warfield, "Unified Program Planning," *IEEE Transactions on Systems, Man, and Cybernetics,* Vol. SMC-2, No. 5 (November 1972), pp. 610-21.

13. R.F. Miles, Jr., ed., *Systems Concepts* (New York: Wiley-Interscience, 1973), pp. 1-11.

14. H.W.J. Rittel and M.M. Webber, *Dilemmas in a General Theory of Planning,* Institute of Urban and Regional Development, Working Paper No. 194 (Berkeley, Calif.: University of California, November 1972).

15. P. Freeman, "Toward Improved Review of Software Designs," *Proceedings of the 1975 National Computer Conference,* Vol. 44 (Montvale, N.J.: AFIPS Press, 1975), pp. 329-34.

16. T.A. Thayer, "Understanding Software Through Analysis of Empirical Data," *Proceedings of the 1975 National Computer Conference,* Vol. 44 (Montvale, N.J.: AFIPS Press, 1975), pp. 335-41.

17. B.W. Boehm, R.L. McClean, and D.B. Urfrig, "Some Experience with Automated Aids to the Design of Large-Scale Reliable Software," *IEEE Transactions on Software Engineering,* Vol. SE-1, No. 1 (March 1975), pp. 125-33.

18. E. Yourdon and L.L. Constantine, *Structured Design: Fundamentals of a Discipline of Computer Program and Systems Design,* 2nd ed. (New York: YOURDON Press, 1978).

19. L.J. Peters, "Relating Software Requirements and Design," *Proceedings of the Software Quality and Assurance Workshop* (New York: Association for Computing Machinery, 1978), pp. 67-71.

20. _____, "Software System Specification and Design," unpublished presentation at the 1980 National Computer Conference panel session on User Requirements and Software Specifications (Anaheim, Calif.: May 1980).

21. F.P. Brooks, Jr., *The Mythical Man-Month* (Reading, Mass.: Addison-Wesley, 1975).

22. L.J. Peters and L.L. Tripp, "Is Software Design Wicked?" *Datamation,* Vol. 22, No. 5 (May 1976), pp. 127-36.

CHAPTER 2
Defining Design

*I do not sketch or design a work,
I merely begin.*
—Joan Miró

In an interview, Spanish-born artist Joan Miró was asked how he came up with his ideas — how he sketched, refined, and finally developed them. He responded that he did not design his works, but that they were spontaneous expressions of his feelings or mood. His explanation may be a little hard for us to accept, but other artists and architects have made similar comments, as have some geniuses among programmers.

The trouble with geniuses is that they are not always consciously aware of the creative force at work within them. They come up with original approaches and do not tell us why or how they were developed. We have all seen some rather elegant solutions to seemingly intractable programming problems published in journals. How often did the author tell us how he arrived at that solution, or how many were proposed and rejected and for what reasons?

Unfortunately, the world is only sparsely populated with geniuses. There is no reason to believe that the software engineering community has an inordinately large proportion of them. Unable to rely on strokes of genius to sustain a programming effort, and needing some controllable way to proceed from problem statement to ready-to-build "blueprints," we are forced to depend on procedural and conceptual guidance. This guidance is design technology. It externalizes for us the process of creating the blueprint.

Producing a blueprint of the system to be built is not as easy as utilizing one. Although many design methods exist for each of the engineering disciplines, each method reflects a particular view of the role of design in system development. These views are often divergent, causing a good deal of heated debate. However, basic agreement exists on a few fundamental issues. One agreed-upon point is that design is not a formulatable activity. It does not lend itself to prescriptive or sequential steps that will ensure success, like the directions for assembling a bicycle. Another agreed-upon issue is that design is not a deterministic process: It is not possible to exhaust all reasonable variations and avenues of inquiry to reach an acceptable design. One could go on essentially forever. In our bicycle analogy, even without the instruction guide there is only a finite number of ways in which the parts could be assembled, and an even smaller number (or subset of these) that would result in a functioning bicycle, but design has no such limit.

This chapter describes several fundamentally different views on just what design is, apart from the issues specific to software design.

2.1 The problem of defining design

Design is a human activity that has eluded definition for some time. It dates back to the time of the Romans [1], and people have been trying to describe design adequately and to provide guidelines on how to design ever since. Since design involves human ingenuity and creativity, there exist widely varying opinions on how to define it. Matters are further complicated by the fact that the results of the design activity are not experienced directly; what is experienced is the resultant implementation of the design. It is widely accepted that quality (or lack of it) inherent in a design largely determines system quality. But the source of design quality may be personal experience, opinion, and individual heuristics.

The next six sections contain as many explanations of design by different authors, each one in the form of a model, and each offering a particular insight. Taken as a whole, they provide a multi-faceted view of design, designers, and the fundamental issues that need to be addressed.

2.2 Design as a process

The first definition views design as a problem-solving process [2], in which the designer proceeds from some perceived problem through a series of activities to a model of a solution for that perceived problem (Fig. 2.1). The three phases or classes of activities — called divergence, transformation, and convergence — are interdependent in the sense that a progression is made from a poorly defined, unstable problem to a well-defined model of a solution. Performed in an iterative manner, each of the three phases is described in detail in the following subsections.

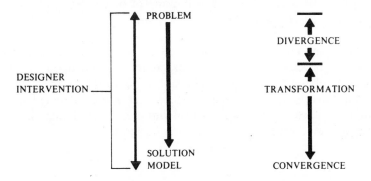

Figure 2.1. Model of design as a phased process.

2.2.1 Divergence

The divergence stage is characterized by change and instability. During this phase, the designer or design team identifies the true objectives of the system and restructures the requirements to reflect these objectives. This phase is marked by the characteristics listed on the next page.

- The system's objectives are tentative and subject to change.*

- The context and dimensions of the design problem are unstable and subject to re-definition.

- Requirements may exist but are subject to change.†

- All factors bearing on the problem are considered, even if they are in-compatible.

- The designer makes a conscious effort to divorce himself from past experience and preconceived notions about solutions in order to understand the problem fully.

The divergence phase can be successfully completed (through one iteration) if questions have been raised that reveal the nature of the problem in a way that will be effective in later stages, and if the original requirements have been reorganized to identify characteristics of the design that will ensure flexibility.

2.2.2 Transformation

The transformation stage is critical to the design process in bridging the gap between the redefined problem and several alternative solutions. It is in this stage that the contending economic and technical factors must be resolved by experience, judgment, and politics. The instability added during the divergence phase is decreased in the transformation phase; since it selects a single, narrowed design view, this phase offers the greatest opportunity for error. Transformation may be characterized by the following:

- failure of a design-by-committee approach

- ego and personality clashes

- stability as evidenced by the definition of constraints and of critical variables, the identification and ranking of objectives, and the recognition of the system's limitations

The success of the transformation phase depends upon the degree to which secondary objectives may be changed to reduce disagreement, and upon the definition of a value set (a ranking of the relative importance of system properties or qualities) specific enough to permit convergence to a single design that will be detailed in a later phase. The transformation phase is not only critical but the most demanding for designers since it requires delicate balancing of contending design factors.

---

*Here the term *objectives* refers to the overall reasons for having the system developed, for example, to reduce the time to process a customer's withdrawal request from the current four minutes (average) to less than two minutes (average); the objectives relate to the external system behavior.
†Here the term *requirements* refers to the internal means used to attain an external end. For example, to meet the system's objective, the following requirement may be in order: The system will respond to user requests within three seconds or less, provided normal operating conditions are present.

2.2.3 Convergence

By the convergence phase, the problem has been stabilized, requirements reorganized, objectives defined and ranked, and several alternative designs identified. It is at this point that one or a combination of the alternatives is selected and refined for eventual implementation. Two basic strategies are utilized in the convergence phase: out-in (top-down), and in-out (bottom-up). Architects, for example, use out-in when they define the exterior size, shape, and style of a structure before they specify the interior or floor plan.

In the in-out approach, the floor plan is first defined and detailed, then the exterior. There must be an interplay between the two strategies to take into account the effects an interior decision has on the exterior, and vice versa.

Success in this phase is a function of the degree to which discipline, precision, and attention to detail are employed, how well critical problems discovered at the sub-problem level are addressed, and the degree to which abstract concepts have been eliminated from the portrayal of alternative designs.

2.2.4 Comments on the process model

The process model presents a view of design characterized by a good deal of uncertainty: Much unstructured activity and information-gathering takes place at the outset; then, the numerous design views and the abundance of information are reduced through judgment; and, finally, a single design is identified and refined. Furthermore, this model points out that the designer is often forced to jump forward in time so as to imagine that the system has been implemented and is in use. He scrutinizes the system, evaluates its role and effectiveness, and utilizes this information in the present to avoid making serious mistakes. Successful design is viewed in this model as relying upon the designer's self-discipline and professional judgment to ensure that design decisions are not based on speculation or premature selection of alternatives.

2.3 Design as a wicked problem

The model of design as a wicked problem [2, 3] is useful for understanding the role of the designer and many of the challenges that he must face. A "wicked" problem is a particularly elusive one, in that the solution of one of its aspects may reveal an even more serious difficulty. Some of the properties of wicked problems follow.

☐ *A wicked problem cannot be definitively stated.* Whenever an attempt is made to formulate a wicked problem, such as a specification, there are always more refinements to be added, more information requested, and other issues raised.

☐ *There is no rule or guideline to determine when a wicked problem is solved.* When working on an equation or a heat transfer problem, for instance, the problem solver knows when a solution has been reached. Criteria such as energy balance, boundary conditions, and/or mathematical relationships indicate the solution is valid. But no such criteria exist for wicked problems, because the process of understanding a wicked problem and the process of solving it are inextricably linked. Each proposed solution aids our understanding of the problem, which provokes the proposal of a more refined solution, which further aids our understanding of the problem, and so on. It seems that a better solution can always be found if we just put in a little more time. Ultimately, the designer stops designing not because he is convinced that the design cannot be further improved, but because of factors that lie beyond the immediate logic or nature of the problem. For example, the schedule may call for the design to be completed at a certain date, the budget for the design effort may be used up, or the designer may be tired of working on this problem.

☐ *Wicked problems do not have right or wrong solutions, only good or bad ones.* In mathematics and other fields, logical, objective criteria are available with which to judge a design to be right (in agreement with the criteria) or wrong (in disagreement). In the case of design as a wicked problem, such criteria are not available; for example, in designing an automobile, no amount of analysis and market surveys can objectively tell the designer whether the design is right or wrong.

☐ *A wicked problem cannot be definitively tested.* Unlike less challenging design problems, wicked problems tend to result in systems that may be subject to significant, unforeseeable difficulties. These difficulties essentially invalidate the conclusion that the problem was solved and wipe out any presumed or hoped-for benefits from the designed system. Moreover, not all difficulties can be eliminated by advance testing.

☐ *Solutions to wicked problems are too significant to be experimented with.* In other disciplines such as science and mathematics, the problem solver can experiment with various strategies and learn on a trial-and-error basis without repercussions. But with wicked problems, experimentation is ill advised. For example, if the wicked problem involves transporting people in and around a large city, one could not very easily build a trial freeway system, determine that it does not solve the problem, tear it down, and try a monorail! The logistics and expense are obviously prohibitive. The problem solver gets essentially one shot at solving a wicked problem.

☐ *Neither the number of possible solutions nor the means of obtaining them is limited.* There is no prescribed set of steps to which the wicked problem solver must limit himself. Any means at all is acceptable. Similarly, any solution is potentially acceptable. For example, the number of ways of solving a transportation problem in a large metropolitan area is essentially without bound, as is the number of methods by which these solutions could be achieved.

☐ *Each wicked problem is a singularity.* Wicked problems each have their own unique set of properties. For example, are any two major airports identical? No, if for no other reason than that each meets a unique set of criteria beyond the mundane function of providing a place for planes to land, dispatch passengers, refuel, load passengers and cargo, and take off. These criteria often have nothing to do with building style but a great deal to do with economic, social, and ecological impacts.

☐ *Wicked problems can be viewed as symptoms of other higher-level problems.* How many times have designers wrestled with seemingly unsolvable problems only to find later that they were seeking a solution at the wrong level of thinking? For example, one design solution after another may be rejected because the estimated cost exceeds the budget. Before long, the higher-level issue must be addressed — specifically, either by allocating a bigger budget or by relaxing requirements to reduce the delivered system cost to within the original budget. Just because we want a certain system at a given price does not mean it is within the realm of possibility. The selection of an explanation for a wicked problem depends upon one's world view; the explanation also determines the solution to the problem.

Comments on the wicked-problem model of design

Anyone who has been involved in the design of at least one non-trivial system should agree that the wicked-problem model of design has captured the essence of this activity. But this model is at once troubling and comforting: It is troubling in the sense that it does not paint a very rosy picture of design, although this does seem to agree with the experience of many. It is comforting in the sense that it provides some verification that there is no easy way to reduce these problems even if we are diligent.

2.4 Design as definition and response to critical issues

The model of design as a set of issues [4] operates from two distinct points of view: The designer must identify the issues critical to the success of the design effort, and then he must define design elements necessary to meet the critical issues adequately. This duality in viewpoint causes the designer to effectively link what is normally considered problem definition (or specification) to solution definition. The limited number and global nature of critical issues set the overall structure of the design. For example, in designing a life-support system, a critical issue would be reliability; nearly all design decisions made after this becomes a recognized critical issue will be influenced by it. All too often systems are specified, designed, and implemented without any knowledge of the customer's real feelings until system delivery. Design based on critical issues can help overcome this phenomenon.

2.4.1 Critical issues

The model of design as a set of critical issues was originally developed in the field of architecture. Even though architects have thousands of years of history and heuristics at their disposal, they still disagree about what design is and how to practice it. One of the more prominent architects of this century was Eero Saarinen, whose works include IBM's Thomas J. Watson Research Center, the St. Louis Freedom Arch spanning the Mississippi River, the TWA terminal at Kennedy International Airport, and Dulles International Airport. The basic scenario he used for all of these projects (Fig. 2.2) is deceptively simple: Gather data; identify factors or issues deemed critical to the success of the project; define a design approach aimed at addressing these issues; reach agreement with the customer; make adjustments in the issues and/or approach based on customer feedback; and refine the design to the point of implementation detail. Let's see it in action during the early stages of the design of Dulles International Airport:*

> "As an airport, the Washington international airport is unique . . . in one way because it is the first commercial airport really to be planned from the start for the jet airplane."

Problem identification and design envelope

> "We sent out teams with counters and stop-watches to see what people really do at airports, how far they walk, their interchange problems. We analyzed special problems of jets, examined schedules, peak loads, effect of weather. We studied baggage handling, economics, methods of operations, and so on. We reduced this vast data to a series of about forty charts.

---

*The following is extracted from *Eero Saarinen on His Work*, revised ed., edited by A.B. Saarinen, © 1968, Yale University Press, p. 102. Reprinted by permission.

"We found there were three very critical areas. One was the time and inconvenience of getting passengers to and from planes. We discovered the already tremendous distances passengers walk through terminals and the 'fingers' extending from them would become as nothing compared to the distances they would have to walk in jet terminals. Another critical area was the heavy cost of taxiing jet planes. A third consideration was the increasing need for greater possible flexibility in operations and servicing of aircraft."

Solution formulation

"We became convinced that some new method of passenger handling had to be found. The soundest system seemed to be one which brought the passenger to the plane rather than the plane to the passenger. . . . Gradually, we arrived at the concept of the mobile lounge: a departure lounge on stilts and wheels, a part of the terminal which detaches itself from the building and travels out to wherever the plane is conveniently parked or serviced."

Conceptual integrity

"As we investigated further, we became convinced the mobile lounge was a logical solution to the critical problems. We were aware that, like any prototype vehicle, it would be expensive and might have 'bugs.' But we believed it a sound system. We think we have made a real contribution. The mobile lounge can have large application. It can be used in new terminals and it has obvious advantages for the economic, efficient expansion of existing ones."

Enhanced customer communication

"After the Federal Aviation Agency accepted the idea, we had the formidable job of explaining or 'selling' it to many people within twelve airlines. We worked with Charles Eames, who did a marvelous job, to reduce our data and thinking to a short movie. . . ."

Four insights from this and other similar descriptions of Saarinen's design method are most pertinent to later discussions related to software design: matching problem with solution, enhancement of customer communications, conceptual integrity, and creation of a design envelope. Each is described more fully in the sections that follow.

Matching problem with solution

Matching problem with solution is intuitively sound: If the problem is to drive a nail, a hammer and not a saw would be appropriate. But in the case of design, the appropriateness of a tool — an approach to a solution — is not as obvious. Note that Saarinen's airport design effort never even considered the architecture of the building until the higher-level, more critical issues had been identified and a means of addressing them composed. Thus, in this model of design, a conscious effort is made to abandon preconceived and premature notions, in favor of addressing the design problem on its own terms, with suitable tools. Once established, these critical issues set the context within which all secondary and detailed issues will be discussed. It should be noted that in 1958 Saarinen felt that this airport would set the style of future airports [4]. What he did not foresee was the fact that few airport designers (and perhaps airport authorities) were willing to divorce themselves from preconceptions and let the problem dictate the solution. The miles that air travelers have to walk through airports and the high cost of increasing the number of airlines servicing airports using the extending "finger" tunnel are living testimony to the practice of having a defined solution looking for a problem to solve.

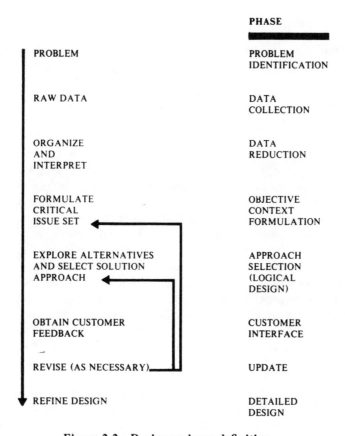

Figure 2.2. **Design as issue definition.**

Enhancement of customer communications

Some designers have a recurring nightmare of delivering an elegant system to a customer and only then discovering a communication gap so great that the customer is immediately unhappy with the system. Saarinen's use of critical issues actually enhances communication with the customer by providing insight into the designer's view of the customer's problem, enabling the customer to establish that the designer truly understands the problem. But, more importantly, the customer better understands the remaining details of the design since they fit into an overriding rationale. In a sense, critical issues act as a filter through which all aspects of the customer's and designer's perceptions are passed. Any of these not related to fundamental issues in the system are trapped in the filter. This tends to reduce the amount of information cluttering communication paths, and to bring discussions down to a basic level. This effectively draws the customer and designer together on the simplest of terms.

Conceptual integrity

To illustrate the idea of conceptual integrity, Brooks [5] draws an analogy between software designs and many European cathedrals. As Brooks points out, because it typically required several generations to construct a cathedral, technical advances, changes in fashion, and replacement of chief architects each with his own personal style, caused the resulting structure to display a mixture of architectural styles. Similarly, today's software systems seem to defy understanding, due to the viewer's lack of insight regarding the designer's intentions. Saarinen's model provides us with a means of establishing the overall conceptual view at the outset. Much like the artisans of old, those working on the details of a software system are faced with a myriad of decisions; if their decisions are informed by knowledge of the system's critical issues, there will be a coherence throughout the resulting system that could not be otherwise attained.

Design envelope

The aircraft industry, like many other engineering-oriented industries, utilizes the concept of a design envelope. The so-called envelope defines boundaries for the design. These boundaries may vary from subsystem to subsystem; in the case of an airplane design, they may include such factors as weight, current flow, and noise level. These local boundaries are derived from more global ones, which are usually few in number and deal only with gross vehicle constraints such as takeoff weight, fuel consumption, and operating cost per passenger-seat-mile. In software engineering, the design envelope is less exact, because precise, deterministic procedures are not available. Hence, software designers are left on their own to figure out what is or is not reasonable, and to compete with other designers for resources. This destabilizes the design environment, resulting in sacrifices of quality and cost-effectiveness. An envelope of critical design issues helps the designer to stay in control of his task, rather than being tempted to increase the problem's boundaries and devote inquiry to irrelevant areas.

2.4.2 Required design elements

This second portion of Saarinen's model is related to the critical issues portion in a hierarchical way (Fig. 2.3). The critical issues that are established at the beginning of design act as limits to the problem at hand. In a sense, these issues put the problem into an overall perspective within which secondary, more detailed issues can be effectively addressed. The basic design elements of function (what the system does), structure (how it does it), and style (why it is done that particular way) are detailed issues and are required of any successful design. However, they should not dictate the overall structure or intent of the system. Both critical issues and design elements serve to direct and limit design of a system, but each should be confined to its own role.

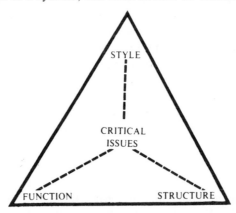

Figure 2.3. Relationship of critical issues to required design elements.

2.4.3 Comments on the model of design as a set of issues

The view that some high-level, non-implementation-oriented thinking is required at the outset is not altogether foreign to design [1]. What is novel is the idea of reaching agreement with the customer as to what issues are most important and how best to resolve them. Note in the quotation from Saarinen that the actual details of the building were not even considered until the system's goals had been established. How often have we seen a system that required a great deal of work to build and refine but whose purpose remains unclear? The utilization of the design model as a set of critical issues ensures not only that a "theme" will be apparent throughout all levels of the system, but that the customer will have agreed to it before the detailed design effort had been committed.

This approach has several advantages, particularly when one considers that no system can fully meet a customer's needs because his perception of them is in a state of flux. When the customer receives the system, he must understand why it is the way it is and why certain features he may have originally wanted are not present. Dissatisfaction and hostility are minimized if the customer is in agreement from the start. Employing this model of design goes a long way toward arriving at this agreement.

2.5 Design as goal attainment

The model of design as goal attainment views design as a process of establishing and reaching goals [6, 7].* It effectively establishes what the system will and will not be expected to do. Defining goals with a good deal of precision enables objective evaluation to establish the degree to which a system does what it is supposed to do: If, for example, an accounting system is required to be reliable, the percentage of wrong answers that is acceptable must have been established in order for the system to be evaluated. In this model of design, the objectives are stated in terms of measurable units, a mechanism by which they can be measured is suggested, and a level of acceptability is established. Hence, communication between designer and customer is made more productive since discussions are focused on narrower, objectively evaluated issues. As shown in Fig. 2.4, the model contends that five tasks are essential to design: identification of goals, establishment of priorities among goals, statement of goals in measurable terms, identification of a measurement mechanism, and definition of a level of acceptability. These are discussed below.

☐ *Identification of goals:* Why does the customer want a system designed and built? What it is intended to accomplish is crucial to responsive design. For example, a customer may say he wants a billing package designed in order to reduce bad debts when, in fact, improving credit-checking procedures might solve his problem. Without knowing the customer's motivation, the designer may well deliver a design that does what it is supposed to do, but does not address the customer's problem.

☐ *Establishment of priorities among goals:* Not all features of the system will be of equal benefit to the customer. When detailed design decisions or schedule or budget issues come up, designers need to have ex-

---

*This model is employed to define a software design method, Design By Objectives (DBO), discussed in more detail in Chapter 9.

plicit guidance on which goals are expendable and which must be met at all costs. This option should be stipulated for the designer; the customer should not assume that the designer will instinctively make the correct choice.

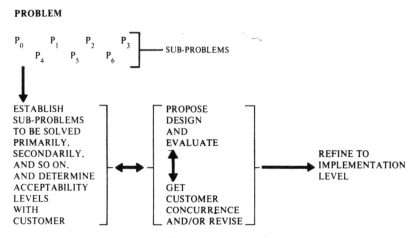

Figure 2.4. Design by goal attainment.

☐ *Statement of goals in measurable terms:* A goal serves a useful function in that it focuses and coordinates effort on a limited set of design issues. However, we also need to know whether we have reached our objective. For example, a goal such as "Improve customer service" sounds fair enough, but how will we know that the system (let alone the design) will do this? We need to know both the level of improvement and how it will be measured.

☐ *Identification of a measurement mechanism:* The means of evaluating the system and its design obviously will affect both the design itself and implementation. The measurement mechanism should be objective in the sense that, given some instruction, anyone could take the measurement. For example, a bank's goal to improve customer service may be measured by timing how much time the average customer spends at a teller's window.

☐ *Definition of a level of acceptability:* Establishing a goal and knowing how to measure it are important, but they are only two-thirds of the issue. The remaining one-third is the minimum level of improvement that is acceptable. Defining logical and objective acceptance levels reduces recriminations that can occur upon system delivery due to political and other pressures on the customer.

Comments on the goal-oriented model of design

The goal-oriented model presents design in an almost scientific light. Issues are explicit and rational, and acceptance criteria are logical and objective. However, for this model to be effective, customers must accept the high level of day-to-day involvement in the design process. Not all customers can accept this, nor can they put their intuitive evaluation mechanisms into objective formulae.

2.6 Design as a viewpoint

Design as a human activity has recently attracted a good deal of research by cognitive psychologists [8, 9, 10]. They have sought to understand how people approach the design problem, what sorts of aids they employ, and, basically, what thought processes go on during design. The psychologists' initial idea was that design is a type of problem. However, as study in this area continued, opinion shifted to favor a model of design as a way of looking at a problem.* Different ways of approaching a problem can reveal significantly different, not necessarily mutually exclusive, packets of information.

For example, to an insulation contractor, the problem of losing heat in a house would be greatly clarified by photographs of the house taken in the ultraviolet, visible, and infrared regions of the electromagnetic spectrum. Each view would tell him something different, yet they would all be related.

Similarly, the way in which we "see" a design problem will affect the type of solution we propose. Our view depends upon several factors, but relates primarily to our own world view: If we are process-control oriented, for example, then we tend to see all design problems in terms of this aspect.

The psychological studies have identified a series of six states through which designers pass in defining and refining designs:

- goal statement
- goal elaboration
- solution outline
- solution elaboration
- solution testing (evaluation)
- acceptance or rejection

These states represent a procedure-like attempt (although the designer may not be aware of it) to understand what the customer is saying and to temper his statements with what is possible.

The basic contributions that this model of design makes are that design is first and foremost a human activity, which means that it will not be easily understood; that aids to the designer will have to be carefully selected and evaluated; and that a great deal more work must be done in order for us to understand how to be more effective designers.

2.7 Design as an integral process of problem definition and solution

The sixth model of design views it as a related process of defining and solving a problem. Software design and design in general have each been described as a discovery process [11]: As the design or solution to a problem is refined, new aspects of the problem are discovered. As these are addressed, further problems are

---

*The idea that design is a way of viewing problems [8] is a key to the discussion of software design methods in Part III. Each method represents a response to the implications of a particular view. The relevance of such responses is also discussed in Part III.

discovered, and so on. The implication is that if we could adequately define a problem, then no discoveries would interrupt the design process.

An accepted means of adequately defining problems in the software field is applying the concept of functional requirements, which merely state the functions or the "what" of the system. The task of design then is to define and detail how these functional characteristics will be accomplished.

The key rule in defining functional requirements is that no information relating to the design solution can be stated. In other words, state the problem but do not state the expected solution. Is this practical? Can it work? Let's use the analogy of building a home. If a person told a building designer that the functional requirements for a physical structure must include the capability of protecting a family of four from the elements, a means of ingress and egress, a way of disposing of human wastes, and a means of heating and cooling the interior, he might be shocked at the design solution: The designer may propose a 14-foot-diameter storm culvert, propped on blocks to prevent rolling, with flooring, ends blocked with doorways . . . all functional requirements being met, but not quite what the customer wanted. After many frustrating sessions with the designer, the customer may finally include some design detail, stating that the functional requirements are to be met in the form of a house. Perhaps the style of the house might even be included. As this example illustrates, one cannot state a problem without some rudimentary notion of what the solution should be [12].

The message for designers is that the means of defining a problem should lend itself to the definition of the solution. The use of wordy, function-oriented requirements documents inhibits, rather than helps, communication between the customer and the designer [13]. The remedy, suggested by this model of design, consists of several recommendations:

- expressing or modeling the problem with the notation that will be used by the designer

- planning for "discoveries" of problem aspects during design rather than assuming that the requirements are complete and frozen

- utilizing prototyping* and a software engineering discipline [12] as a means of looking ahead without the heavy investment of full development

- establishing system objectives and utilizing them to define an abstract system model

The basic utility of this view is that it reflects the approach used in the definition, design, and development of systems in other engineering disciplines. But the model of design as an integral process of problem definition and solution is not without its complications. One of the most serious is that it may lead to premature implementation. The design/development teams may view the prototype as a first version of the delivered system, and may have a tendency away from modern programming practices and toward the "code first and design later" approach. Also, the customer may become enamored with the prototype and not wish to support the remainder of the project.

---

*In this context, a prototype is a working model in which only some of the features of the final system are supported.

These and other problems associated with this approach can be controlled and overcome with a prudent, persistent, and flexible management approach. It has proved successful in other engineering fields and is establishing a place for itself in today's software engineering environment.

2.8 Conclusion

In this chapter, we have briefly described six models of design. Although they appear quite different, the following common ideas pervade the set:

- Design is a "good" thing to do prior to implementation.

- Design involves abstraction, including the use of graphics, mock-ups, prototypes, and physical analogies, to strip away detail and to get at the essential character of the system.

- Some rationale is necessary to focus design activity, make it more effective, and ensure that successors will understand what was done.

- Design is inexact in that it does not lend itself to the use of formulae or precise estimates.

- Design is a creative act, uniquely suited to people rather than automata, in that people can bring their entire experience to bear on a new problem.

- Design is a discovery process, in that, as we refine our understanding of the problem and enrich our design to address this new knowledge, we often discover subtle nuances.

- Design and analysis (or specification) are inextricably linked and only artificially separable.

In the remainder of this book, three key issues are addressed: software design representation (Part II); software design composition (Part III); and selection of a method or technique that will be effective in a particular design situation (Part IV).

Many of the design concepts discussed in this chapter will reappear in a different form when we examine software methods and techniques. Despite its newness, there is nothing fundamentally unique about software design.

EXERCISES: Chapter 2

1. Briefly describe what you are doing when you are designing. With which of the six models of design does this activity most closely coincide? With which do you most agree? Are these two sets of views synonymous? If not, why not?

2. Describe an activity that you believe to be design. Describe one that is not design. Compare these activities.

3. Assuming that design is a form of problem solving, why do people often resist criticism of their efforts?

4. Make two lists, one containing those technical, job-related tasks and activities you like most and the other containing those you dislike. Which list contains more activities closely related to design? Why?

5. Briefly describe the last major design effort for which you had trouble meeting the deadline. If you could turn back the clock, re-assemble the same design team, and work an additional three months, how would the results be different? Even with the additional effort, would there be areas in need of improvement? Is the wicked-problem view applicable to your case?

6. Have you ever needed to modify a system and wished you had been told why the system was the way it was? How would this have helped? Do you communicate such information to your successors? Why? How?

7. Describe a design problem in which the requirements are clearly separable from the design. Describe one in which they are not separable. Compare the two problems. Are they intrinsically different?

REFERENCES: Chapter 2

1. W.R. Spillers, ed., *Basic Questions of Design Theory* (New York: American Elsevier, 1974).

2. J.C. Jones, *Design Methods* (New York: Wiley-Interscience, 1970).

3. H.W.J. Rittel and M.M. Webber, *Dilemmas in a General Theory of Planning,* Institute of Urban and Regional Development, Working Paper No. 194 (Berkeley, Calif.: University of California, November 1972).

4. A.B. Saarinen, ed., *Saarinen on His Work,* revised ed. (New Haven, Conn.: Yale University Press, 1968).

5. F.P. Brooks, Jr., *The Mythical Man-Month* (Reading, Mass.: Addison-Wesley, 1975).

6. T. Gilb, "Design by Objectives: A Structured Systems Architecture Approach," *Infotech State of the Art Reports* (Maidenhead, Berkshire, England: Infotech Information Ltd., 1980).

7. J.P. Herzog, "System Evaluation Technique for Users," *Journal of Systems Management,* Vol. 14, No. 5 (May 1975), pp. 30-35.

8. J.C. Thomas and J.M. Carroll, "The Psychological Study of Design," *Design Studies,* Vol. 1, No. 1 (July 1979), pp. 5-11.

9. A. Malhotra, J.C. Thomas, J.M. Carroll, and L. Miller, *Cognitive Processes in Design,* IBM Corp., Research Report RC-7082 (Gaithersburg, Md.: 1978).

10. J.M. Carroll, J.C. Thomas, and L. Miller, *Aspects of Solution Structure in Design Problem Solving,* IBM Corp., Research Report RC-7078 (Gaithersburg, Md.: 1978).

11. P. Freeman, "Toward Improved Review of Software Designs," *Proceedings of the 1975 National Computer Conference,* Vol. 44 (Montvale, N.J.: AFIPS Press, 1975), pp. 329-34.

12. L.J. Peters, "Relating Software Requirements and Design," *Proceedings of the Software Quality Assurance Workshop* (New York: Association for Computing Machinery, 1978), pp. 67-71.

13. T. DeMarco, *Structured Analysis and System Specification* (New York: YOURDON Press, 1978).

PART II

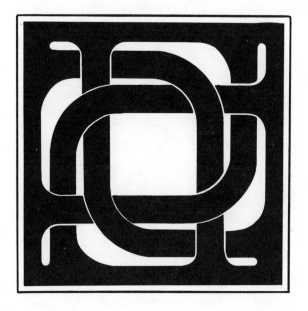

Design Representation Techniques

PART II
Design Representation Techniques

*To successfully communicate
a software design to others,
one must think deep
but speak, write, and draw shallow.*
                                        —L.P.

The phrase "a picture is worth a thousand words" sums up what software design representation is all about. So why go on? Because the picture and the words it connotes differ from design to design and from audience to audience. In fact, to reviewers of designs — any designs, not just software — the pictures *are* the design. Consider the approach taken by great painters: Each work possesses various qualities consciously integrated into the piece to contribute to the overall theme. Subtle shadings, distortions, textures, colors, and poses are contrived to elicit a specific response from the viewer.

Now consider how blithely the means of communicating software designs are selected — sometimes merely out of habit or ignorance of other, potentially more effective techniques. Each design representation scheme will prompt different responses from different viewers and emphasize a different aspect of the system; no single approach is totally suitable for representing all designs, or even representing all aspects of a single design. Selecting a design representation scheme involves several categories of factors, including the objectives of the design, its intended audience, and the ability of the scheme to integrate the results of the design effort into the overall project. For example, how often is the intended audience considered? Have you ever portrayed a software design in more than one way in order to reach both technical and managerial personnel?

Fields of endeavor outside the data processing industry have had to face the problems associated with system depiction for some time. In many fields, such as architecture, this challenge is addressed in two ways. One way depicts the system with very little detail, or with details presented as disjoint, independent entities. The blueprints and artist's drawings of a building are examples of this first approach. Note that although the blueprint contains large amounts of detail, the detail is de-coupled from the environment and other classes of detail (e.g., the superstructure is separated from the facade). This separation of factors makes it difficult for the customer (and even the engineer or architect) to perceive what the entire building will be like.

The second approach is the practice of combining the detail contained in a blueprint-like depiction with the gross characteristics identified in the artist's conception to form a scale model. Such models provide the observer with insight into how the various pieces of the system fit together and gives him a sense of what it will be like. Although much of the fine detail is obscured by the model, the overall effect is noticeably more informative than either the blueprint or the artist's conception.

Many of the software design representation schemes described in this part are also integral components of their respective software design methods. They are discussed separately here because Part III concentrates on the software design issues associated with each method and would be overly lengthy if individual representation schemes were included. Also, as design representation is generally separated from design formulation, the reader may select a system of design representation apart from the corresponding method.

Part II surveys typical software design representation schemes currently practiced. The basis for each is described together with its use. Techniques ranging from depiction of system architecture to diagrams of database structure and flow are discussed. Each technique is discussed from different viewpoints. The first is the notation itself, totally apart from a particular application. The second is the use of a common example by which the reader can compare schemes. Thirdly, since the example may not be well suited to all of the techniques, some techniques are also demonstrated by an example highlighting that technique's strong points. In this way, the relative strengths and weaknesses of each technique are made apparent.

The techniques described in this section have been organized into four categories: architectural, structural, behavioral, and database.* Architectural techniques are primarily concerned with the depiction of the major subsystems and functional elements that compose the system. Structural techniques depict the hierarchical relationships and functional mapping into individual modules. Behavioral techniques depict the processing or dynamic properties of the system elements. Database techniques are used to describe the information environment within which the system will do its job. Finally, the characteristics of each technique within each category are summarized. This will permit a software designer to combine complementary, compatible techniques to form an effective hybrid representation scheme for a particular system.

---

*Although a particular technique is discussed within only one of these categories, it may also be useful as a means of displaying information in another category.

CHAPTER 3
Representing System Architecture

*The world cannot be understood
from a single point of view.*

—Eleanor Roosevelt

The depiction of system architecture is the least understood and most poorly addressed issue of software design representation. The objective of this type of representation is the communication of primary conceptual issues upon which the remainder of the design is based. This is accomplished by depicting major portions or functions of the system, and their relationships to one another; and by demonstrating that this choice of functions so related addresses the critical issues of the design problem.

The primary reason system architecture is unaddressed is that such a global conceptual issue disturbs designers, who are much more at ease in the mode of identifying and addressing small, deterministic problems. The comfort level of users or customers is just the opposite: They are much more confident of success when the software designer appears to understand the large issues that they face every day. Instead, a typical design presents the user or customer with design review materials that spell out in excruciating detail precisely how the proposed system will eventually work. It gives him what the system will do, but not why it is done that way. For example, if a non-architectural scheme was used to document an electronic switching system, it may depict the executive controller as just another module. An architectural scheme would clearly highlight its broad span of control and relative importance to the health of the system. This will tend to put other aspects of the design into perspective.

A secondary reason for the lack of attention to architectural issues in software design is the difficulty of composing this "conceptual map" or undetailed abstract model of the system. The problem lies in identifying critical issues and in contriving a conceptual approach to addressing them. As described in Chapter 1, critical issues are at the heart of the system's architectural design. After these are addressed, lesser issues are addressed. However, if the architecture is not effective at resolving these high-level critical issues, then the quality of the solutions for the lesser problems is not important.*

---

*For example, in the design of an on-line checking account inquiry system, critical issues might include the timeliness and accuracy of the information obtainable from the system, rapid response time, and the ease with which inquiries can be made. Less important or non-critical issues might include output format, availability of back-up and recovery capability, and expansion of capabilities.

But, as we have seen, what is important to the software designer is not likely to be the same as what is important to the customer. The review and design information will be based on one set of values, while the customer's perspective is based on another. The customer is frustrated, because he does not relate well enough to what is presented to ask meaningful questions. His ignorance embarrasses him, but he intuitively feels some part of the design must need re-work. So, he searches for some aspect of the design that he can understand and perhaps question. As a result, such reviews often consist of a seemingly endless string of nit-picking questions. The designers come away from such exercises in futility feeling that the customer really did not seem to understand the overall design. The customer leaves feeling that the designer does not really understand his problem, but has done a lot of work, and maybe things will work out — maybe not. This situation inhibits communication between customer and designer and tends to create some mistrust and disbelief. An effective depiction of the system architecture provides an information pipeline at the highest conceptual level. This represents the first step in a continual process of refinement down from the concept to the implementation level.

There are only two schemes presented in this section. Although other schemes may be viewed by the reader as qualifying as architectural schemes based on the foregoing discussion, the reader should withhold judgment until these are presented. The first of these is the Leighton diagram. It was originally developed to address precisely the needs described above. It is significant in that its originator is the son of an architect and is himself an artist (as well as a software engineer) — two very creative, conceptual, and structurally oriented areas of endeavor. The Leighton diagram strips away most of the detail of the system, leaving the scope of control, hierarchy, and external interfaces. HIPO (Hierarchy, plus Input, Process, Output) is the second scheme presented. It contains much of what is in Leighton diagrams but adds other information (e.g., flow of data and implied sequence of operation) as well. Even though their information content is similar, the geometric appearance of the two schemes is quite different. Since they are so different in what they attempt to show, a single, common example might not accurately portray their relative effectiveness. Hence, each scheme is presented using an example which highlights its strong points.

3.1 Leighton diagrams

The Leighton diagram addresses the problem of depicting software system architecture in an easy-to-read and understandable format. The approach generally avoids many of the communication problems (such as complexity and detail) associated with employing tree-like diagrammatic forms while displaying sources of inputs, processing levels, precedence relationships, and destinations of outputs.

3.1.1 Concept

Leighton diagrams were originally developed to serve a function analogous to that of the blueprint in engineering [1], and have the following characteristics:

- employing some of the characteristics of tree-like structures, including two-dimensionality and hierarchy
- clearly depicting sources of input and destinations of output

○ being easy to present and copy using standard-size forms and allowing sequential presentation to avoid repetitive backtracking

○ clearly depicting the complexity associated with what is being presented and the occurrence and use of common routines

○ permitting the incorporation of textual information

○ being compatible with modern programming practices

○ being effective on a broad spectrum of system types

○ being automatable in a cost-effective manner

The primary goal in developing Leighton diagrams was to enhance communication among customers, users, software architects, and software development personnel concerning design and development issues. This is accomplished by incorporating some notational concepts from such diverse disciplines as management science, engineering, and computer programming, specifically highlighting the control hierarchy and user interface with a graphic technique described in the next section. The levels within the control hierarchy are explicit on Leighton diagrams, but their implications are somewhat context-dependent. For example, a return to MAIN has a different meaning in a batch system than in a real-time or operating system.

3.1.2 Notation

Leighton diagrams utilize combinations of rectangles, directed line segments (vectors), standard flowchart device and media symbols,* and connecting lines. A rectangle is used to portray a module (a contiguous set of instructions that may be addressed by name). The presentation of these graphic symbols is nearly three-dimensional in nature. The horizontal dimension is used to display the control hierarchy in terms of call levels, with the main program at the leftmost of the diagram and each subsequently called module appearing to the right in turn (see Fig. 3.1).

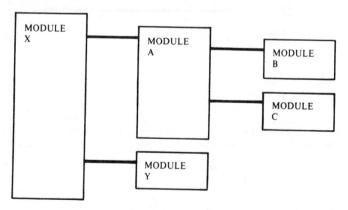

Figure 3.1. Use of graphic elements in Leighton diagrams.

---

*See N. Chapin, "Flowcharting with the ANSI Standard: A Tutorial," *ACM Computing Surveys*, Vol. 2, No. 2 (June 1970), pp. 119-46.

In Fig. 3.1, the scope of control of module X includes modules A and Y, while that of module A includes modules B and C. Module X calls module A, which in turn calls module B and/or C. The returns from B to A and to X are implicit.

The horizontal dimension portrays the overall hierarchy, but not the scope of control of a module; this latter is shown on the vertical axis, as the height of each rectangle used to represent a module is proportional to its respective scope of control. The third "dimension" of these diagrams relates to the portrayal of external interfaces, shown at the rightmost or lowest control level in the hierarchy using standard flowchart device symbols (for example, keyboard, disc, and magnetic tape) and vectors. An annotated example of a Leighton diagram is presented in Fig. 3.2.

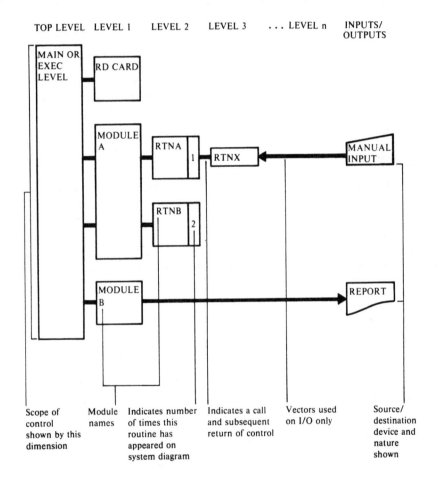

Figure 3.2. Notational conventions used in Leighton diagrams.

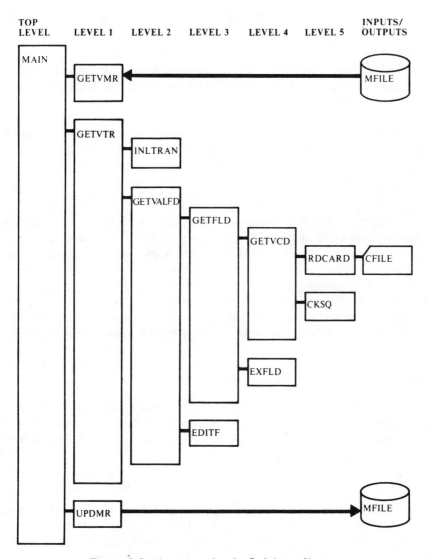

Figure 3.3. An example of a Leighton diagram.

3.1.3 Use

Follow these rules to generate Leighton diagrams:

☐ Represent all (including repeated) modules with labeled rectangular boxes.

☐ Make sure that subroutine calls proceed from top to bottom and from left to right.

☐ Make box sizes as long as is necessary to portray required relationships. They may extend onto successive pages as indicated by a dotted line. Other off-page references, such as connectors, are not allowed.

- ☐ Indicate the number of times a subroutine appears in a set of diagrams in the right side of its box.
- ☐ Show control interfaces with horizontal lines.
- ☐ Display input sources and output destinations on the right side of the diagram using standard flowchart symbols, which are repeated for each source or destination.

An example of the physical appearance of the Leighton scheme is presented in Fig. 3.3 on the previous page, showing a master file update program. Although used in relatively few firms, this scheme is enjoying increased interest and popularity [2].

3.1.4 Discussion

Of the schemes currently available, the Leighton diagram provides the most effective starting point for displaying system architecture. It shows precedence and dependency relationships while relating the system to user interfaces. Although it presumes that all or most of the modules composing the system are known, the approach aids in the refinement of the system architecture through the identification of other modules. The Leighton diagram is useful both in its published form and in modified versions that retain its basic conceptual intent. It is the first scheme to capture architectural issues graphically, and will probably be followed by others in the future.

3.2 HIPO

HIPO (Hierarchy, plus Input, Process, Output) is an informal and highly flexible scheme for capturing the hierarchical and interdependent relationships in a system in an undetailed manner [3]. It was developed and refined by IBM, and its use is aided by the availability of a special IBM template.

3.2.1 Concept

This software design representation scheme is based on the view that software (and other) systems can be adequately modeled as processes with distinct inputs and outputs. HIPO captures the essence of top-down decomposition by enabling its users to decompose a top-level view of a system into lower, more refined, and more detailed views without having to include logic details. It also provides a gross description of data input and output from processes and aids in defining data flow composition.

3.2.2 Notation

HIPO utilizes a set of simple, easy-to-draw symbols. Individual HIPO diagrams consist of three parts (input, process, and output) with their respective position in the overall hierarchy (Fig. 3.4). The use of large, vector-like symbols between processes clearly defines the data communication taking place (Fig. 3.5). The order in which processes are placed in the process section of the diagram implies the sequence of execution, although exact details of execution cannot be depicted with the basic notation.

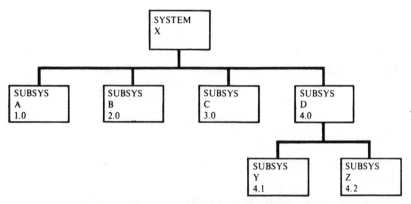

Figure 3.4. Example of HIPO notation and organization.

In Fig. 3.4, system X consists of four subsystems — A, B, C, and D. Each is described by a HIPO diagram.

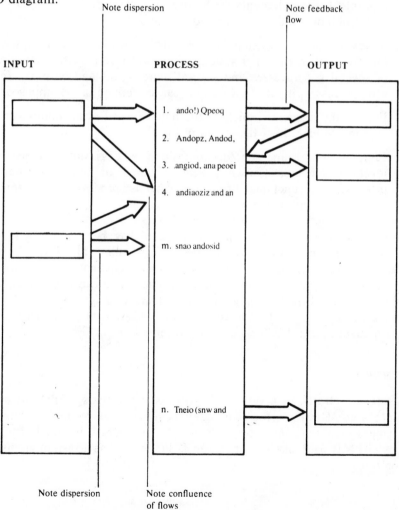

Figure 3.5. Examples of notational conventions in HIPO.

Note: Nonsense type is used to represent actual variables supplied by the user of the method.

3.2.3 Use

HIPO is an easy scheme to use, for it has few notational requirements. The basic procedure by which HIPO diagrams can be generated is straightforward:

☐ Begin at the highest level of abstraction (little detail is present).

☐ Identify the inputs to the system and the outputs from it in aggregate terms.

☐ Identify the major processing steps by which input is transformed into output.

☐ Associate each input and output with the appropriate process or processes (that is, one or more using the input or producing the output).

☐ Document these elements of the overall system design using HIPO diagram notation and the associated tree-like structure.

☐ Repeat the above five steps, but this time consider each process and its input/output as the total system. This will result in the identification of several subprocesses and several more inputs and outputs. In this way, processes, inputs, and outputs can be refined or decomposed.

☐ Expand the diagram to include the newly identified elements using the appropriate identifiers (as shown in Fig. 3.4).

☐ Continue the refinement/decomposition process until an acceptable level of decomposition has been attained or until the identified processes are functional primitives (that is, processes that cannot be decomposed any further).

The use of the HIPO technique in projects has been published [4], and is described at greater length in Katzan's book in particular [5]. Two of its strongest features are its simplicity and the ease with which customers can learn it, aiding contractor/customer communication. Users and customers can comprehend the terms used in the notation. However, large systems of HIPO diagrams are very difficult to change manually and to verify for consistency. Also, data feedback is difficult to describe. An example of a HIPO diagram is presented in Fig. 3.6.

3.2.4 Discussion

For software efforts, in a variety of business applications, HIPO has proved itself to be a useful tool. However, the rippling effect (changes in related diagrams) associated with changes to systems described with HIPO can render it impractical for very large applications. This is particularly acute when HIPO is used as a system architecture documentation tool.

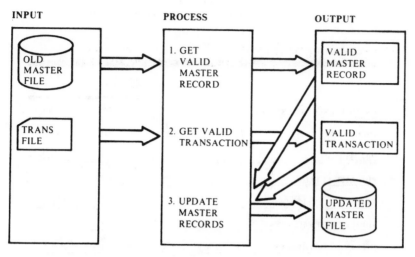

Figure 3.6. An example of a HIPO diagram.

3.3 Summary of characteristics

The primary goal of an architectural representation scheme is to portray the software system in such a way as to communicate these categories of information:

- *Philosophical:* The basis for the particular system organization chosen can be of critical importance in communicating with customers and users alike. If they understand it, they can identify and resolve any reservations. Users are much more likely to accept minor problems with a system if they understand why the problems are there and if they agreed to the overall approach that promulgated them.

- *Organizational:* The structural properties of a system may help or hinder the observer in understanding its various pieces. The reviewing process is best served if the system's structure permits each subsystem to be considered in and of itself because its relationship to the rest of the system is known and understood.

- *Contractual:* The ability of the software system to meet or exceed the legal obligations in the contract with the customer is often the primary concern at reviews. Even when systems are developed within the user organization, some working agreement is usually present in order to judge the system.

Neither of the schemes discussed in this chapter will meet all of the needs in each category. But each scheme has provided, and will continue to provide, much of what is needed in a particular software development situation. A summary of the types of information depicted by each scheme is presented in Table 3.1, and the information categories are defined below.

Table 3.1

Types of Information Depicted by the Architectural Schemes

CATEGORY OF INFORMATION	APPROACH	
	LEIGHTON DIAGRAM	HIPO
CRITICAL ISSUES/SYSTEM PHILOSOPHY	IMPLICIT	IMPLICIT
HIERARCHY	EXPLICIT	EXPLICIT
PRECEDENCE	EXPLICIT	IMPLICIT
PRIORITY LEVELS	–	–
EXTERNAL INTERFACES	EXPLICIT	IMPLICIT
MODULE INTERACTIONS	IMPLICIT	–
INTERNAL INTERFACES	EXPLICIT	–
OVERALL SYSTEM ORGANIZATION	EXPLICIT	IMPLICIT
USER REQUIREMENTS	IMPLICIT	IMPLICIT
PROCESS LOGIC	IMPLICIT	IMPLICIT

Definition of Information Categories

Critical issues/system philosophy the key or essential properties that have been built into the design; viewed as the minimum, high-level requirements by the software system designer

Hierarchy the grouping or arrangement of system elements into a set of successively subordinate/superordinate classes

Precedence the concept of events that must take place before other, subsequent events or processes can occur

Priority levels the relative importance of one process or sequence of processes over another, given that the required precedent events have occurred successfully

External interfaces the means by which the world (e.g., user, graphics terminals, or tape drives) outside of the system boundaries and internal computing environment communicates with the software system and vice versa (see definition of internal interface)

Module interactions   exchanges of information between or among modules within the system

Internal interfaces   the relationships between the software system's modules and the operating system

Overall system organization   the configuration in hierarchy, precedence, and priority of all elements internal to the software system and those that it interfaces with, internally and externally

User requirements   the legal, contractual, specificational, or otherwise required functions that the software system is expected to perform

Process logic   the internal workings of the identified modules in the software system

EXERCISES: Chapter 3

1. When you review a design, what is the primary documentation you use to understand it: typewritten text, diagrams contained in the design documentation, or some figures you drew to help understand the text? Is this the same form that you emphasize when you document your software design? Elaborate.

2. Have you ever been involved in the review of a software system design in which a coherent theme was present throughout? If so, what mechanism was used? What was the theme? If not, how could such a thematic description be accomplished?

3. How do you (or would you) currently display overall system architecture? Using the format of Table 3.1, list the types of information that your approach highlights as well as the types that it does not display. Are these two sets compatible with the conceptual nature of architectural design?

4. Regarding the impact of design representation on procedures, how would design activities be affected by the use of the Leighton diagram versus the HIPO approach? For what type of customer, user, or designer would each be better, and why?

REFERENCES: Chapter 3

1. L.R. Scott, "An Engineering Methodology for Presenting Software Functional Architecture," *Proceedings of the Third International Conference on Software Engineering* (New York: IEEE Computer Society, 1978), pp. 222-29.

2. *The Computer Program Development Specification for IDEF Support Tools — Build 1,* Boeing Computer Services Co., Document No. BCS-40254, Appendix D (Seattle: April 1979).

3. *HIPO — A Design Aid and Documentation Technique,* IBM Corp., Manual No. GC20-1851 (White Plains, N.Y.: IBM Data Processing Div., 1974).

4. F.E. Gatewood, ed., *A Structured Requirements Process Using the Improved Programming Technologies,* IBM Corp., Technical Bulletin GG22-9011-00 (Gaithersburg, Md.: September 1977).

5. H. Katzan, Jr., *Systems Design and Documentation: An Introduction to the HIPO Method* (New York: Van Nostrand Reinhold, 1976).

CHAPTER 4
Representing Design Structure

*Understanding a system
depends more heavily
on perceiving relationships
than on memorizing details.*
−L.P.

The term *structure* refers to the organizational relationships present in a software design. Hierarchy, inclusion, and equivalence are examples of relationships that are most often depicted explicitly. But structural properties are not easily presented without the inclusion (at least implicitly) of other information, such as precedence, execution sequence, and scope of control. Hence, the representation of software design structure includes secondary issues, regarding what correlative information is acceptable, misleading, or best hidden. The main issue is, How does the system operate on a macroscopic scale, and what must be depicted for the reader to understand this? Armed with such a perspective, he can feel free to explore other parts of the design, always knowing the way back to the starting point. Structural representation acts as a link between detailed information and the reader's curiosity.

Many approaches have been developed to accomplish this. Each was developed with its own set of problems, audiences, and intended message. In this chapter, we will examine several software design structure representations. They vary in their approach, ranging from a derivative of mathematics to schemes developed to support specific software design methods. Each was based on its author's view of the world. For instance, a graph theorist would be more concerned about depicting the details of control, transitive closure, and planarity, than about the structure of the database and the implications for the eventual code. In reviewing these, note the degree to which each scheme depicts non-structural information.

4.1 Design tree

The design tree approach for depicting design structure is directed at externalizing the decomposition of a system [1]. It is based on mathematical concepts used in top-down design.

4.1.1 Concept

Two notions are fundamental to the use of the design tree: containment and hierarchy. Containment refers to the fact that a concept includes (or contains) other concepts. For example, the concept of airplane includes the concepts of propulsion system, body, wing, and tail (Fig. 4.1). Hierarchy explicitly portrays concepts as being subordinate or superordinate to one another; that is, some concepts do not just include other concepts, but are greater or higher on a scale than they are. Used since the time of the Egyptians and possibly earlier, the design tree approach to ordering systems is inherent to all top-down approaches. This ancient idea must have some merit or it would not have lasted this long. It graphically portrays groupings of concepts within some overall framework in two dimensions, and has proved a convenient adjunct to the use of decomposition strategies.

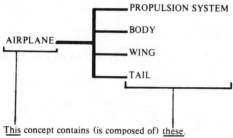

This concept contains (is composed of) these.

Figure 4.1. Example of containment.

4.1.2 Notation

The design tree uses a simple, flexible notational scheme. Only two basic graphic elements are used: a straight line and a node symbol. Examples of commonly used node symbols include circles, squares, and rectangles. Each node symbol contains textual information. The user of this scheme can employ any node symbol that is convenient, or choose not to enclose the text associated with each node; it has been incorporated into many of the methods and techniques in this book, and there is no rigid standard. The scheme is flexible in that it can be used to depict complex or simple systems to the desired level of decomposition.

4.1.3 Use

The key concept to bear in mind when using design trees is that of logical abstraction: This technique is useful in the construction of abstract graphic models of systems. The procedure for doing this is deceptively simple:

- ☐ Begin by defining a single node to be "the system" (as illustrated by "airplane" in Fig. 4.1).

- ☐ Identify the largest conceptual "chunks" of which the system or parent node is composed.

- ☐ Define these to be the next level of decomposition (see Fig. 4.2).

- ☐ Make sure that the level of detail present in this decomposition level is consistent and correct as necessary (Fig. 4.3).

- ☐ Select a node as a new parent and proceed as in steps 2 through 4, until an acceptable level of detail is obtained.

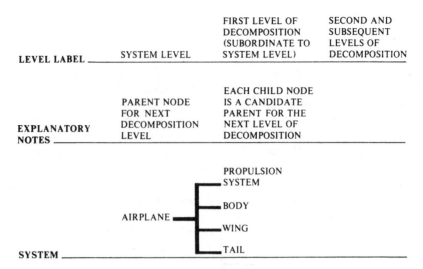

LEVEL LABEL	SYSTEM LEVEL	FIRST LEVEL OF DECOMPOSITION (SUBORDINATE TO SYSTEM LEVEL)	SECOND AND SUBSEQUENT LEVELS OF DECOMPOSITION
EXPLANATORY NOTES		PARENT NODE FOR NEXT DECOMPOSITION LEVEL	EACH CHILD NODE IS A CANDIDATE PARENT FOR THE NEXT LEVEL OF DECOMPOSITION

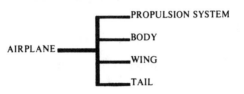

SYSTEM

Figure 4.2. Containment issues expressed hierarchically.

The new decomposition level from Fig. 4.2 is checked in the three parts of Fig. 4.3.

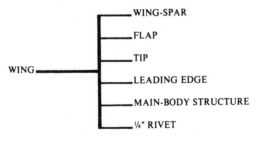

Figure 4.3a.

Examining "wing" in more detail, we might have

WING — WING-SPAR / FLAP / TIP / LEADING EDGE / MAIN-BODY STRUCTURE / ¼" RIVET

Figure 4.3b.

But "wing-spar" and "¼" rivet" are not at the appropriate level of detail (decomposition level). The figure should look as follows.

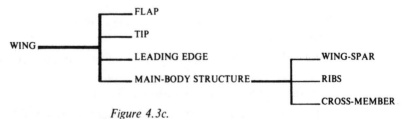

Figure 4.3c.

Figure 4.3. Consistency and correctness issues.

In the figure, the term "¼" rivet" will appear in more than one subtree and at a very low level. Not all potential parents will be decomposed to the same level, since they differ in complexity.

In this approach, not all parts of a system have the same level of complexity. Hence, instead of ending up with a design tree like the uniform model of a tree at the left in Fig. 4.4, we often produce a design tree that looks like the one at the right. Also, not every node is a real subsystem or procedure module. In fact, many of the nodes are merely mental placeholders, created to allow the designer to control the number and kind of things with which he has to deal. Thus, the implementation of a system is such that the logical design tree will have to be reconfigured to an implementable form.

There are other difficulties with using this approach. For example, how does one know when to stop decomposing? One suggested guideline is to stop when the level of detail is such that coding could begin. However, a more serious problem is present. At issue is the very concept of decomposition: How do we know that we have a true decomposition, and not just a series of apparent decompositions that do not introduce any new information? The classic organization of a software system is in the form of three functional areas or nodes: input, process, and output (as in HIPO, discussed in Section 3.2). At the first decomposition level, each node can, in turn, be subdivided into input, process, and output, and so on until as many decomposition levels had been attained as the designer desired. The following guidelines seem to be in order:

- Use each parent node as a statement of *what*.
- Derive the child nodes by describing *how* the *what* will be accomplished.
- Bear in mind that there exists an implied sequence of operations as one reads the node descriptions from left to right.
- Do not include decision or control information on the diagram.
- Use simple declarative verb-object combinations to describe nodes.
- Define all terms to be used by customer, user, and designer.

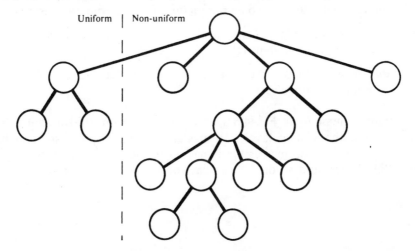

Figure 4.4. Models of design trees showing uniform and non-uniform subsystem complexity.

All things considered, the design tree concept is probably the simplest and easiest means of graphically depicting the hierarchical relationships inherent in a designer's conceptual view of a system. It also permits sufficient flexibility to enable designers to tailor the syntax of their design tree to suit the intended audience. Its utility is attested to by its adaptation in one form or another by several other representation schemes and design methods, including structure charts and Jackson's method.

4.2 Structure charts

Structure charts were originally developed by Stevens, Myers, and Constantine [2, 3] to specify modular characteristics of software design. The charts are an integral part of the structured design methodology [4].

4.2.1 Concept

The notational basis for the structure chart is the design tree. Here, the concept of one node including another has been replaced by each node being a module that may invoke subordinate modules or be invoked by superordinate modules. The information communicated between modules is graphically depicted. As defined in Section 3.1, a module is a set of lexically contiguous program statements that can be referred to by name. The relationships and interactions depicted include data flow, activation, and communication of control parameters. This scheme specifically identifies modules that will compose the software system, but permits design quality to be evaluated by the criteria of coupling and cohesion (see Section 7.3).

4.2.2 Notation

Structure charts can be drawn in several different ways. The approach proposed by Constantine et al. utilizes three basic graphic forms, shown in Fig. 4.5:

- the rectangle, used to contain a module name or module descriptor

- the vector that highlights control relationships between modules (such as a call and subsequent return)

- the arrow with a circular tail, used to depict the transfer of data between two modules

The graphic elements in Fig. 4.5 are assembled to form the structure chart in Fig. 4.6. In this case, the system level is a master file update processor that has several subordinate functions. The master file is passed to the edit module, which returns errors and valid entries, and so on. Note that control flags are represented by filled tail circles.

a) Module Call Notation

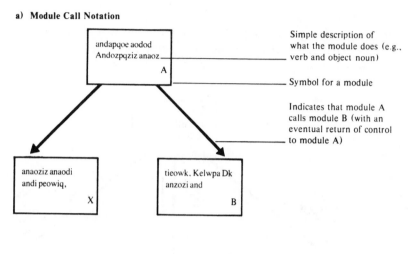

b) Module Couple Notation

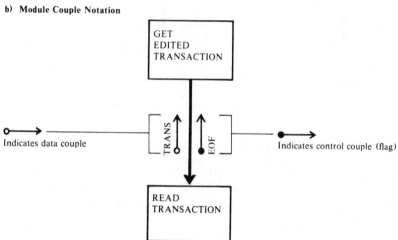

Figure 4.5. Graphic elements of structure chart notation.

Note: Nonsense type is used to represent actual variables supplied by the user of the method.

4.2.3 Use

As a design like Fig. 4.6 is refined, new modules are identified and added to the structure chart. When the chart contains very little detail, each module appears to be a black box to the design reviewers and, perhaps, to the designer, in that little is known about the processes it contains. As the designer's thinking matures and refinements are made, such modules are depicted as calling other, subordinate modules. Hence, if a reviewer wishes to find out how a particular module does its job, he can get a rough idea from inspecting the modules it calls. A more accurate and extensive information set is available in pseudocode, which is often used in conjunction with this technique. The initial version of the structure chart used by the designer, as well as some of its refinements, is derived from an analysis tool called a data flow diagram [4, 5], which is described in Chapter 7.

This representation scheme externalizes many of the implementation issues associated with a design. Although it does not permit the documentation of detailed decision information, the sequence of execution is implied in reading from left to right. It is a valuable means of depicting the segmentation of a system into modules and the interfaces that exist. The relative amount of information traffic between modules depicted in this way is symptomatic of the merit of the partitioning of system activities into modules.

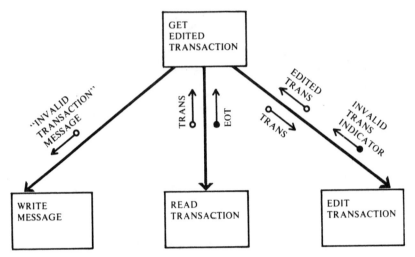

Figure 4.6. Example of a structure chart.

4.3 Structured analysis and design technique

Structured analysis and design technique, usually referred to as SADT®, was originated and trademarked by SofTech [6].* Its representation scheme includes a data model and an activity model. We will limit our discussion here to the activity model form of this scheme.

4.3.1 Concept

The SADT scheme uses two graphic forms: One is a design tree that serves as a road map for the system model; and the second is the system model used to describe a single program or a group of programs, and composed of one or more activity charts or diagrams. The activity chart depicts the flow of data and control information between activities or processes. The basic idea is to provide the user of the technique with a means of graphically portraying his analysis of an existing system or his perception of a system under design.

---

*SADT was derived from work by Hori [7] and as a result of development experience acquired in the AED, APT, and CAM efforts at the Massachusetts Institute of Technology. It is still undergoing development at SofTech, and a version of it has been adopted by the U.S. Air Force Integrated Computer Aided Manufacturing project (ICAM) [8].

4.3.2 Notation

SADT employs labeled rectangular boxes, arrows, labels, and a tree-like structure to maintain decomposition traceability. Distinctions are made both in what is represented and how it is represented. For example, the basic distinction between data flow and activities is made, but data are also classified as input, output, or control (see Figs. 4.7 and 4.8). Execution sequences are not explicitly shown.

Note that some data flows in Fig. 4.8 split into separate data flows; for example, the REQUESTS flow forks into SORT KEYS and REPORT TYPE. The case of two data flows becoming one is called a *join*. Although other notational subtleties are part of this scheme, only the basic symbols have been presented here.

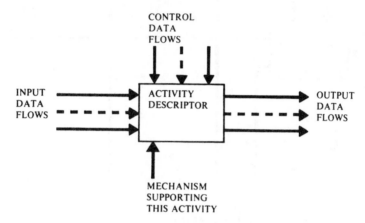

Figure 4.7. Basic notational conventions for the SADT approach.

4.3.3 Use

SADT utilizes a hierarchy of diagrammatic schemes to form system designs. The basic building block is the activity diagram or chart. These can be combined to form one or more models by using the design tree concept (see Section 4.1). Each model, which depicts a major subsystem, is evaluated by a mechanism called a kit (a coherent collection of diagrams). Issues of correctness and consistency are addressed through the use of review cycles, in which authors of diagrams critique each other's diagrams.

The primary disadvantage with using the SADT approach is its richness: That is, because an SADT diagram contains so much information, it is difficult for customers to be comfortable about approving such a model as correct. It is subject to wide latitudes in interpretation by those reviewing it. Without the direct participation of the author of such diagrams, reviewers are forced to make many assumptions. But assumptions will not always answer all of a reviewer's questions, such as why the designer/analyst interpreted a particular type of data as control data. These issues have a disquieting effect on the reviewer, particularly reviewers, such as managers or customers, who are only casually familiar with this notation. This uneasiness can reduce the success of identifying and correcting errors and consequently the value of the review.

The strong dependence of design quality on the establishment and maintenance of effective communication between the design team and the customer raises the question of whether such a rich notation is useful in design. Some customers may possess the technical skill to interpret this notation correctly, but the majority probably do not. It is a potentially powerful notational scheme for analysis, but much of its potential may be blunted by the difficulties previously mentioned. Using it in design carries the risk of imposing the designer's view on the customer with a predictable, negative outcome.

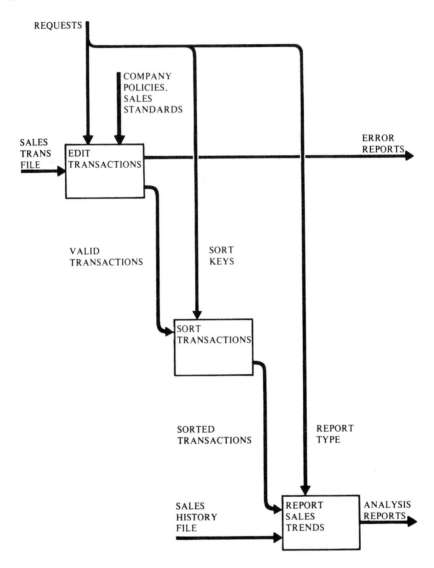

Figure 4.8. Example of an activity diagram.

4.4 Systematic activity modeling method

The Systematic Activity Modeling Method (SAMM) was originated by the Boeing Company and developed by Boeing Computer Services Company [9, 10]. Like SADT, it is based on the work of Hori and resulted from a desire to improve communication between customer and software development personnel through a simple, easy-to-use diagrammatic technique. Recently, the use of this method was simplified further through the development of an interactive graphics software tool by Boeing Computer Services [11].

4.4.1 *Concept*

SAMM is based on the depiction of activities and data flows as the primary means of understanding system design. It is essentially a manufacturing modeling tool, whose properties lend themselves to software design. Manufacturing engineers think in terms of flows, both forward and feedback, and processes. SAMM utilizes both. Interface problems with the analysis phase are reduced since the same notation can be used for both analysis and design.

Activity Cell

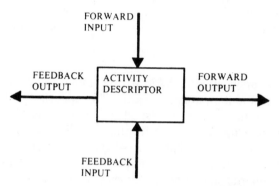

SAMM Diagram (Composed of Activity Cells)

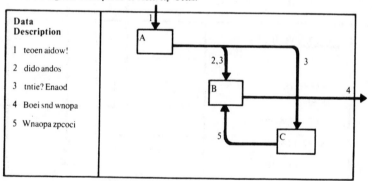

In the above diagram,

	INPUT TO	OUTPUT FROM	DESTINATION/ SOURCE
1	A	–	EXTERNAL
2	B	A	INTERNAL
3	B,C	A	INTERNAL
4	–	B	EXTERNAL
5	B	C	INTERNAL

Figure 4.9. Notational conventions in SAMM.

Note: Nonsense type is used to represent actual variables supplied by the user of the method.

The basic building block of a SAMM diagram is the activity cell. An activity cell may contain several processes or may itself be a single process. Several activity cells, related by data flows, together form an activity model. Individual activity cells can be expanded into other, subordinate activity models, thus forming a hierarchy of activities and data flows. This hierarchy implies data structure, and makes functional decomposition explicit. Data flows are classified into several categories — forward, feedback, input, output, internal, and external. The activity model information is supplemented by tables that detail activities and data.

4.4.2 Notation

The basic notational considerations for the SAMM activity cell and activity model are shown in Fig. 4.9. In examining the figure, note that the intersection of data flow lines does not in and of itself indicate a confluence or "bussing" of data flows. Rather, numbers are used at each intersection to define the destination of data flows explicitly.

4.4.3 Use

Figure 4.10 depicts the application of SAMM to a simple problem and shows how a table and other supportive notation enhance its use. The application of this scheme to larger systems utilizes the design tree concept (see Fig. 4.11). Note that the underlying function of this scheme is showing data flow, with the identification of functions almost incidental. This emphasis is particularly apparent when one considers how to identify data structure in this approach. Each activity model must be internally consistent, as well as consistent with its superior and subordinate models in the hierarchy at the time the analyst composes it. Unlike SADT (described in Section 4.3), SAMM requires correctness and consistency from the start.

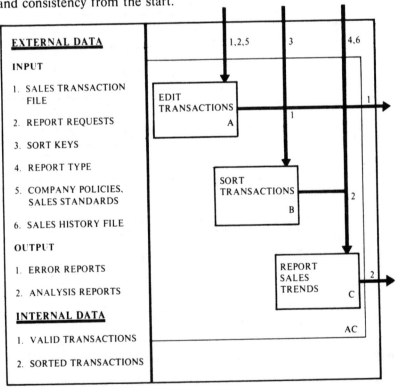

Figure 4.10. An example of the use of SAMM.

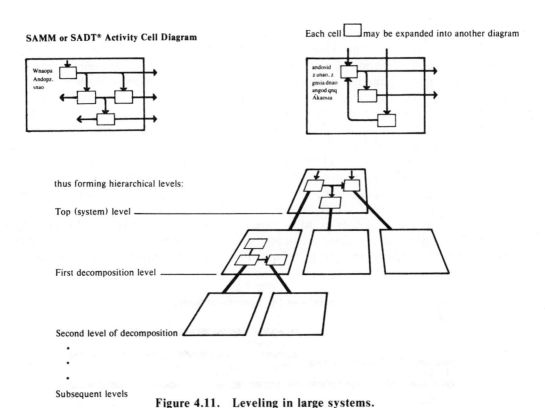

Figure 4.11. Leveling in large systems.

Note: Nonsense type is used to represent actual variables supplied by the user of the method.

4.5 Summary of characteristics

The four representation schemes — design tree, structure chart, SADT, and SAMM — possess several common features, although they are based on different viewpoints on what is and is not important in software design. All four utilize some hierarchical representation and indication of data flows, but distinction between different types of flows, and what is represented in the hierarchy, vary. Structure charts portray relationships among software modules, while SADT and SAMM are more generalized in that they can portray module functions and existing manual systems as well as physical software modules.

The process and philosophy used to derive and evaluate these charts show the individuality of their proponents. For example, SAMM requires the analyst and designer to force-fit the information they encounter into a specific, inherently consistent structure. If the analyst finds some inconsistency within a diagram or between one diagram and another at any level of decomposition, the problem must be resolved before any further refinements are developed. This forces him to filter his results in a continuous manner, which may result in a distorted model. The reason for the distorted model is that SAMM documentation of a system cannot have inconsistencies and is presumed to be complete to the level of detail reached.

In the case of SADT, the analyst or designer snapshots what he finds without regard for consistency issues, necessitating further investigation later. As in SAMM, reviews are used, but for an additional purpose — to resolve interface and inconsistency problems. The thought process of analysis or design does not have to be artificially structured, and problems or mysteries inherent in the analyzed system become evident. Systems are analyzed as they actually are, with few presumptions.

Which of the four approaches is "best" cannot be determined a priori. The resolution of this issue depends heavily on the type of system being analyzed or designed, the objectives of the analysis or design task, and the characteristics of customer personnel. A matrix of some characteristics of design structure-oriented representation schemes is presented in Table 4.1; definitions of those characteristics follow the table.

In selecting and using a structured approach, recall the diametrically opposed views of the designer and the customer. The designer usually wants to investigate local, detailed issues, which are closely related to the actual operation and execution of each module, and which are more comfortable to deal with than the global issues related to overall system organization, objectives, and philosophy. The customer and user, by contrast, are concerned about interface issues, global issues, and system organization, and not with details of its eventual execution and other local issues. In selecting a structural representation scheme, customer and user needs and interests are critical. These needs must be met in a manner compatible with other representation approaches.

Table 4.1
Comparison of the Structural Schemes

| | APPROACH | | | |
CHARACTERISTIC	DESIGN TREE	STRUCTURE CHART	SAMM	SADT[*]
HIERARCHY	YES	YES	YES	YES
PRECEDENCE	NO	IMPLIED	IMPLIED	IMPLIED
PROCESS LOGIC	NO	NO	NO	NO
MODULE COMMUNICATION	NO	EXPLICIT	IMPLIED	IMPLIED
TRAINING NEED	NONE	MODERATE	LOW	HIGH
TRAINING AVAILABILITY	–	YES	–	BY ARRANGE-MENT
TUTORIAL MATERIAL	(NOT ESSENTIAL)	YES	LIMITED	YES
AUTOMATED SUPPORT	–	NO	YES	MAY BE REQUESTED
PROLIFERATION	HIGH	HIGH	VERY LIMITED	LIMITED
EVALUATION CRITERIA	–	YES	NO	SOME
NOTATIONAL COMPLEXITY	LOW	MODERATE	MODERATE	HIGH
ANALYSIS COMPATIBILITY	–	HIGH	MODERATE	HIGH
GENERALIZED MODELING TOOL	–	SPECIFIC TO SOFTWARE DESIGN	YES	YES

Characteristics of Design Structure Representation

Hierarchy
the grouping or arrangement of system elements into a set of successively subordinate/superordinate classes; it can be treated in two primary ways: data and control

Precedence
the concept of events having to take place before subsequent events or processes can occur

Process logic
the description of the internal workings of the identified modules in the software system

Module communication
explicit depiction of the modules that constitute the system and the information that passes between/among them

Training need
the degree to which special instruction is required in order to use the technique

Training availability
the existence of publicly offered courses (not just custom-tailored in-house instruction) in the use of the scheme

Tutorial material
the existence of publicly available (in the literature) concise descriptions of use of the scheme

Automated support
the availability of an automated tool that makes the use of this scheme feasible on large projects

Proliferation
the degree to which the scheme has been utilized in software development by companies other than the firm that developed it

Evaluation criteria
the availability of objective heuristics with which to evaluate the quality of the software design structure

Notational complexity
the richness or diversity of the scheme's notation

Analysis compatibility
correspondence between this design scheme and one or more notations utilized in deriving a system specification, and hence the relative ease with which the consistency between design and specification can be established

Generalized modeling tool
flexibility for use in other than strictly design efforts

EXERCISES: Chapter 4

1. Re-examine a design document you recently had to work with. Estimate the percentage of the total effort that was devoted to describing the overall system structure. Assuming this implies the relative importance given by the designers to this issue, do you agree with them? Elaborate. How does their/your view stand up to the kind of scrutiny described in Chapters 1 and 2?

2. Jot down the types of questions asked by customer, user, and technical personnel (combine customer technical personnel with contractor technical personnel) at the last few design reviews in which you participated. Are the categories such that a single representation approach could adequately communicate with all three groups? Does your firm use an approach? If so, how effective is it? Why?

REFERENCES: Chapter 4

1. L.C. Carpenter, A.S. Kawaguchi, L.J. Peters, and L.L. Tripp, "Systematic Development of Automated Engineering Systems," unpublished paper delivered at the Second Japan-U.S.A. Symposium on Automated Engineering Systems (Tokyo: August 1975).

2. W.P. Stevens, G.J. Myers, and L.L. Constantine, "Structured Design," *IBM Systems Journal,* Vol. 13, No. 2 (May 1974), pp. 115-39. [Reprinted in *Classics in Software Engineering,* ed. E.N. Yourdon (New York: YOURDON Press, 1979), pp. 207-32.]

3. L.L. Constantine, "Structure Charts — A Guide," unpublished material from YOURDON inc. *Structured Design* course (New York: November 1974).

4. E. Yourdon and L.L. Constantine, *Structured Design: Fundamentals of a Discipline of Computer Program and Systems Design,* 2nd ed. (New York: YOURDON Press, 1978).

5. T. DeMarco, *Structured Analysis and System Specification* (New York: YOURDON Press, 1978).

6. *How to Increase Programmer Productivity Through Software Engineering Using PL/I,* unpublished SofTech Inc. course notes (Waltham, Mass.: 1973).

7. S. Hori, *CAM-I Long Range Planning Final Report for 1972,* Illinois Institute of Technology Research Institute (Chicago: December 1972).

8. *The Computer Program Development Specification for IDEF Support Tools — Build 1,* Boeing Computer Services Co., Document No. BCS-40254 (Seattle: April 1979).

9. *SAMM (Systematic Activity Modeling Method) Primer,* Boeing Computer Services Co., Document No. BCS-10167 (Seattle: October 1978).

10. S.A. Stephens and L.L. Tripp, "Requirements Expression and Verification Aid," *Proceedings of the Third International Conference on Software Engineering* (New York: IEEE Computer Society, 1978), pp. 101-08.

11. S.S. Lamb, V.G. Leck, L.J. Peters, and G.L. Smith, "SAMM: A Modeling Tool for Requirements and Design Specification," *Proceedings of COMPSAC 78* (New York: IEEE Computer Society, 1978), pp. 48-53.

CHAPTER 5
Representing Database Structure

*Models do not occur by accident,
but are the result of the application
of our world view.*
—L.P.

Early attempts at software design representation tended to dwell on representing those aspects of the program considered most important at that time: sequence of operation, decision and control flow, precedence, hierarchy, and the details of execution, for example. The volume and organization of data to be processed were almost incidental to logic definition. But the nature of the problems being addressed since those early days has changed drastically; commercial, scientific, and engineering applications are challenging the technology from both computational and informational standpoints.

For example, the databases currently used by major credit card firms were so much science fiction only a generation ago. Whereas emphasis was formerly placed exclusively on the representation of executable code, with database treated as an afterthought or stepchild, database design and representation is now considered a necessary task.* Even in apparently simple database efforts, a careful, rational database design will reduce both response time and the costs of change. Although some of the approaches discussed in this chapter have evolved over a period of years, the synchronization of program design with database design is a relatively recent and still maturing phenomenon.

In other areas of software design technology development, the dichotomy between logical and physical models is becoming increasingly accepted. The idea of a logical design or model of a computer program is not very new or foreign to most software designers. Similarly, the idea of having to modify, adjust, or "package" a logical design before it can be prudently implemented is also growing in acceptance. But it is especial-

---

*In the context of this discussion, database design refers to the abstract or logical organization and representation of database elements, totally without regard to the characteristics of a given database management system. This approach is the equivalent of abstract program design in the sense that implementation issues are considered only at the very end.

ly difficult to distinguish the logical aspects of data; it is relatively common to hear a designer speak of some aspect of a logical design in one breath, and of the details of the database management system file structure needed to support it in the next.

Logical database definition, then, presents the software designer with a problem similar to that of the designer of executable code: The designer must create a design that, when implemented, will result in a system that behaves *as though* it had been constructed exactly as depicted in the logical design. Logical designs, then, play the role of specifications or requirements.

In the following sections, we will examine schemes currently in use for representing data. Our primary concern is the representation approach, and not the database management system or automated aid that supports one scheme or another. In particular, we will concern ourselves with two basic classes of database representation schemes: One is for cataloging information about data (data about data). This type of scheme implies a certain hierarchical ordering of data elements. The second type of representation scheme depicts relationships in addition to hierarchical ones, and can portray file organization and access keys as its end result.

Since each specific representation scheme is integral to a particular school of thought on database design, considerable attention must be paid to both the concept and the "semantic richness" of the scheme. Hence, we will focus on these aspects when discussing each approach.

5.1 Chen entity-relationship approach

The Chen entity-relationship approach [1] is one of several schemes to recognize that database as well as code needs to be designed in two stages — logical and physical. As in other cases we've seen, the database representation scheme supports a particular database design method.

5.1.1 Concept

This design representation scheme contains three classes of things: entities, relationships, and attributes. Entities are objects that can be uniquely identified. Groups of entities may constitute an entity type, such as *employee* or *automobile*. Relationships are conceptual links that exist between or among entities. Relationships also can be classified into different types, such as *marriage* or *project-employee*. Attributes are properties possessed by entities and relationships, and have corresponding values. For example, *age* is an attribute or property of all employees. For a given employee, the corresponding value may be 29. Relationships also may have values. For example, the relationship *marriage* has the attribute *anniversary date*. The value associated with this attribute, for example, 06/11/66, is the date on which the marriage relationship began.

The basic scenario in using the Chen scheme involves identifying and documenting entities and relations and their interaction, identifying and documenting attributes and values, and, finally, combining these results into the form of a data structure that may be implemented on any database management system (DBMS). The process used to produce Chen entity-relationship diagrams is shown in Fig. 5.1.

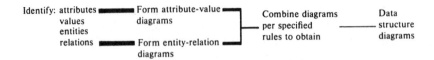

Figure 5.1. The process used to obtain a Chen entity-relationship diagram.

5.1.2 Notation

Each concept used in Chen's approach is represented by an individual building block in the diagram. Several blocks of the appropriate type may be combined according to a set of conventions. The individual forms of this notation are as follows:

○ Entity types are depicted by rectangles (see Fig. 5.2).

○ Relationship types are depicted by diamonds with lines connecting them to the appropriate entity types. Note the introduction of the symbols n and 1, which document the nature of the interaction between the relationship type and the entity type. In Fig. 5.2, the n and 1 indicate that a buyer may be the registered owner of several automobiles, but each automobile may have only one registered owner. In addition, tables are used to document values and attributes.

Figure 5.2. Depicting relationships using Chen's approach.

5.1.3 Use

The Chen entity-relationship approach incorporates many of the features of the data dictionary (such as data composition and organization), while providing the software designer with a flexible means of depicting information-based (as opposed to processing-based) problems. For example, the problem of representing some of the information contained in a state automobile registration accounting system. Cars are purchased by buyers but are owned by a bank (or other lending institution) until the lien against the automobile is paid in full. To begin our application, we list the entities and the relationships present within this limited system.

As a first cut, we can depict this information using the Chen diagrammatic scheme as shown in Fig. 5.3. The representation scheme basically says that cars are related to buyers by the registered owner relationship. It also shows that the nature of this relationship is $1:n$ in that each car may have only one registered-owner entity (even though the registered owner can be two or more people), but that a given registered owner may own more than one car. A similar situation exists between the bank entities and cars through the legal owner relationship.

Banks and buyers, however, have an *n:m* relationship, because there may be many different buyers dealing with one bank and, conversely, each buyer may deal with more than one bank. This situation does not necessarily represent a database problem to the designer or to the user of Chen's representation scheme. However, implementation into a database management system like CODASYL would be greatly aided if only 1:*n* relationships existed. In this case, the problem can be quickly remedied by creating a debtor/creditor entity in place of the debtor/creditor relationship, as shown in Fig. 5.4.

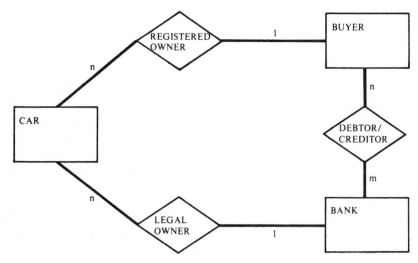

Figure 5.3. Initial view of entities and relationships.

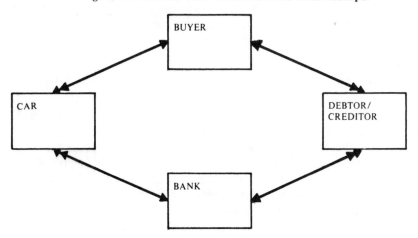

Figure 5.4. Revised, file-oriented view.

Note that from the outset the Chen approach forces the software designer to view data not as a hierarchical arrangement, but as a set of entities, each possessing certain attributes, and each having relationships of one kind or another with other entities. This shift in view is somewhat analogous to the data flow view of software systems. In that view, design is based on what is thought to be the most stable characteristic of a system — the flow of data. Content may change, but communication lines are stable. Similarly, in database modeling, the relationships between and among entities will be quite stable, although new entities and new or modified attributes may be incorporated over time. Such changes may affect hierarchical structure more profoundly than relational structure.

5.2 Data dictionary

The data dictionary has proved itself to be a useful adjunct to other software design representation schemes, particularly when it is developed in parallel with the software design rather than as an afterthought. Although there are different views on the role and content of the data dictionary [2, 3], the approach presented here provides the reader with a basic tool that can be modified to suit a specific problem.

5.2.1 Concept

The data dictionary is a requisite tool in successful software design. It enables the designer to establish the same sort of compositional relationships for data that are employed for functions and modules in the executable portions of the software. The dictionary is analogous to the design structure-oriented representation schemes. The basic goal is to create a catalog that identifies each data item, the data items of which it is composed (if any), any aliases by which it is known, and (when practical) the values it may take on.

Although the data dictionary's more popular role has been as an aid to database design, it has recently become prominent in software systems analysis and design [3]. Its role in analysis has been one of aiding communication between analyst, customer, and user by ensuring that they are speaking a common language. Its role in design has been to clarify to the designer the flow and content of data items through the system. The purpose of a data dictionary during design is to define composition and formulation rules for data items, not to chronicle that such-and-such will be a 24-bit integer or an inverted list. Such characteristics are not related to software design, but reside in the realm of implementation.

5.2.2 Notation

Different software shops and authors have favorite schemes for representing data dictionary information. However, some schemes are inconvenient to use or require an automated tool. For these reasons, a representation scheme is presented in Table 5.1 that is easy to use manually and can be typed or entered into a text processor, since it expresses relationships linearly without the use of special characters. In the scheme, the types of relationships that occur in programs or executable code are reflected in the data. The basic set of constructs — sequence, selection, and iteration — correspond in data dictionary parlance to concatenation, selection, and iteration, respectively. A shorthand notation of these constructs, together with definitions and examples, is presented in Table 5.1.

5.2.3 Use

The notational scheme presented in Table 5.1 may be employed in any one of several different ways, and many designers prefer to use notational variants that can be implemented on text processors or line-printers. Examples of the linear form of this notation are presented in Fig. 5.5.

Table 5.1
Basic Data Dictionary Notation

SYMBOL	DEFINITION	EXAMPLE
=	IS EQUIVALENT TO IS COMPOSED OF	CUST-NAME = SURNAME AND FAMILY-NAME CUST-NAME = SURNAME + FAMILY-NAME
+	AND	ADDRESSEE = CUST-NAME + ADDRESS
[ ]	EITHER-OR[†]	ADDRESS = $\begin{bmatrix} \text{PO BOX NO} \\ \text{STREET ADDRESS} \end{bmatrix}$ + STATE + ZIP
{ }	ITERATIONS OF[‡]	PLAYER-ROSTER = { PLAYER-NAME + PLAYER-NO }
( )	OPTIONAL	PLAYER-NAME = SURNAME + (MIDDLE- INITIAL) + FAMILY-NAME

[†]You may use a vertical bar between items to express the definition on a single line (see Fig. 5.6).
[‡]Default limits are 0 and ∞; that is, { X } means there may be as few as zero or an undefined number of X's. Use " " to denote literals, and * * to denote comments.

<pre>
MAILING-LIST   = { CUSTOMER-NAME + MAILING-ADDRESS }

CUSTOMER-NAME = (TITLE) + GIVEN-NAME + FAMILY-NAME

TITLE   = ["MR." | "MS." | "MRS." | "RESIDENT"]
                    * THE USE OF "RESIDENT" AS A TITLE
                    WILL BE DELETED AS OF DEC. 1, 1980 *

GIVEN-NAME   = 1 { ALPHABETIC-CHARACTER } 16

FAMILY-NAME   = 1 { ALPHABETIC-CHARACTER } 32
</pre>

Figure 5.5. Examples of data dictionary notation in linear format.

5.3 Data structure diagrams

Use of data structure diagrams as a database representation approach was developed by Bachman in the 1960s [4]. It is aimed at portraying data items through the relationships that exist between them and at representing a database in a way that lends itself to rapid implementation in any database management system.

5.3.1 Concept

This approach uses graphics to depict data as classes of entities and classes of sets by which the entities are related. For example, houses and banks are entities. Taken as groups, they make two very different entity classes. However, all the houses owned by a bank compose a set of entities that are subordinate to the owner entity.

Data structure diagrams portray four types of information: entities, entity classes, entity sets, and set classes. The term *entity* refers to the specific object being considered. *Entity class* refers to a group of entities whose attributes are similar enough for them to be considered together. The term *entity set* refers to a hierarchical relationship that exists between some entities in one entity class and one entity of a different entity class. Entity class and entity set are independent concepts. *Set class* refers to a group of entity sets that are similar enough to be considered together. In the case of set classes, the same entity-to-entity relationship must exist. The classic example of these relationships is the case of a corporation that has many departments and employees. Considered as a group, the employees of the corporation would compose one entity class, while the departments taken as a group would constitute another entity class. These are, obviously, independent groupings, but in some applications (e.g., in cost accounting) certain employees are "owned" by one or more departments (an employee may be shared by certain departments). Hence, a department may be considered as the owner of the set of which its employees are members. Considering such sets together results in a set class.

5.3.2 Notation

The data structure diagram employs two graphic symbols: the rectangle, and the directed line segment or vector. The rectangle is used to depict entity classes. The vector represents set classes and the inherent owner-member relationship (see Fig. 5.6).

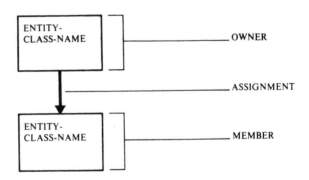

Figure 5.6. Notation used in data structure diagrams.

5.3.3 Use

Data structure diagrams have been employed in a wide range of applications. Recently, they have been utilized in the description of database requirements during the systems analysis and specification phase [3]. They have proved to be particularly useful in such applications since they basically represent how the database is supposed to behave and not how it should be constructed. For example, in the course of our software design effort for a bank, we may find that we need to be able to obtain the name and address of the registered owner if we supply the license number to the system. The user or the software designer may view the system as a rather simple arrangement with a single file consisting of owner information indexed by license number. In actual fact, there may be several intermediate accesses involved when the system is implemented. However, the software designer need not worry about how the implementation will be accomplished.

The basic ideas upon which the data structure diagram is based require patience and self-discipline to utilize fully. This approach remains a powerful tool particularly when used in conjunction with the data dictionary. It can result in a non-redundant statement of the minimal, logical database requirement. The example used in Section 5.1 is presented in the form of a data structure diagram in Fig. 5.7. Note that this is identical to Fig. 5.4 graphically but differs conceptually in that BUYER and BANK are owners and satisfy certain constraints. Also, if we were to factor $m{:}n$ relationships as in Fig. 5.4, we would obtain a data structure diagram from the entity-relationship diagram.

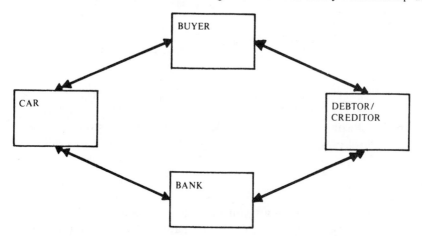

Figure 5.7. An example of a data structure diagram.

5.4 DeMarco's data structure diagram approach

Data structure diagram information can be expressed in a much more explicit manner than that described in Section 5.3, and DeMarco's approach [3] uses graphics to accomplish this.

5.4.1 Concept

The concepts upon which this database representation scheme is based are identical to those in Section 5.3.1.

5.4.2 Notation

The primary difference between the data structure diagram approach described in Section 5.3 and that described here is the richness of the notation. This scheme was developed as a means of supporting systems analysis through the classic progression from modeling the current physical system, through its logicalization and subsequent replacement with a new logical model.

Although rectangles and directed line segments are used as before, access key information is added. Also evident is a close working relationship with the data dictionary (see Fig. 5.8). Two types of files are described in the data dictionary: attribute files and correlative files. Attribute files have a single accessing key and contain all the attributes related to that key. Correlative files define relationships or correlations between keys.

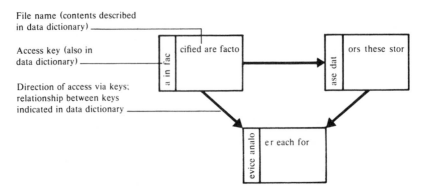

Figure 5.8. Basic notation used in DeMarco's form of data structure diagrams.

Note: Nonsense type is used to represent actual variables supplied by the user of the method.

5.4.3 Use

DeMarco's approach is based on the same ideas as those of Bachman's scheme [4], but in this case they are strongly supported by a nuts-and-bolts procedure for deriving the diagrammatic elements, and the explicit nature of the graphics, and coordinating all of this effort through the use of the data dictionary [3]. The procedure is aimed at distilling out of the confusion of data procedures, policies, and existing systems the essence of the database requirements to support the system. The basic scenario of DeMarco's approach is as follows:

☐ Identify all references to stored data by inspecting a logical model of the system. List these accesses, assigning each a number for future reference, and noting the direction of the data flow, the reason for the access, and the direction of the access.

☐ Replace each procedural data flow identified in step 1 with the minimum set of data entities needed to accomplish the reason for the access. Identify the keying information required for each access.

☐ Reorganize the file structure into an alternative set of files, called private component files (PCF), such that only one private component file exists for each logical access.

☐ Delete those portions of PCF keys that do not relate directly to the contents of the file.

☐ Examine the resulting keys. Create a new set of files wherein no key is duplicated by incorporating the contents of files with identical keys and having the key unchanged.

☐ Normalize (reduce to a common denominator) the results of step 5 by linearizing (removing non-linear characteristics such as repeating groups) the resultant files. Do this by iteratively creating new files for each repeating group within a given file, and assigning each an access key derived by concatenating the original key plus a new key representing the internal repeating group.

□   Eliminate any entities that can be derived by accessing one or more other files.

This approach produces models that describe how the database should *appear* to be constructed, not necessarily how the database administrator will construct it. An example of the application of this technique showing the nature of the relationship and the access mechanism is presented in Fig. 5.9.

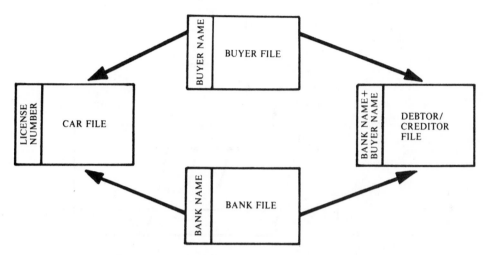

Figure 5.9. An example of DeMarco's notation.

Remember that this data structure diagram must be accompanied by a data dictionary that shows the relationships of the keys and the contents of the files.

5.5 Flory and Kouloumdjian approach

The Flory and Kouloumdjian database representation scheme is an integral part of a logical database design methodology developed in France [5].

5.5.1 Concept

The approach has two sets of objectives: One set is for the modeling or representation scheme, the other set concerns the method used to generate the model. The representation scheme is directed at retaining as much of the real-world semantics as practicable and at aiding the database administrator. The method is aimed at structuring the designer's understanding of the database and enhancing the database designer's ability to depict this understanding. Since the conceptual basis for this approach could not be explained without utilizing an undue amount of space, we will limit our discussion in this section to the representational aspects of this approach. Three concepts are fundamental to the use of this scheme: The *characteristic,* also known as an attribute, refers to the smallest unit of information that can be treated independently. The second concept, the *entity type,* is also known as a class of entities; entities compose the conceptual schema. An entity may be a real-world entity (an actual object) or a conceptual entity (an abstract image of a real-world entity). The third fundamental concept is the *association* or relation type. The representation scheme deals with conceptual modeling issues.

5.5.2 *Notation*

Entity types and association types are depicted by rectangular boxes. Directed line segments or vectors portray functional relationships (see Fig. 5.10).

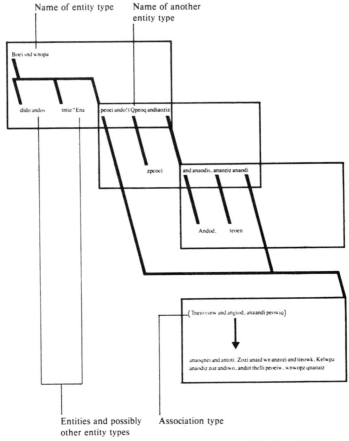

Figure 5.10. Basic notation used in the Flory and Kouloumdjian approach.

Note: Nonsense type is used to represent actual variables supplied by the user of the method.

5.5.3 *Use*

Applying Flory and Kouloumdjian notation to our automobile registration-legal ownership database example, we obtain Fig. 5.11. Note that we have added the requirement that some relationship between what each registered owner owes to each lending institution must have also been addressed as an association type. A great deal of theory backs up the use of the representation scheme (as with other database representation schemes), and it can be utilized effectively in portraying design-associated database issues. It has much in common with other entity-relationship type approaches and provides yet another means of representing a database as an abstract specification, and not as an implemented database; it still leaves the implementation job to the database administrator.

However, the notational approach can be awkward to use when dealing with even a small to moderate database problem, due to the interlinking of many of the entity classes. The lack of repetition and selection information on the diagram simplifies graphics, but forces the user to refer to the data dictionary for details.

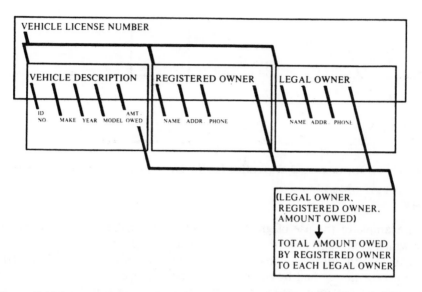

Figure 5.11. An example of the use of the Flory and Kouloumdjian approach.

5.6 Graph model of behavior data charts

The graph model representation scheme is part of the SARA (System ARchitects Apprentice) system [6]. Although this approach is not strictly a means of depicting data structure, it does represent an alternative, flow-oriented view.

5.6.1 Concept

Graph model of behavior data charts utilize a notation designed to depict data inputs, outputs, transformations of data, and the control processes associated with these data processes. Four basic concepts are inherent in this scheme:

- *controlled data processor,* a transformation of data that is activated whenever a particular control node is activated

- *uncontrolled data processor,* a transformation of data whose outputs are dependent only upon stated functions to be performed on the inputs and independent of the state of any control node

- *data set,* a collection of data at rest that may or may not have a specific structure associated with it

- *data arc,* a vector, which defines static relationships of read/write access between data sets and data processors

5.6.2 Notation

These data charts utilize one symbol for each of the conceptual entities employed, as well as another symbol to accommodate random delays (Fig. 5.12). The symbols can be hand-drawn but are also available on a standard flowchart template.

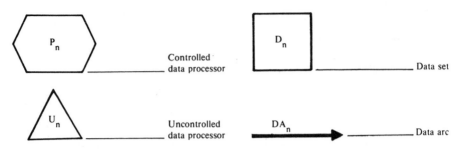

Figure 5.12. Notational convention for the graph model of behavior data charts.

5.6.3 Use

An example of the use of graph model of behavior data charts is presented in Fig. 5.13, in which controlled processor P_1 is initiated whenever one of nodes N_1, N_2, or N_3 is initiated. When initiated, processor P_1 reads data sets D_1 and D_2, performs the operation on them specified by the designer, and produces data set D_3. Processor P_2 is initiated only by the initiation of node N_4. It reads data sets D_3 and D_4, performs a specified operation, and outputs data set D_5. Uncontrolled processor U_1 reads D_5 and produces D_6.

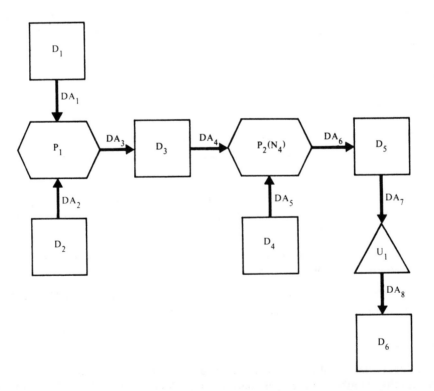

Figure 5.13. An example of a graph model of behavior data chart.

5.7 Jackson's data structure approach

Jackson's notational scheme represents a useful way of depicting database characteristics [7].*

5.7.1 Concept

The basis for Jackson's approach is the premise that a well-structured program design must parallel the structure of the data. Hence, this approach utilizes concepts from programming in order to depict data structure. The basic notions of sequence (or concatenation), selection, and iteration are employed using the containment or composition concept from the design tree (see Chapter 4, Section 4.1).

5.7.2 Notation

Jackson's notation is as simple and straightforward as are his conceptual notions. Rectangles are used to represent data (e.g., files, arrays, and individual data items), while connecting lines describe ownership or composition (see Fig. 5.14). An asterisk and a degree symbol are used to denote selection and iteration, respectively.

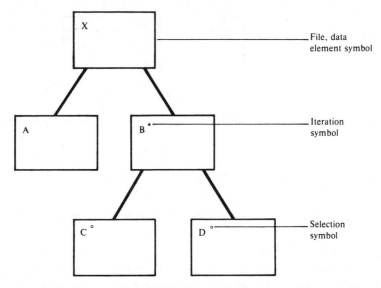

Figure 5.14. Notation used in Jackson's approach.

In Fig. 5.14, sequence is indicated by position such that X is composed of a single A followed by iterations of B, and B consists of C or D.

5.7.3 Use

An example of the use of Jackson's scheme is presented in Fig. 5.15. Notice the similarity between the graphics of this approach and those of other program design-oriented notations, such as structure charts. As simple as it may be, the notation is effective at capturing the database characteristics associated with a single program; but it

---

*Jackson's scheme is also utilized in program design, as we will examine in Chapter 8.

may fall short on representing systems of programs. The approach certainly is an aid to understanding data and programs, but it does not address the relational issues present in most large systems. Jackson's notation provides a graphic means of depicting the information possibly found in a data dictionary.

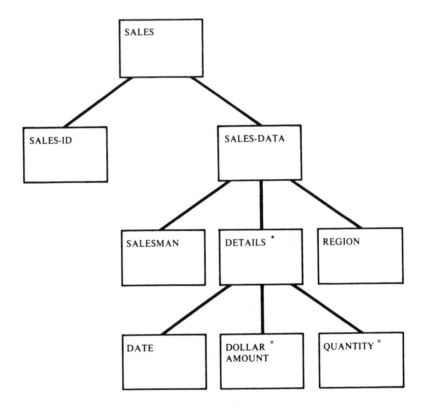

Figure 5.15. An example of the use of Jackson's approach to depict data.

5.8 Problem analysis diagram

The Problem Analysis Diagram (PAD), which is part of a software design method that will be described in Chapter 9, utilizes graphics to represent data and employs the same sort of constructs associated with program design [8].

5.8.1 Concept

PAD describes data in terms of sequence, selection, and iteration. This aids its use in conjunction with a similar program design notation, such as Jackson's approach, in that relational concepts are not depicted or addressed.

5.8.2 Notation

PAD employs rectangles, triangles, and connecting lines to describe data structure. The notation that represents iteration, sequence, and selection is shown in Fig. 5.16.

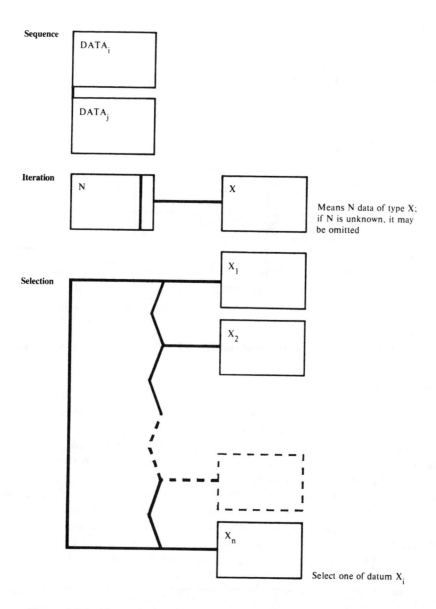

Figure 5.16. Notation used by PAD to depict database structure.

5.8.3 Use

PAD is a relatively straightforward scheme to use. The notation is simple and is not as intertwined and awkward to use as the Flory and Kouloumdjian scheme (see Section 5.4). However, PAD does not address the issue of relational characteristics, but does detail some characteristics of iteration. This form of data structure representation will require interpretation by the database administrator in order to implement it within a given system. However, it is a useful adjunct to many software design representation schemes directed at program design. An example of the application of PAD is presented in Fig. 5.17.

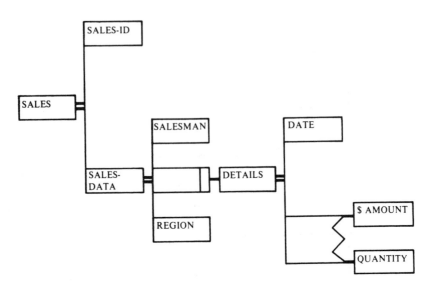

Figure 5.17. An example of the use of PAD to describe data structure.

5.9 Summary of characteristics

The development of representation schemes for database structure has somewhat paralleled that of software representation. In program design, the transition from large, monolithic programs to modularized ones has raised representation issues, while the transition in database technology and hardware support has resulted in databases of ever-increasing size and complexity. Similarly, the issues in system design have migrated from procedural and sequential ones to structural ones, while database issues have remained focused squarely on the relationships between or among data. The necessity of coordinating program design and development with database design is becoming widely accepted. The value of database representation may lie in the potential it provides for narrowing the gap in perception between program design and database design to one of information system design. Many of the schemes presented in this chapter are forerunners of this next stage in software design technology development.

EXERCISES: Chapter 5

1. How do you now depict database design models or problems? How was this approach selected? If you do not use one now, why not?

2. Which appears to be more natural when designing a system: dwelling on the process/procedural aspects, or on the inherent database issues? Describe how the two might be synchronized.

3. Depict the database associated with a recent program design using either the Chen or Bachman approach, and again using either the PAD or Jackson approach. Which looks more like the structure of the program?

4. Would it have been helpful, during design, to have depicted the database associated with a system using one of these representation schemes? Why or why not?

REFERENCES: Chapter 5

1. P. Chen, *The Entity-Relationship Approach to Logical Data Base Design,* The Q.E.D. Monograph Series on Data Base Management, No. 6 (Wellesley, Mass.: Q.E.D Information Sciences, Inc., 1977).

2. J. Martin, *Principles of Data-Base Management* (Englewood Cliffs, N.J.: Prentice-Hall, 1976).

3. T. DeMarco, *Structured Analysis and System Specification* (New York: YOURDON Press, 1978).

4. C.W. Bachman, "Data Structure Diagrams," *Data Base, The Quarterly Newsletter of the Special Interest Group on Business Data Processing of the ACM,* Vol. 1, No. 2 (Summer 1969), pp. 4-10.

5. A. Flory and J. Kouloumdjian, "A Model and a Method for Logical Data Base Design," *Proceedings of the Fourth International Conference on Very Large Data Bases,* ed. F.B. Yau (New York: IEEE Computer Society, 1978), pp. 333-41.

6. G. Estrin, "A Methodology for the Design of Digital Systems — Supported by SARA at the Age of One," *Proceedings of the 1978 National Computer Conference,* Vol. 47 (Montvale, N.J.: AFIPS Press, 1978), pp. 313-32.

7. M.A. Jackson, *Principles of Program Design* (London: Academic Press, 1975).

8. Y. Futamura, T. Kawai, H. Horikoshi, and M. Tsutsumi, "Development of Computer Programs by PAD (Problem Analysis Diagram)," *Proceedings of the Fifth International Software Engineering Conference* (New York: IEEE Computer Society, 1981), pp. 325-32.

CHAPTER 6
Representing Software Behavior

*Which most quickly leads
to understanding a system:
a description of how it works,
or of what it does?*

−L.P.

One of the first tools for documenting software − the flowchart − was developed from the belief that a program should be documented *after* it was written. Today, with the benefit of a quarter-century's experience, our view is that program design and documentation must precede coding. But, even with the proliferation of modern programming practices, we still tend to support the use of the flowchart and its derivatives as tools for software design representation.

In this chapter, we will examine several software design representation schemes that capture the behavior or dynamic properties of the design, and, presumably, the code. As with other inventions, the needs of the particular problem environment prompted the creation of each scheme; hence, each addresses problems about which its own creator was most concerned. The suitability of a scheme to problems in other environments is an issue not often addressed by its author, but the issue is of primary concern to the users. In this chapter, we will summarize the attributes of each approach and provide guidelines on its use, potential modifiability, and compatibility with other schemes.

The software design representation schemes described in this chapter will be demonstrated using two types of examples. One will illustrate the way in which the scheme represents basic constructs. The other type will show the application of the scheme to a simple SORT algorithm. In this way, a comprehensive view of the capabilities of each scheme will be provided. The SORT algorithm used throughout this chapter is presented first in the form of pseudocode in the next section.

6.1 Pseudocode

Pseudocode may be the oldest software design representation scheme still in widespread use today. It has undergone considerable changes with the advent of more modern software design and development practices. Many forms of pseudocode have been suggested [1, 2, 3], but no standard or unique form of pseudocode has been widely adopted. Hence, the form used in this book possesses the traits of several schemes.

6.1.1 Concept

Any sort of an English-like statement of a program that does not require the same degree of syntactic and semantic restriction as a programming language is a potential candidate for pseudocode. The basic idea is to permit the designer to capture rapidly and conveniently the important elements of the design, and to do so in such a way as to give him maximum flexibility. This flexibility is important, for the demands of the semantics and syntax of a programming language inhibit the creation and translation processes involved in transferring a concept from the designer's mind to paper. The myriad of illogical restrictions, such as variable naming conventions, restricted use of keywords, and maximum statement length, inhibit this information transfer. The use of a relaxed, almost casual, medium of expression enhances this process. Later, such undisciplined meanderings will be refined, reviewed, and coded or put into a codable form. Each designer/programmer has personal preferences that result in pseudocode of one form or another. Many software designers employ pseudocode whose syntax and semantics are identical to some programming language preprocessor, but this practice has several potential hazards that will be discussed in Section 6.1.3.

6.1.2 Notation

There is currently no pseudocode standard notation equivalent to the American National Standards Institute (ANSI) standards for programming languages. Some specialists in software design have chosen to utilize the Pascal, Algol, or other programming language syntax and semantics as a standard, while others have proposed their own. However, nearly all of these possess the following common characteristics:

- o keywords to denote specific constructs (e.g., IF-THEN-ELSE, UNTIL-DO, SELECT, or CASE)

- o delimiters to specify the range or extent of a construct (e.g., ENDIF, ENDDO, or ENDSELECT)

- o free-form naming of variables and process descriptions (e.g., IF x < SIGNAL-THRESHOLD, ADJUST AMORTIZATION-SCHEDULE-B-VERSION-1.6)

- o elimination or minimal use of GOTOs or GOTO-like constructs, such as EXIT-BLOCK

- o visual delineation of the extent and nesting-level of pseudocode statements, usually by a fixed amount of indentation per level of nesting

- o restriction of the number of lines of pseudocode that any single module or process can contain

- o hierarchical organization of blocks of pseudocode via calls, co-routines, or other mechanisms

- o syntax and/or semantics that approximate a programming language; features akin to PL/I, FORTRAN, and COBOL are probably the most popular at this time

One set of pseudocode formatting conventions is presented in Fig. 6.1.

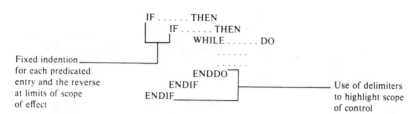

Figure 6.1. Some common notational conventions for pseudocode.

6.1.3 Use

Pseudocode does not involve a specific syntax and/or semantics, the use of a special template, or other inhibitions of the designer's imagination. But all of this freedom does produce some difficulties: First, the proximity of pseudocode's appearance to that of code can lead to coding under the guise of designing, unless much self-discipline is exercised. The lack of universal standards can lead to communication difficulties within the design team unless team members have a working set of guidelines. Individual styles have to be made subservient to overall project needs.

This design representation scheme does provide a relatively easy means of employing modern programming practices without the designer's getting bogged down in language details. It communicates the complexity contained in a program design on a local, segment-by-segment basis. Overall system structure can be communicated using some other more global scheme such as the design tree. An example of one form of pseudocode is presented in Fig. 6.2. The SORT algorithm in Fig. 6.2 will be used throughout the remainder of this chapter to demonstrate the use of dynamic software design representation schemes.

```
UNTIL NEXCH = 0 DO
    NEXCH = 0
    FOR I = 1 UNTIL NITEMS - 1 DO
        IF ITEM(I) > ITEM(I + 1) THEN
            EXCHANGE ITEM(I) WITH ITEM(I + 1)
            NEXCH = NEXCH + 1
        ENDIF
    ENDDO
ENDDO
```

Figure 6.2. A version of pseudocode to depict our SORT algorithm.

6.2 Flowcharts

The flowchart is probably the most widely used, misused, and misunderstood design representation scheme in use today. It has resulted in many derivatives, some of which are presented later in this chapter. The flowchart was originally developed by John von Neumann, who intended it to be an accurate means of documenting a completed program, not a design representation scheme. Since von Neumann's time, the use of the flowchart has been further legitimized through the efforts of the ANSI [4]. The flowcharts presented here employ the ANSI format.

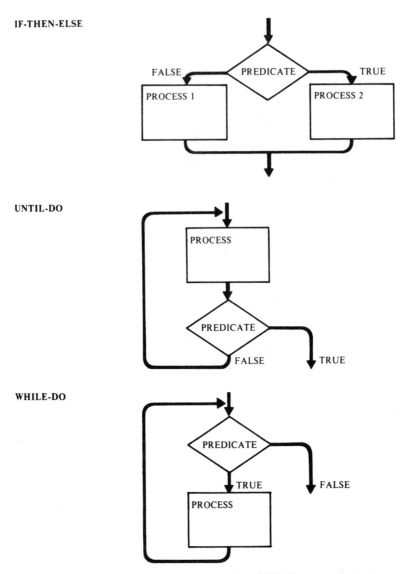

Figure 6.3. Some basic constructs using the ANSI flowcharting scheme.

6.2.1 Concept

The ANSI flowchart depicts the details of control flow by using different symbols for processes, decisions, and entry and termination points. There are no requirements that some specific set of constructs be employed. Hence, any type of control transfer supported by a programming language or algorithm may be represented by the flowchart.

6.2.2 Notation

Primarily, this scheme uses three symbols: the rectangle, the rhombus or diamond, and a directed line. Other symbols are used to depict manual operations and external or hardware interfaces. The rectangle is used to represent arithmetic operations or processes, such as $n = n + 1$, $x = ab$, and *reset end-of-file flag*.

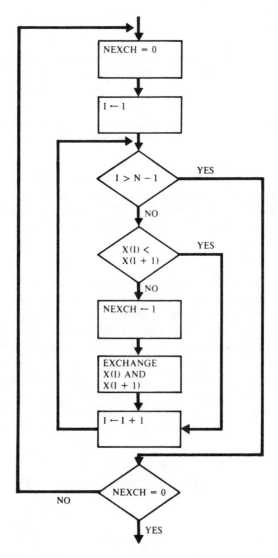

Figure 6.4. SORT **example using an ANSI flowchart.**

The diamond shape is used to stand for decision points, for example, *end-of-file flag set?, n = 0?, x − ab?*. The directed line indicates the flow of control or precedence in a flow sequence.

6.2.3 Use

Several of the basic control constructs in a flowchart are shown in Fig. 6.3. Some of these can be combined to portray our SORT algorithm (Fig. 6.4).

Like pseudocode, the flowchart requires self-discipline on the part of the software designer, for the designer must know all of the details about the execution or behavior of the system before he can effectively use this scheme. This can present a dilemma, because often the design problem being solved is not yet fully understood, let alone the details of the program to solve it. Hence, the designer is usually forced into making decisions and assumptions concerning the details of system execution before he can accurately do so. Such assumptions may often disagree with reality as the user knows it, and the rest of the scenario is all too familiar.

Flowcharts are very effective at depicting the execution details of a single code segment within a system. The charts tend to be somewhat monolithic, however, and only imply data flow and data structure. In today's environment, these data issues are more important than ever and need to be expressed explicitly. Thus, flowcharts enhance our understanding of the control logic on a small, local basis at the expense of a more global perception of a system. Perhaps von Neumann was right, and we should not use flowcharts until after the program is running!

6.3 Control graphs

An adaptation of concepts from automata theory, control graphs have proved useful in program design and development [5, 6, 7], particularly in making explicit the execution details of the design (and of the eventual program).

6.3.1 Concept

The basic notion utilized by control graphs is that a program can exist in any one (and only one) of several possible states at a given time. The transfer of control or transition from one state to another must have a cause, and may have an effect, which is external to the state (see Fig. 6.5). From a software design standpoint, the concept of state can be thought of as equivalent to that of a process, with causes and effects as the controlling factors associated with a process acquiring or relinquishing control. Under certain conditions, these diagrams are also referred to as transition diagrams. Beginning with a high-level, control-graph description of a process, we can add more detail through decomposition. The hierarchy developed in this way allows users of this technique to effectively control the level of detail and complexity with which they must deal.

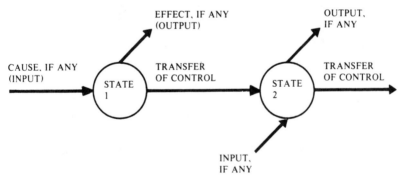

Figure 6.5. Cause and effect relationship in control graphs.

In the figure, control may be transferred from state 1 to state 2 merely because state 2 is the next in a sequence and not necessarily because of some input to state 1. The output of state 1 is not necessarily the input to state 2. Also, conditions encountered in a state are the basis for transfer of control and for inputs and outputs (the potential causes and effects, respectively).

6.3.2 *Notation*

The design tree is typically used in conjunction with this scheme to describe the hierarchy, as shown in Fig. 6.6. The figure also depicts a common labeling convention. The label given the parent node is used as a root and the label of the child node is concatenated with it. Hence, a label depicts the lineage or roots of a node. Often, the decimal point or some other symbol is used to demarcate each ancestral generation or hierarchy level contained in the label. Letters or numbers may be used, depending on the designer's preference. The effect is the same, however, in that the resulting node has a unique label that precisely states its position in the hierarchy.

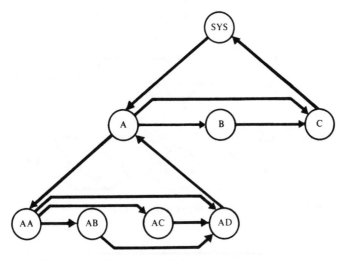

Figure 6.6. Design tree form of a control graph.

The control graph is composed of node symbols, directed arcs, and labels (Fig. 6.6). Combinations of these can be used to depict constructs such as SEQUENCE, IF-THEN-ELSE, loops like WHILE-DO, and CASE or SELECT (Fig. 6.7). Arc labels (as in Fig. 6.8) provide the designer with a means of documenting the reasons, causes, and effects associated with each transfer of control. The associated reason is referred to as a condition, such as *end-of-flag set*. The associated cause is referred to as the associated input to the node from which control is being relinquished, while the associated effect is referred to as the associated output from the node relinquishing control.

6.3.3 *Use*

The main advantage of using control graphs is that concepts from automata theory can be applied to establish that all nodes in a system of graphs can be reached, and that, once any graph is entered, it can be exited. An example of the use of this scheme, including the basic elements of the control graph, is shown in Fig. 6.8. Applying this scheme to larger, more complex problems will involve several levels of decomposition.

In actual practice, this scheme results in an abstract program model, and not necessarily one that represents the physical or implementable characteristics of the design. The reason is that many of the nodes in the control graph and design tree are conceptual entities, introduced to further clarify and document the design without a corresponding element in the delivered system. This is a reasonable approach for the logical design of software, but not, however, for the physical design.

Other factors present serious difficulties. For example, data flow and data structure issues are masked nearly as well in a control graph as in a flowchart. Also, the mathematical analysis of such charts only serves to ensure the absence of certain classes of errors, not to show whether the design will meet the user's needs. Because this scheme is not palatable to most users, we cannot effectively establish through the user that perceived needs are going to be met. However, the control graph approach has proved effective when used on small, complex executive routines whose reliability is essential.

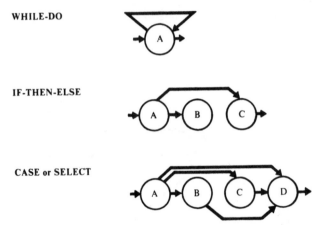

Figure 6.7. Basic constructs represented in the form of control graphs.

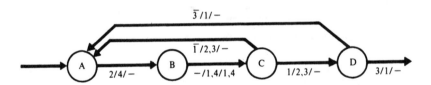

Notation convention:
condition/input/output

PROCESS DESCRIPTIONS

A EXAMINE PAIRS OF ITEMS FOR EXCHANGE
B EXCHANGE I^{TH} AND I^{TH} + 1 ITEMS AND BUMP EXCHANGE COUNTER BY +1
C CHECK IF ARRAY HAS BEEN COMPLETELY EXAMINED
D CHECK IF ARRAY IS NOW IN ORDER

CONDITION DESCRIPTIONS

1. ALL OF THE ITEMS HAVE BEEN EXAMINED
2. I^{TH} AND I^{TH} + 1 ITEMS MUST BE EXCHANGED
3. NO EXCHANGES HAVE BEEN MADE

DATA ELEMENT DESCRIPTIONS

1. NUMBER OF EXCHANGES
2. ITEM NUMBER (INDEX)
3. NUMBER OF ITEMS
4. ITEM ARRAY

Figure 6.8. SORT example using control graph approach.

6.4 Decision tables

Decision tables have been used in other engineering applications to analyze and describe deterministic systems and to sort out confusing decision-making problems. Their use in programming dates back to the days of wired logic and telephone-switching problems [8]. Although other forms of the decision table are useful, for the sake of brevity we will limit our discussion to the most common form of decision tables: limited-entry decision tables.

6.4.1 Concept

Decision tables have been shown to be useful in program design and can take many different forms [9, 10]. These all stem from the same basic notion that, for each possible combination of situations that a system (or program) can encounter, the system's response is known. These situations are referred to as *conditions,* while system responses are referred to as *actions.* For every condition or set of conditions that can occur, one and only one action or set of actions is possible: The response of the system is known with certainty.

6.4.2 Notation

The basic decision table consists of two portions — the condition stub and the action stub. Conditions are collected, and optionally labeled, in the condition stub, while actions are collected, and optionally labeled, in the action stub. Conditions and actions are most often described horizontally. Vertical columns in the condition stub are used to identify the conditions that apply in a given instance. A corresponding column in the action stub describes the system's response (see Fig. 6.9).

Condition stub

Condition 1	Y	N	Y	—	—
Condition 2	N	—	—	Y	Y
.	.	.	.	.	.
.	.	.	.	.	.
.	.	.	.	.	.
Condition n	Y	—	N	—	Y

Action stub

Action 1	X	—	X	X	—
.	.	.	.	.	.
.	.	.	.	.	.
.	.	.	.	.	.
Action n	—	—	X	—	X

KEY

Y = Yes

N = No

— = Does not apply or is logically precluded due to other conditions

X = Action initiated

Figure 6.9. Condition and action stubs in decision tables.

6.4.3 Use

An example of the use of a decision table to describe the dynamics of a program design, specifically to portray the actions of a real-time executive, is presented in Fig. 6.10. In such applications as this, the importance of accounting for all possibilities justifies the tedium of developing and maintaining even large tables. Although it has been used successfully to provide an exhaustive (and perhaps exhausting) portrayal of a program, it does so at the expense of comprehension. Moreover, there is no general indication of execution flow, data transfer, or database interaction; only the cold, binary documentation of system responses to stimuli is shown. Although such deterministic attributes are a definite plus in certain applications, the decision-table user would do well to augment this scheme with a complementary one or to use it only in carefully chosen design applications.

		1	2	3	4	5
A	Start	Y	N	N	N	N
B	Number of exchanges = 0	–	–	N	Y	–
C	Array index within limits	–	Y	N	N	Y
D	Indexed pair out of order	–	Y	–	–	N
E	Reset start flag	X	–	–	–	–
F	Initialize number of exchanges = 0 and set array index = 1	X	–	X	–	–
G	Exchange array elements and set exchange flag	–	X	–	–	–
H	Increment array index	–	X	–	–	X
I	Exit	–	–	–	X	–

Figure 6.10. SORT example using decision table.

6.5 Dill, Hopson, and Dixon approach

The Dill, Hopson, and Dixon design representation approach originated at Brown University as an aid for students learning programming techniques [11]. It has been used as the standard format for flowcharting in such introductory courses.

6.5.1 Concept

The basic concept employed in the Dill, Hopson, and Dixon approach is not unlike that of a flowchart. Flow is generally from top to bottom with loops, sequences, and decision points graphically depicted. However, this scheme explicitly portrays levels of nesting (in which a process is conducted within or subordinate to another), the extent or range of loops, and the point at which a loop is exited. Loop exiting is not restricted. A loop may be exited at any point within a nesting level. As in the case of flowcharts, data flow and data structure are only implied by this technique.

6.5.2 Notation

The notational elements used in this scheme are nearly identical to those of the flowchart (Section 6.2.2). An element unique to this scheme is the explicit loop exit, which consists of a triangular textual notation to identify the point at which a loop is exited and at what level of nesting. This notation more clearly depicts those points in the flow at which processing "pops" to the next higher level of nesting.

6.5.3 Use

The use of the Dill, Hopson, and Dixon approach is similar to that of the flowchart, with two important differences: One is that the range of each explicit or implicit loop and the point at which it is exited must be identified before or during diagramming. The second is that each level of nesting must be identified. Once these two aspects of the diagram have been established, they are arranged and displayed in hierarchical order. That is, the outermost process (e.g., a DO-LOOP) is diagrammed first on the leftmost portion of the page, the next outermost, and so on. The extent of each level is graphically portrayed on the diagram (see Fig. 6.11). An example of the use of this technique is presented in Fig. 6.12. Note how this technique communicates the relative level of complexity and explicitly portrays the effects of specific results from nested processes.

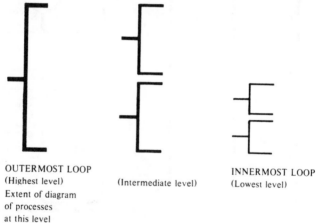

OUTERMOST LOOP
(Highest level)
Extent of diagram
of processes
at this level

(Intermediate level)

INNERMOST LOOP
(Lowest level)

**Figure 6.11. Displaying nesting and loop extent
in the Dill, Hopson, and Dixon approach.**

6.6 Ferstl diagrams

The Ferstl software design representation scheme was developed to support program development by stepwise refinement and to aid in coding and testing [12].

6.6.1 Concept

The Ferstl diagram is a derivative of the ANSI flowchart [13]. The intent of this particular derivative is to extend flowchart notation by introducing an additional control symbol. The overall effect is to depict a program in a tree-like structure, which aids in its construction and testing.

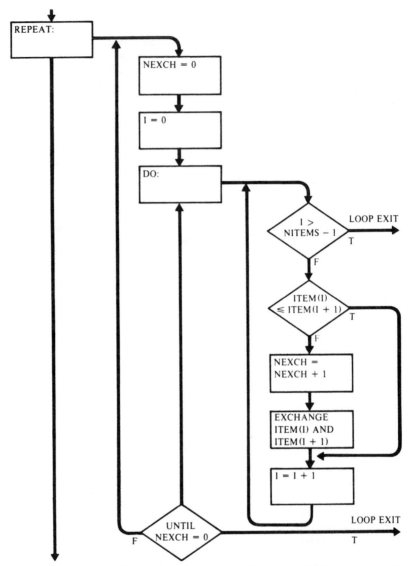

Figure 6.12. SORT **example using the Dill, Hopson, and Dixon approach.**

The claimed advantages of using the Ferstl approach are the parallel development of the control structure and the refinement of a program task; the emphasis on the use of basic control structures and only restricted use of GOTO statements; the improved definition of the scope of data; the relatively easy translation of these charts into code; and the simplified correctness-checking.

6.6.2 Notation

The notation used in Ferstl diagrams is identical to the ANSI flowchart symbols for input/output, process, predefined process, connector, and decision. However, a hexagonal symbol is used to describe conditions, as shown in Fig. 6.13. Parallel processes and the restricted use of GOTOs are also addressed in this technique (refer to Fig. 6.14).

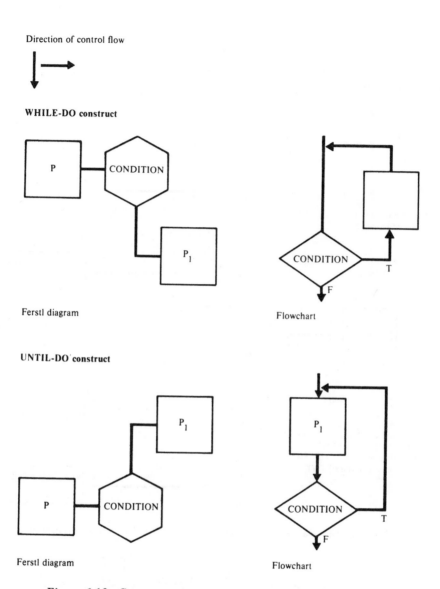

Figure 6.13. Some notational conventions in Ferstl diagrams.

6.6.3 Use

Ferstl diagrams provide many of the same features as the flowchart. The adaptation of some symbology to aid the representation of parallel processes and multiple exit loops is helpful in such applications, but the absence of a means of explicitly depicting data flow is a shortcoming. The heavy emphasis on control structure and flow make it a likely candidate for localized (program-level, not system-level) problems that emphasize control issues. An example of the use of this scheme is presented in Fig. 6.15.

Parallel processing

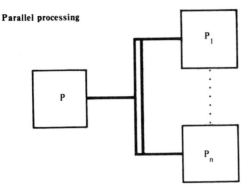

P is composed of $P_1, \ldots, P_n$, which are
executed in parallel.

Iteration

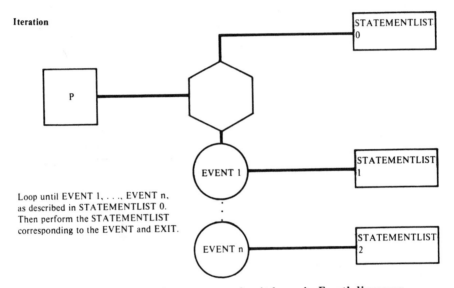

Loop until EVENT 1, . . ., EVENT n,
as described in STATEMENTLIST 0.
Then perform the STATEMENTLIST
corresponding to the EVENT and EXIT.

Figure 6.14. Parallel processes and exit loops in Ferstl diagrams.

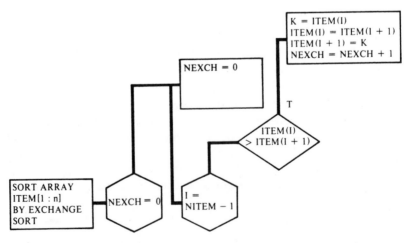

Figure 6.15. SORT example using Ferstl diagram approach.

6.7 GREENPRINT

GREENPRINT is a block-structured diagrammatic approach to modeling programs, which was originally developed as an aid to program maintenance. It has been shown to be an effective means of enhancing a programmer's understanding of code developed by others, and has been used successfully as a program design tool [14].

6.7.1 Concept

GREENPRINT provides the designer with the graphic means to depict not only the basic constructs but also the GOTO construct. It greatly facilitates the reduction and possibly the elimination of the GOTO, if that is desired, but also depicts the structural implications of such a restructuring of the design. Basic concepts such as scope of control and nesting levels are addressed by GREENPRINT. The emphasis in this scheme on rapid assimilation and explicit depiction of the implications of proposed structural changes closely parallels the issues of software design. The need for a graphic means of capturing and externalizing the structural essence of the existing program has resulted in a notation well suited to program design.

6.7.2 Notation

GREENPRINT's notation of boxes, connecting and directed line segments, and some special symbols was designed for ease of implementation on a line printer. Nesting levels are indicated by a shift of position from left to right. Unlike many of the schemes presented in this chapter, GREENPRINT separates the graphic or symbolic portrayal of the design from the actual description. Specifically, the graphics appear to the left of the textual description of the process so as to facilitate synchronization of existing code with graphics in maintenance programming, but also to enable the software designer to inspect the structural characteristics almost completely apart from the procedural ones. This separation is definitely an advantage when one considers that the most troublesome (and probably expensive) type of design problem to remedy is of a structural, rather than a procedural, nature. The symbols for the basic constructs and the GOTO are shown in Fig. 6.16.

6.7.3 Use

The initial use of this approach was in program maintenance, where it helped fill the need for an easy-to-use notation that would reveal the structure of existing programs to maintenance programmers. GREENPRINT supports the concepts inherent in current software design technology, while recognizing that not all applications or target programming languages will support strict adherence to basic constructs. It addresses this flexibility in construct and complexity by including a formulated measure of program complexity. The comprehension complexity is given by

$$c = \frac{S}{P_{total}} \sum_{p=1}^{P_{total}} N_p$$

where N is the total number of occupied columns in row ρ, ρ_{total} is the number of rows in the GREENPRINT, and S is the total number of program statements. Hence, for our SORT algorithm,

$$c = \frac{9}{7} \sum_{\rho=1}^{7} (1 + 2 + 3 + 3 + 4 + 5 + 5) = \frac{207}{7}$$

The GREENPRINT formula provides the designer with yet another way to evaluate the relative quality of a program design in its pseudocode form.

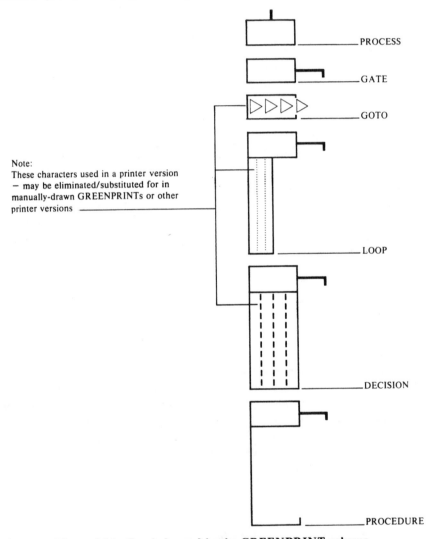

Note:
These characters used in a printer version
— may be eliminated/substituted for in
manually-drawn GREENPRINTs or other
printer versions

PROCESS

GATE

GOTO

LOOP

DECISION

PROCEDURE

Figure 6.16. Symbols used in the GREENPRINT scheme.

GREENPRINT is an excellent example of an "engineered" notation, in that it was designed to be effective within a certain set of operating parameters. However, when used manually, it can require a lot of horizontal and vertical space to depict relatively simple modules. Its use in maintenance has been enhanced by the development of a program that can generate GREENPRINTs from PL/I code. An example of the application of GREENPRINT is shown in Fig. 6.17.

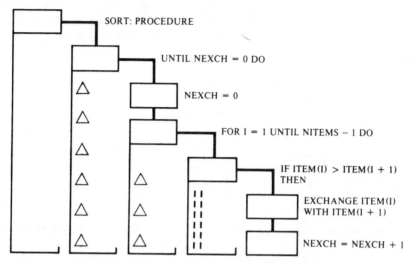

Figure 6.17. SORT example using GREENPRINT.

6.8 Hamilton-Zeldin approach

The Hamilton-Zeldin scheme was originally devised in support of the National Aeronautic and Space Administration's Space Shuttle software development [15]. It has been further refined and enhanced and is now supported by an automated flowcharting tool [16]. Hamilton-Zeldin diagrams are called structured design diagrams (not to be confused with the *structured design method,* discussed in Chapter 8).

6.8.1 Concept

Although the original intent of the Hamilton-Zeldin approach was to support the use of high-level languages, it can be employed in other applications. The objectives of this scheme include

- explicitly depicting the levels of nesting (and, hence, complexity) inherent in the design structure

- depicting all processes in an algorithmic manner (as opposed to employing explanatory text)

- demonstrating the extent, or scope of control or effect, of all loops

- supporting and encouraging the use of the basic constructs and their alternative forms

The basic effect of this scheme is that both the software designer and his customer can follow sequences of equations to determine whether they are appropriate, while gaining an appreciation for the relationships between different parts of a software system.

6.8.2 Notation

Structured design diagrams are composed of rectangles, directed lines, and a pentagonal combination of a rectangle and triangle. Execution is generally from top to bottom in the diagram, with the exception of IF tests and DO-LOOPS, which proceed from left to right with each occurrence. This arrangement clearly shows the level of nesting. Each of the graphic forms contains an algebraic statement or test, as appropriate. The notational conventions used by this scheme are shown in Fig. 6.18.

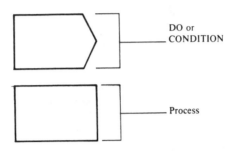

Figure 6.18. Notational conventions used in the Hamilton-Zeldin approach.

6.8.3 Use

The Hamilton-Zeldin approach is used in a manner similar to the Dill, Hopson, and Dixon scheme: Levels of nesting and the sequence of operations occurring within each level are established at the outset and then the diagrams can be drawn. In the Hamilton-Zeldin approach, though, the diagram semantics have been simplified, so that only two basic types of symbols are employed. One symbol depicts control transfers restricted only to IF and DO constructs or their derivatives. The other symbol depicts processes (Fig. 6.19). But note that the flow of data is not explicitly portrayed. As in the case of the flowchart, this is a worthwhile attribute if the primary issue lies in the control structure and flow. However, most present-day applications necessitate the use of a scheme that can aid the designer in addressing data-oriented problems.

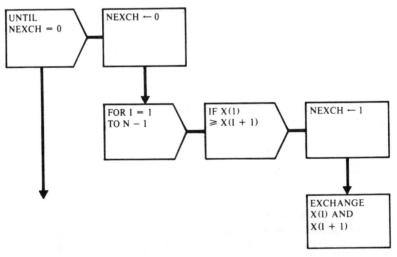

Figure 6.19. SORT example using Hamilton-Zeldin approach.

6.9 Nassi-Shneiderman approach

The Nassi-Shneiderman diagram was introduced as a means of syntactically enforcing the use of three basic program constructs: sequence, decision, and loop. Since its introduction [17], it has been modified [18, 19] and incorporated into an interactive graphics system to aid software design [20].

6.9.1 Concept

Nassi-Shneiderman diagrams are a conceptual departure from flowchart-based techniques. They aid in the adherence to the use of programming structures other than the GOTO. A single process is completely contained within a rectangular box, which is subdivided into sections. Each section denotes a specific sub-process (e.g., an assignment or decision). A hierarchy of such diagrams can be established and maintained using subroutine calls or dummy processes that refer to other diagrams. The range of a loop, the basis and effect of a decision, and the general sequence of the process flow are all explicit in this scheme.

6.9.2 Notation

Nassi-Shneiderman diagrams consist of rectangles and triangles. These each contain a statement of the operation performed and are arranged so as to define process flow. The use of these symbols is shown in Fig. 6.20 and an example is presented in Fig. 6.21.

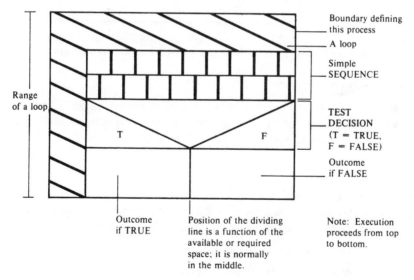

Figure 6.20. Use of symbols in the Nassi-Shneiderman approach.

6.9.3 Use

As with other diagrammatic techniques, the use of Nassi-Shneiderman diagrams should begin with a high-level description of the program. Distinct processes may be identified and refined by developing more detailed diagrams. Although the notation itself is quite simple and unrestrictive as to diagram size and complexity, this approach has several practical shortcomings. For instance, the very nature of software design is change; most of all, our design diagrams change. This approach is such that seemingly insignificant changes in an algorithm will necessitate an entire diagram (and perhaps related diagrams) to be redone. If this scheme is not supported by an automated aid, even a small project will have logistics problems utilizing it as the primary means of expressing software designs. Also, the programming languages most commonly used in industry today support the GOTO. Hence, the use of this approach may lead to awkward modifications of the notation, either in the design or implementation. However, this design representation scheme is easy to learn and understand, and it aids in the rapid and effective validation of designs.

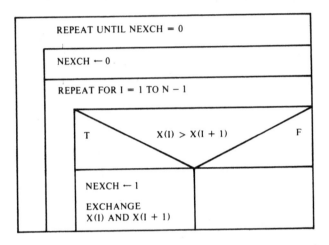

Figure 6.21. SORT example using Nassi-Shneiderman diagram.

6.10 Problem analysis diagram

The Problem Analysis Diagram (PAD) was intended as an improvement over Warnier diagrams (see Chapter 8). It was developed and has been utilized in software development at the Hitachi Corporation, Japan, since 1973 [21].

6.10.1 Concept

The PAD representation scheme is designed to be a two-dimensional, tree-structured representation of programs that lends itself to easy and rapid translation into code. It offers the following advantages over Warnier diagrams:

- more flexible control structure
- easier coding directly from the diagram
- flow-oriented, less flowchart-like diagrams

PAD notation restricts the software designer to a basic set of programming constructs consisting of sequence, repetition, and selection. PAD recognizes that the GOTO or its equivalent is an intrinsic part of many programming languages, and addresses the problem through the use of extensions to PAD, as well as the possible incorporation of some flowchart-like notation. Use of these variations within the PAD notational framework is up to the user. PAD can also be used to describe data relationships (see Section 5.8).

6.10.2 *Notation*

PAD employs five symbols, one each for depicting repetition, selection, process, statement-label, and definition (Fig. 6.22). It can also be used to show parallel processing (Fig. 6.23), as well as basic constructs (Fig. 6.24).

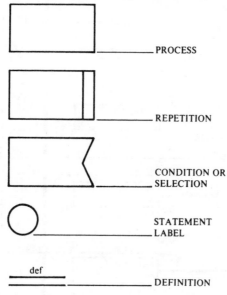

Figure 6.22. Graphic symbols used in PAD.

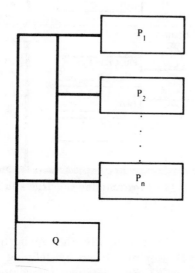

Figure 6.23. PAD meaning "Do P_1, . . ., P_i in parallel, then do Q."

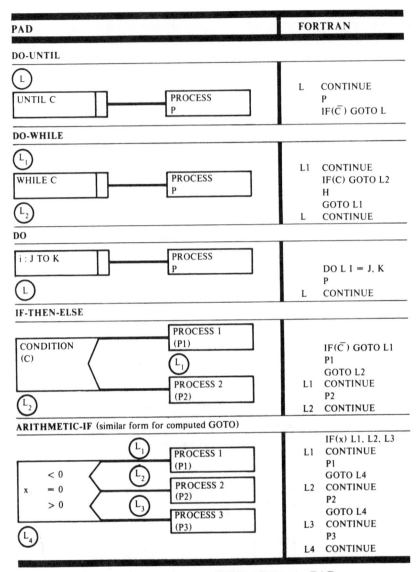

Figure 6.24. Programming constructs in PAD.

6.10.3 Use

PAD notation enhances and supports the application of top-down, stepwise refinement concepts. A PAD user may begin by defining a high-level view of a program or group of programs, adding more detail as it becomes known through the use of the *def* symbol (Figs. 6.22 and 6.25). The combination of the vertical display of sequence information with the horizontal depiction of branching and nesting levels presents a compact view of a program with characteristics similar to those of the Hamilton-Zeldin approach (Section 6.8).

However, PAD explicitly addresses the issue of translating PAD diagrams into code through the use of symbols that indicate GOTOs. Such constructs are integral to the two most widely used industrial programming languages — FORTRAN and COBOL. Any representation scheme that forces the software designer to interpret the graphic design creatively in order to implement it in a programming language may con- tribute to the loss of conceptual integrity in the design. PAD clearly addresses this is- sue, but its graphics may not lend themselves to use as an analysis and customer review tool. PAD represents a unique combination of graphic/conceptual issues, in that the primary graphic emphasis is on basic control structures developed by Böhm and Jacopini [22], while the secondary emphasis is on the realities of implementation. Hence, in viewing the PAD representation of a program such as that of Fig. 6.26, the reader is presented with the control structures of the program in IF-THEN-ELSE and DO-LOOP terms, but is also made aware of implementation implications.

a) Initial PAD Chart

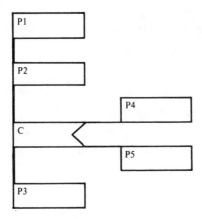

b) Refinement of P2 using the def symbol

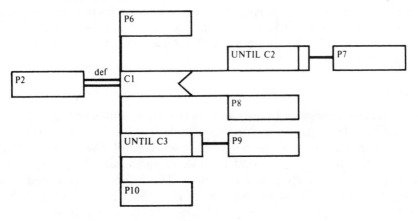

Figure 6.25. Use of the definition feature in PAD.

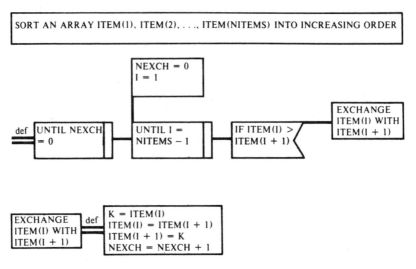

Figure 6.26. SORT **example using PAD.**

6.11 Structured control-flow and top-down

The Structured Control-flow And Top-down (SCAT) approach was developed to support the concept of top-down structured programming, and to aid program implementation and testing [23].

6.11.1 Concept

The SCAT design representation scheme has been classified as a derivation of the flowchart [24], but it retains few characteristics of it, including vertical depiction of control flow, and the use of rectangles to contain and partition subsets of the overall process. Levels of nesting are portrayed explicitly with loop entry and exit points clearly shown. The conditions and actions associated with the IF construct are depicted in a compact manner, which aids readability and comprehension. Data flow and structure are not shown explicitly.

6.11.2 Notation

SCAT utilizes rectangles to contain processes and connecting straight lines to depict control flow. The relative position of a rectangle indicates its position in the sequence of execution. Arrows are not used since control flows from top to bottom. Each rectangle is labeled or numbered for ease of reference. The beginning of a process can be labeled by subdividing a rectangle. The beginning, end, and range of DO-LOOPS are indicated by an auxiliary notation on the rectangles. IF tests and the outcome actions are also given special treatment. The test and the action to be taken if true or if false are shown explicitly. Only the default (e.g., TRUE shown and FALSE not shown) is implicit. Examples of these notational features are presented in Fig. 6.27.

Basic syntax

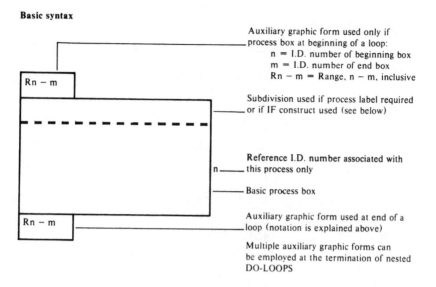

Auxiliary graphic form used only if
process box at beginning of a loop:
  n = I.D. number of beginning box
  m = I.D. number of end box
  Rn − m = Range, n − m, inclusive

Subdivision used if process label required
or if IF construct used (see below)

Reference I.D. number associated with
this process only

Basic process box

Auxiliary graphic form used at end of a
loop (notation is explained above)

Multiple auxiliary graphic forms can
be employed at the termination of nested
DO-LOOPS

Portraying an IF-TEST

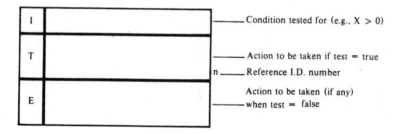

Condition tested for (e.g., X > 0)

Action to be taken if test = true

Reference I.D. number

Action to be taken (if any)
when test = false

Figure 6.27. Notation used by SCAT.

6.11.3 Use

This scheme can be used in the same way one would use the flowchart. The ex-
ceptions are the statement of the range, beginning, and end of loops, the labeled anno-
tation of each process box, and the denotation of IF tests as previously described. The
use of this technique is demonstrated in Fig. 6.28. Note that adherence to a specific set
of constructs is not as strictly enforced as in other schemes (e.g., the Nassi-
Shneiderman approach in Section 6.9).

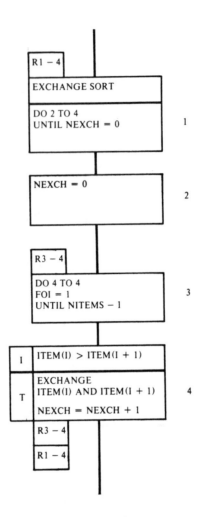

Figure 6.28. SORT **example using SCAT.**

6.12 Structured flowcharting approach

Structured flowcharting is an example of an adaptation of the flowchart to support structured programming concepts [25]. It is representative of many such approaches that are in use.

6.12.1 Concept

The structured flowcharting scheme is designed to reduce labels and unstructured branching, encourage a single-entry/single-exit approach, aid in the use of top-down design techniques, and enhance modularization. The approach encourages the designer to conceive of the system in high-level constructs and not in terms of individual detailed statements. For example, the use of off-page connectors is avoided through the addition of code expansions, which are referred to in a "Remarks" section adjacent to the diagram itself. This section aids the reviewer to understand what is in the diagram. The top-level diagram refers to several code expansions or modules, but there is not a one-to-one correspondence between modules on the diagrams and modules in the system.

6.12.2 Notation

With the exception of the use of a remarks column and references to code expansions, the notation employed by this scheme is identical to the ANSI flowchart. An example of the notation used by this technique is presented in Fig. 6.29.

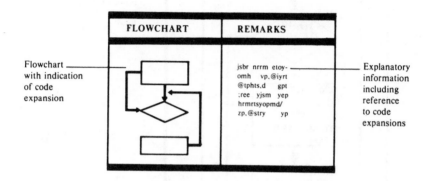

Figure 6.29. Notation used in the structured flowcharting approach.
Note: Nonsense type is used to represent actual variables supplied by the user of the method.

6.12.3 Use

Structured flowcharting has most of the positive and negative attributes associated with the use of the ANSI flowcharting scheme. There is no syntactic enforcement of the more desirable practices and, hence, the designer is left to proceed on his own good behavior. Again, as with flowcharts, the level of detail is clearly too great to provide anything more than local insights, while database structure and data flow are unaddressed. This can lead to a well-proceduralized but not coherent system design. However, when used properly, this approach is superior to the much-maligned flowchart. An example of the application of this technique is presented in Fig. 6.30.

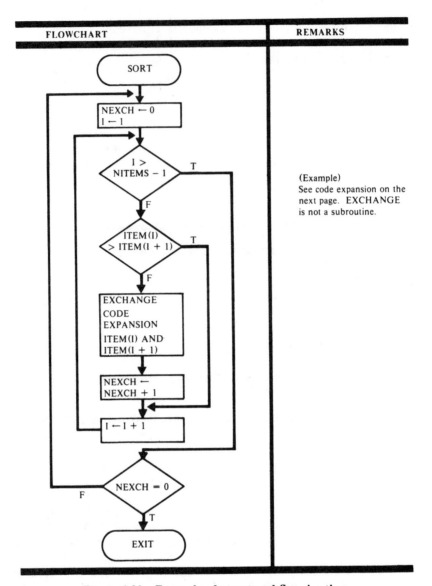

FLOWCHART	REMARKS

(Example)
See code expansion on the
next page. EXCHANGE
is not a subroutine.

Figure 6.30. Example of structured flowcharting.

6.13 Transaction diagrams

After several years of use in England, the transaction diagram was introduced to this country in 1975 [26]. It is intended to create self-documenting program design.

6.13.1 Concept

Transaction diagrams give the software designer carte blanche in utilizing pseudocode-like statements at once to define and to design his program. The narrative statements can be as descriptive or as cryptic as the designer wishes. The nesting of processes or subprocesses is explicit. The sequence of execution is depicted as proceeding from top to bottom in any process. Data flow and data structure are not depicted explicitly.

6.13.2 Notation

Transaction diagrams consist of labeled or, more accurately, titled boxes, each containing some pseudocode-like statement of the details of the process named in the box title. The range of a repeated sequence of statements is indicated by use of a vertical box inside the larger titled box. Nesting is shown explicitly by the relative position of a box on the page — the leftmost being the highest or outer level and the rightmost depicting the lowest or most interior level. A Nassi-Shneiderman-like notation is used to depict the IF construct. The graphics are clarified by Fig. 6.31.

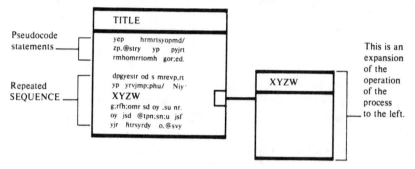

Figure 6.31. Notation of the transaction diagram.
Note: Nonsense type is used to represent actual variables supplied by the user of the method.

6.13.3 Use

Beginning at the highest-level statement of the process, successively add detail to each of the subprocesses by placing refinements (additional details) in boxes to the right. Any type of pseudocode or programming language statements may be used. Be as descriptive and explicit as is appropriate to each level of refinement. An example of the use of this technique is presented in Fig. 6.32. Although the example only depicts expansion of loops, expansions of processes are also possible. In the latter case, the same notation would be used but with the process name in place of the DO-type of statement.

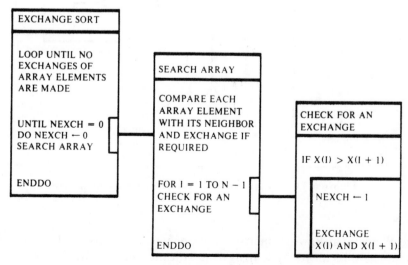

Figure 6.32. SORT example using transaction diagram.

6.14 Weiderman-Rawson approach

The Weiderman-Rawson approach is also a flowchart derivative and is intended to support structured programming concepts [27].

6.14.1 Concept

The Weiderman-Rawson scheme successfully eliminates the use of GOTO constructs in the design phase, providing a syntax that simultaneously depicts nesting levels, the range of loops, and sequence of operations. The approach permits the reviewer to rapidly identify the conditions that must be present in order for a particular portion of the chart to "execute."

6.14.2 Notation

The notation used in this scheme is quite similar to that of the flowchart and other schemes presented in this chapter. However, several important syntactic differences exist. For example, the diagram expands to the right by a fixed amount with each occurrence of nesting in an algorithm. Also, the range or extent of loops — implied or explicit — is indicated with a special termination symbol, as shown in Fig. 6.33.

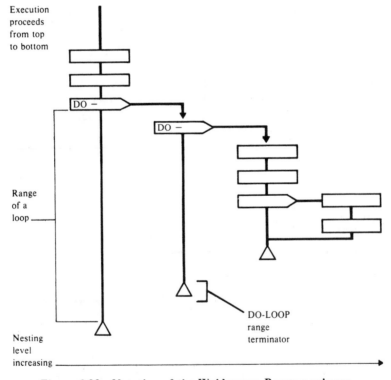

Figure 6.33. Notation of the Weiderman-Rawson scheme.

6.14.3 Use

The Weiderman-Rawson approach does encourage simple, well-structured designs that will be less difficult to implement than with the undisciplined use of the flowchart. However, it does present logistics problems with respect to changes due to the "ripple" or spread of the effects of a change from one part of the diagram to another, and due to the sheer physical size the diagrams can assume. That its notation is similar to that of the flowchart and hence probably familiar to most software designers is an asset. An example of the use of this scheme is presented in Fig. 6.34.

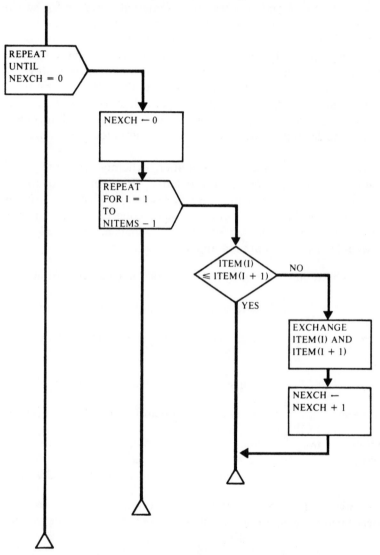

Figure 6.34. SORT **example using the Weiderman-Rawson scheme.**

6.15 Summary of characteristics

The software design representation schemes described in this chapter are composed of graphic and conceptual elements. Each of these factors may be important in a given application. For example, such variables as the information to be displayed and the availability of training all figure strongly in the decision of what representation scheme should be used. A summary of the schemes and their characteristics is shown in Table 6.1. A list of factors related to the efficacy of this chapter's dynamics-oriented software design representation schemes, together with a brief description of each, is presented with the table. Although the evaluations may not agree with the reader's opinion of a favorite representation scheme, the summary chart does provide a basis for comparison. It is best utilized not as an absolute measure but one that provides relative levels to use as a basis for evaluation.

The important role played by these representation schemes for software behavior is underlined by the large number of such schemes that have been proposed. However, this proliferation is most probably due to the fact that it is easier to consider a system design at the microscopic (program) level than at the macroscopic (system) level. Also, it is easier for people to deal with local, specific information than with global, conceptual models. As evidence, consider the small number of system-oriented software representation schemes currently available. Granted, it is important to establish that this detailed view of the system is correct and consistent, but how much more widespread and long lasting are the effects of poor architecture than erroneous implementation?

All of the software design representation schemes presented in this chapter presumably attempt to solve some set of problems. However, few of these schemes are part of a system of representation that depicts system architecture, structure, and database characteristics as well. The benefits of such a coherent set of schemes, capable of cross-checking and aiding development and maintenance, may well prompt the next wave of software design representation approaches.

Characteristics of Software Behavior Representation

Data flow	data communication between program elements
Data structure	organizational and relational properties of the data utilized by a program
Control flow	transfer of control between program elements
Control structure	hierarchy and organization of control relationships
Syntactic adherence to basic constructs	the limitation of program design to sequence, repetition, and decision constructs according to Böhm and Jacopini [22], by means of restricted graphic elements
Distinction between logical and physical form	the ability to represent the program as an abstraction and not in a manner that allows design to approximate coding
Depiction of nesting levels	graphic display of the effects of different conditions and the switches required for a part of the program to acquire control
Real-time interrupts/responses	effects (in real time) of events that may occur during program execution

Table 6.1
Comparison of Software Behavior Representation Schemes

REPRESENTATION APPROACH

REPRESENTATION CHARACTERISTIC	PSEUDOCODE	ANSI FLOWCHART	CONTROL GRAPH	DECISION TABLE	DILL, HOPSON & DIXON	FERSTL DIAGRAM	GREENPRINT	HAMILTON & ZELDIN	NASSI & SHNEIDERMAN	PAD	SCAT	STRUCTURED FLOWCHARTING	TRANSACTION DIAGRAM	WEIDERMAN & RAWSON
DATA FLOW	–	–	I	–	–	–	–	–	–	–	–	–	–	–
DATA STRUCTURE	–	–	–	–	–	–	–	–	–	C	–	–	–	–
CONTROL FLOW	E	E	E	E	E	E	E	E	E	E	E	E	E	E
CONTROL STRUCTURE	I	I	E	–	E	E	E	~	I	E	E	I	E	E
SYNTACTIC ADHERENCE TO BASIC CONSTRUCTS	P	N	N	–	P	Y	N	Y	Y	Y	Y	N	~	Y
DISTINCTION BETWEEN LOGICAL & PHYSICAL FORM	N	N	Y	–	–	~	–	–	–	N	–	N	–	–
DEPICTION OF NESTING LEVELS	Y	N	I	–	Y	Y	Y	Y	Y	Y	Y	Y	N	Y
REAL-TIME INTERRUPTS/RESPONSES	–	–	–	–	–	–	~	–	–	–	–	–	–	–
APPLICATION/BATCH ORIENTATION	~	Y	~	N	Y	~	~	~	Y	~	Y	Y	Y	Y
LINKAGE TO REQUIREMENTS	–	–	–	–	~	–	–	–	–	–	–	–	~	–
TRAINING REQUIRED TO USE EFFECTIVELY	L	L	M	L	L	L	L	L	L	L	L	L	L	L
TUTORIAL MATERIALS AVAILABLE	~	Y	Y	Y	~	~	~	~	~	~	~	~	~	~
ABILITY TO DESCRIBE PARALLEL PROCESSING	P	P	Y	P	P	Y	P	P	–	Y	P	P	–	–
COLLATERAL NOTES	P	P	–	–	–	–	–	–	–	–	–	Y	–	~
AUTOMATED SUPPORT	P	Y	–	–	–	–	–	Y	–	–	–	–	–	–
TRAINING AVAILABILITY	–	–	–	–	–	–	–	–	–	–	–	–	–	–

KEY
I = implied
E = explicit
H = high
M = moderate
~ = somewhat or some
L = low
Y = yes
– = not addressed
C = available in collateral form
N = no
P = potential exists in some cases

Application/batch orientation   the orientation toward depicting single, non-real-time interruptable programs, such as in a batch application

Linkage to requirements   a means of assuring that the design addresses and is responsive to the overall system and program specifications

Training required to use effectively — (self-explanatory)

Tutorial materials available — printed matter, publicly available, that clearly explains the use of the schema

Ability to describe parallel processing — the inherent ability of the schema for graphic depiction of the execution of processes executing in parallel

Collateral notes — a means available to incorporate explanatory material with the graphics

Automated support — availability of a software tool with which to employ a design representation scheme

Training availability — publicly available courses on the use of the technique

EXERCISES: Chapter 6

1.   Analyze the software design representation scheme that you currently use to depict the dynamics of programs, applying the characteristics used in Table 6.1. Given the type of programs developed in your shop, how do its pros and cons compare with those of other schemes that are available?

2.   Each of the schemes described in this chapter possesses a different ability to depict a variety of program design errors. Intentionally insert a bug into a program or pseudocode, and depict this flawed design with three widely different representation schemes. Which displays the bug in the easiest-to-find form? Would this be true of all types of bugs or just the type you chose? Experiment.

3.   Which of the schemes would be easiest for you to transform into code? Why? Which is the hardest? Why? What are the relative assets and liabilities of the use of these?

4.   What software design representation scheme does your shop use the most? Why? Be specific. Which one would you prefer to use? Why? Be specific.

5.   The success of a scheme is dependent in large part on the extent to which it matches the characteristics of the system being designed. Construct a list of properties similar to the one following Table 6.1, but for a specific, non-trivial design problem, preferably one you are currently working on. Set up and use a scoring system to evaluate each dynamic software design representation scheme.

   a.   If the highest-ranking scheme is the one you are now using, what problems or issues does it *not* assist you in solving? What other scheme would be most effective at resolving just those issues? Could these schemes be used in tandem?

   b.   If the highest-ranking scheme is not the one you are currently using, could it be used as an adjunct?

6.   Examine Table 6.1. Draw up a list of properties, based on a current real need, which none of the schemes listed possesses. Incorporate elements of various schemes to form a hybrid scheme with the desired properties.

REFERENCES: Chapter 6

1. R.C. Linger, H.D. Mills, and B.F. Witt, *Structured Programming: Theory and Practice* (Reading, Mass.: Addison-Wesley, 1979).

2. S.H. Caine and E.K. Gordon, "PDL — A Tool for Software Design," *Proceedings of the 1975 National Computer Conference,* Vol. 44 (Montvale, N.J.: AFIPS Press, 1975), pp. 271-76.

3. R.W. Jensen and C.C. Tonies, *Software Engineering* (Englewood Cliffs, N.J.: Prentice-Hall, 1979).

4. N. Chapin, "Flowcharting with the ANSI Standard: A Tutorial," *ACM Computing Surveys,* Vol. 2, No. 2 (June 1970), pp. 119-46.

5. H.B. Burner, "An Application of Automata Theory to the Multiple Level Top Down Design of Digital Computer Operating Systems," Ph.D. Thesis, Washington State University, 1973.

6. L.C. Carpenter, A.S. Kawaguchi, L.J. Peters, and L.L. Tripp, "Systematic Development of Automated Engineering Systems," unpublished paper delivered at the Second Japan-U.S.A. Symposium on Automated Engineering Systems (Tokyo: August 1975).

7. L.C. Carpenter and L.L. Tripp, "Software Design Validation Tool," *Proceedings of the 1975 International Conference on Reliable Software* (New York: IEEE Computer Society, 1975), pp. 395-400.

8. S.L. Pollack, H.T. Hick, Jr., and W.F. Harrison, *Decision Tables: Theory and Practice* (New York: Wiley-Interscience, 1971).

9. H. McDaniel, *An Introduction to Decision Logic Tables* (New York: Petrocelli/Charter, 1978).

10. M. Montalbano, *Decision Tables* (Palo Alto, Calif.: Science Research Associates, 1974).

11. J.M. Dill, R.W. Hopson, and D.F. Dixon, "Design and Documentation Standards" (Providence, R.I.: Brown University, 1975).

12. O. Ferstl, "Flowcharting by Stepwise Refinement," *ACM SIGPLAN Notices,* Vol. 13, No. 1 (January 1978), pp. 34-42.

13. J. Bruno and K. Steiglitz, "The Expression of Algorithms by Charts," *Journal of the Association for Computing Machinery,* Vol. 19, No. 3 (July 1972), pp. 517-25.

14. L.A. Belady, C.J. Evangelisti, and L.R. Power, "GREENPRINT: A Graphic Representation of Structured Programs," *IBM Systems Journal,* Vol. 19, No. 4 (1980), pp. 542-53.

15. M. Hamilton and S. Zeldin, *Top-Down, Bottom-Up, Structured Programming, and Program Structuring,* Charles Stark Draper Laboratory, Document E-2728 (Cambridge, Mass.: Massachusetts Institute of Technology, December 1972).

16.   J. Rood, T. To, and D. Harel, "A Universal Flowcharter," *Proceedings of the NASA/AIAA Workshop on Tools for Embedded Computer Systems Software* (Hampton, Va.: AIAA, 1978), pp. 41-44.

17.   I. Nassi and B. Shneiderman, "Flowchart Techniques for Structured Programming," *ACM SIGPLAN Notices,* Vol. 8, No. 8 (August 1973), pp. 12-26.

18.   N. Chapin, R. House, N. McDaniel, and R. Wachtel, "Structured Programming Simplified," *Computer Decisions,* Vol. 6, No. 6 (June 1974), pp. 28-31.

19.   N. Chapin, "New Format for Flowcharts," *Software — Practice and Experience,* Vol. 4, No. 4 (October-December 1974), pp. 341-57.

20.   P.G. Hebalkar and S.N. Zilles, *TELL: A System for Graphically Representing Software Design,* IBM Corp., Research Report RJ2351 (San Jose, Calif.: September 1978).

21.   Y. Futamura, T. Kawai, H. Horikoshi, and M. Tsutsumi, "Development of Computer Programs by PAD (Problem Analysis Diagram)," *Proceedings of the Fifth International Software Engineering Conference* (New York: IEEE Computer Society, 1981), pp. 325-32.

22.   C. Böhm and G. Jacopini, "Flow Diagrams, Turing Machines and Languages with Only Two Formation Rules," *Communications of the ACM,* Vol. 9, No. 5 (May 1966), pp. 366-71. [Reprinted in *Classics in Software Engineering,* ed. E.N. Yourdon (New York: YOURDON Press, 1979), pp. 13-25.]

23.   J.B. Holton and B. Bryan, "Structured Top-Down Flowcharting," *Datamation,* Vol. 21, No. 5 (May 1975), pp. 80-84.

24.   L.J. Peters and L.L. Tripp, "Design Representation Schemes," *Proceedings of the MRI Symposium on Software Engineering* (New York: Polytechnic Institute of New York Press, 1976), pp. 31-56.

25.   S.C. Dewhurst, "A Methodology for Implementing Structured Flowcharting," *ACM Systems Documentation Newsletter,* Vol. 6, No. 1 (June 1979), pp. 10-11.

26.   D. McQuillan, "Transaction Diagrams — A Design Tool," *ACM SIGPLAN Notices,* Vol. 10, No. 5 (May 1975), pp. 21-26.

27.   N.H. Weiderman and B.M. Rawson, "Flowcharting Loops Without Cycles," *ACM SIGPLAN Notices,* Vol. 10, No. 4 (April 1975), pp. 37-46.

PART III

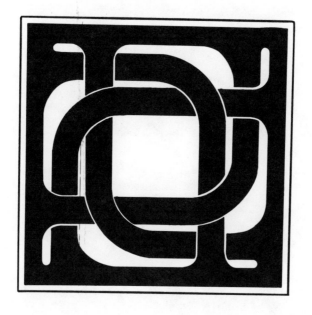

Software Design Methods

PART III
Software Design Methods

*Software design is 99 percent
perspiration and 1 percent inspiration.
The purpose
of a software design method
is to keep the perspiration from
drowning the inspiration.* *

—Mac Alford

In the latter part of the 1960s, software engineering came of age with the realization that discipline was the key to success in software development. Although the initial interest dealt with code (for example, restricting the use of GOTOs and developing a self-modifying code), it quickly spread to software design. If code was to be organized, its design must also be organized. But what form would such an organization take?

In the case of code, the course of action is clear. Many guidelines have been suggested regarding size of modules, types of instructions, commenting techniques, code indentation, and the like. Although hard experimental evidence is sparse, many of these guidelines are widely accepted — at least, in principle. Possibly, they are accepted because they agree with intuition and sometimes experience. But, what about design? As in the case of code, a lot of well-structured programs and systems have been designed and successfully implemented. They must have some qualities in common. Such thinking led several authors to externalize the software design process as they sometimes practiced it or conjectured how others ought to practice it.

Details of these software design schemes vary greatly. Some consist only of a set of guidelines, while others include strict rules, based on experience, and a set of coordinated graphics. But each approach has been developed to respond to the design problem most familiar to its creator. Design problems stem from many sources. The developmental environment, personnel, administration and, particularly, the type of software being developed are some common sources. Based on their publications, few, if any, authors of design methods recognize the uniqueness of their methods, assumptions, and operating environment. Reviewing their papers, we do not find descriptions by these authors of when and where their method is useful and when it is not suitable. Contrast this with other more mature engineering disciplines such as heat transfer en-

---

*Paraphrase of Thomas Edison on genius. Mac Alford is a software requirements engineer affiliated with TRW, Inc.

gineering. There the issue is not whether a heat transfer problem has a design solution, but rather how its solution should be derived. The approach used is to apply some physical constraints to obtain a differential equation. Then a test is applied to identify the appropriate type of mathematical relationship to solve the equation.

The approaches that have been proposed for software design are as diverse as the experience and background of their authors. Many of these approaches qualify as full-fledged software design methods in that they are composed of a set of techniques directed at supporting a common, unifying rationale. Not all of the approaches described in this section qualify as methods. However, the diversity of this discussion is aided by the presence of these procedure-oriented approaches. Hence, a more convenient view of design methods is that they are step-by-step procedures that are taught through the use of written materials and training courses.

In Part III, we will examine thirteen approaches to designing software. In general, the methods discussed in each chapter are presented in alphabetical order. The basis and use of each, as well as its strong points and shortcomings, will be presented together with its area of applicability. These presentations are not intended to be comprehensive tutorials on the use of these methods; rather, they are only an overview. The reader should be able to use any method presented here on simple problems. For complex problems or situations in which the method's subtle intricacies come into play, refer to one or more of the cited references.

The examples used to demonstrate these methods are selected for their relative simplicity, for the ease with which the issues can be communicated to the reader, and, most importantly, for their ability to highlight each method's features. At the end of Part III, guidelines are presented for selection of methods, combinations of methods, or specific elements of methods to apply to a given software design problem.

CHAPTER 7
Data Flow-Oriented Methods

Over the lifetime of a system,
the flow and transformation of data,
not the functions,
remain the least changed.

—L.P.

Software analysts and designers over the last ten or more years have used a number of different approaches to guide their decisions, capture information, and identify natural decompositions of a system. Perhaps the most widely used approaches in industry are those that use data flow as a guide. This approach seems natural when one is designing an automated system to replace a manual one. In such a case, the first step is to build a model of the existing system. At that point, the software designer or analyst can stand back and identify logical economies that will result in an equivalent but streamlined model of the software system. Using this as a starting point, he can often identify further economies. The resulting design may not look functionally very much like the original, but it provides much more flexibility and capability.

Not as clear is the use of data flow-oriented techniques to build a new system that has no similar (manual) predecessor. Then, the software analyst/designer must conjure up what he thinks the system might look like, based on his experience, and on interviews with prospective users, customers, and, rarely, others who have built similar systems. The danger when a manual system exists is that the development team may merely automate the manual system on a one-for-one basis; the danger when there is no predecessor is that without some benchmark to compare the new system to, user needs may not be adequately met.

The data flow-oriented methods that we will examine in this chapter have been used widely for several years. They represent alternative formulations of this single basic concept. The use of these methods is enhanced by several texts (referenced in each section) and professional classes given by independent firms that describe analysis techniques based on data flow.

The representation schemes used by all three of the methods described in this chapter were described in Part II. As stated there, this enables us to examine the representation approach apart from the concept inherent in the method. In this way, both can be objectively examined and not influenced by shortcomings in one area or the other. Approximately half of this chapter is devoted to structured design. This reflects two characteristics: One is the degree of refinement it has undergone since its introduction in 1974. The other is the richness and utility of the evaluation scheme it includes. This scheme can be applied to any software design.

As these methods are presented, the reader should reflect on the basic differences among these approaches, in what they emphasize and in what they choose to ignore. This reveals something about the origins of each method and their relative domain of effectiveness.

7.1 Structured analysis and design technique

Structured Analysis and Design Technique (SADT®), originated and promoted by the SofTech Corporation [1], is based on the results of studies into computer-aided manufacturing [2]. Like computer-aided manufacturing, SADT takes a data flow view of the analysis and design problems, but utilizes an original notational scheme and a distinct project organization approach. Although employing the organizational approach is not absolutely required in order to use this method successfully, we will describe these roles in Section 7.1.2 to provide insight into how analysis and design were perceived by the originators of SADT.

7.1.1 Concept

SADT is based on the following concepts:

- Precise models capable of providing an understanding of complex problems are the best means of obtaining effective solutions.

- Analysis should be conducted in a top-down, structured, modular, and hierarchical fashion.

- The system model should be represented graphically in such a way as to highlight the interfaces between component parts and the hierarchical structure that they compose.

- The modeling approach must be able to depict objects (e.g., data, people, devices, and modules) and events or actions of the various parts of the system, as well as the relationships between objects and events or activities.

- A clear differentiation must be made between the functions to be performed by the system (the "what"), and the means by which these will be accomplished (the "how").

- The analysis and design method must provide coherent discipline between participants.

- Documentation and review of all decisions and feedback related to the analysis and design effort is essential.

The above concepts sound reasonable enough and imply attainment of goals or requirements. The approach to accomplish these goals has several unique characteristics, as explained in the next section.

7.1.2 Approach

SADT goes beyond the mere specification of the proper steps of software design. As indicated by its name, SADT recognizes the inextricable link between analysis and design. But SADT also recognizes the need for an environment conducive to effective, successful analysis and design activities. Hence, SADT sets forth the goals of the analysis and design activities, the required personnel roles to attain them, and the procedures deemed necessary to successfully conduct a project [3]. Following are the roles in SADT.

Table 7.1
Personnel Titles and Descriptions Within SADT

Title	Description
Author	one who performs data gathering and analysis tasks and organizes this material using SADT models
Commenter	one who reviews models by authors and who comments in writing; usually is another author
Reader	one who reads SADT diagrams constructed by others but is not required to document (write) these comments; in a sense, one who receives the models for his own information or verbal comment only
Expert	one who provides technical guidance to authors concerning the resolution of unique or troublesome problems
Technical Committee	a group of expert personnel who review the results of the analysis effort on a level-by-level basis; they can identify or resolve technical problems and coordinate with project management
Project Librarian	one who archives and controls versions, releases, updates, and feedback from reviewers
Project Manager	one who has overall responsibility for the project
Monitor (or Chief Analyst)	one who provides technical assistance and guidance in SADT use
Instructor	one who trains authors and commenters to use SADT

The above participants contribute to the definition and design of the system [1, 3]. Heavy emphasis is placed on user involvement. The results of such efforts are described in the next section.

7.1.3 *Discussion*

The notational conventions and use of SADT activity diagrams will not be repeated here; refer to Section 4.3, especially the example of a simple report generation problem shown in Fig. 4.8. The notational conventions distinguish between control data (e.g., SORT KEYS) and mere input data (e.g., SALE TRANSACTION FILE). In a system involving many such diagrams arranged in a hierarchical order, the usual comprehension problems for the design team and customers are compounded by the addition of the dimension of control information to the diagrammatic scheme. Also, the advocated policy of permitting each designer or analyst to develop independent diagrams and resolving integration problems via the review cycle may cause additional difficulties. That is, interface problems between a designer's portion of the system and the rest of the system are only considered after he has developed this independent model.

The activity diagram model clearly depicts the interaction between modules. Although the notational scheme may add some complexity, its utility in real-time process control systems is apparent.

7.2 Systematic activity modeling method

Systematic Activity Modeling Method (SAMM) was originated and refined by the Boeing Company [4] and is based on concepts contained in the human-directed activity cell model [1]. Its data-flow perception of the world concerns the notion that distinct, separable activities are related to each other by means of data flows. SAMM resulted from a desire to develop a means of modeling processes (e.g., manufacturing or computer programs) that would be simple and straightforward enough to be understood by a broad spectrum of customers and would lend itself to being automated.

7.2.1 *Concept*

SAMM is based on the integration of several conceptual themes. Some of these are common among the data flow-oriented methods, but the forward/feedback data flow, absence of control flow, and data decomposition set SAMM apart. The following concepts are included in SAMM:

- ○ The use of hierarchies to organize collections of objects or activities into subordinate and superordinate rankings is an important part of any successful modeling technique.

- ○ Data flow (data can be bits of information, sheets of aluminum, finished sub-assemblies, and so on) between individual activities is the key to understanding processes or sets of related activities.

- ○ Data flow and activity information should be presented in as simple a manner as possible. Specifically, the complexity limit of 7 ± 2 should be observed [5].*

- ○ The use of syntactic standards in the graphic depiction of a model will aid clarity. Hence, a model consisting of several hierarchical levels and many separate, but related, diagrams will be constructed according to the same strict formatting rules.

---

*Studies by psychologists have shown that humans can comprehend approximately 7 ± 2 distinct things at one time, thus establishing a comprehension limit.

○ Understandability of a model is aided by keeping control-oriented information separate from data flow information. In the data flow form of SAMM diagrams, no distinction is made between data flows that influence sequencing or branching and those that provide an activity with the data needed to do its job.

○ As decomposition of the system proceeds, a link or tracing capability is needed to ensure that the composition of data flows (and activities) implied by the decomposition is shown explicitly. For data, this feature supports the same sort of concept as the data dictionary.

The primary objective of the SAMM approach is to facilitate communication between customer, user, analyst, and designer as simply as possible. Hence, the notation (see Section 4.4.2) does not have the richness associated with similar methods such as SADT. SAMM is also intended primarily for use in the system definition, requirements analysis, and design phases. It has proved to be particularly useful in modeling existing systems.

7.2.2 Approach

Experience with the use of SAMM has shown its utility from problem definition through software design [6]. The basic building block is the activity cell, which was described in Chapter 4 (Fig. 7.1). The adherence to specific rules about the intrinsic meaning of a flow associated with the side on which it enters the cell enables readers of SAMM diagrams to ascertain rapidly the nature of the flow. Also, the simplistic portrayal of the four data flows aids in the assessment of the impact of proposed changes.

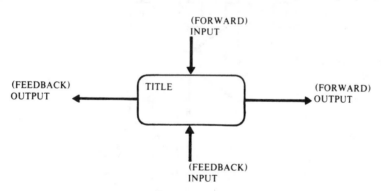

Figure 7.1. Example of an activity cell.

In the figure, FORWARD INPUT/OUTPUT refers to a source/destination that is outside of the activity-data flow diagram containing the activity cell. FEEDBACK INPUT/OUTPUT refers to a source/destination that is within the activity-data flow diagram containing the cell.

Activity cells that are immediate subordinates, or "children," of another activity cell are depicted on a single activity-data flow diagram (Fig. 7.2). Labels designating cells are composed of the letters of the alphabet starting with A, except for the root node or cell, which is designated 0 (zero). The complete label for a cell is arrived at by concatenating its own label within its own family (i.e., children of a single parent) with the labels of its ancestors. Hence, a label such as ABCCA indicates that this cell is "child" A of a parent node whose label is ABCC. Similarly, ABCC is child C of the parent ABC, and so on (Fig. 7.3). Activity cells are described by simple combinations of verb and object, as in SADT and structured design (see Sections 7.1 and 7.3).

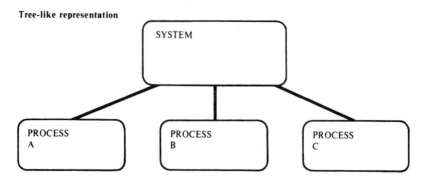

Figure 7.2. Relationship between activities and cell boundaries in SAMM.

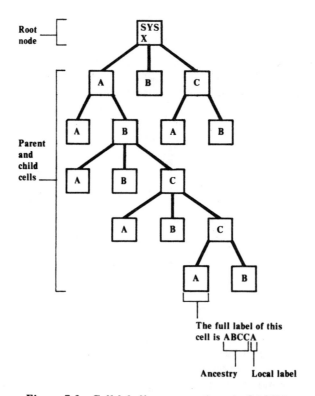

Figure 7.3. Cell labeling conventions in SAMM.

7.3 Structured design

Structured design is based on concepts developed by Stevens, Myers, and Constantine [7].* In structured analysis, the same notational schemes (data flow diagrams) and concepts are used to model problems and eventually to produce a specification and a software design using this method. Structured design is probably the most widely used of the methods described in this book. Part of the reason for its popularity is the ease with which it can be used, and the evaluation criteria it includes.

7.3.1 Concept

Conceptually, structured design may be unique among software design methods, in that it consists of three rationales: One aims at the composition and refinement of the design; another separates issues into abstract and implementation; and the third enables the user of the method to evaluate the results of his efforts. Each of these will be discussed separately in the following sections.

7.3.1.1 Composition rationale

Structured design views systems in two complementary ways: One is the flow of data, and the other is the transformation that such data flows undergo from input into output. Together, these views form a network model of a system showing data entering as input; undergoing a transformation; perhaps undergoing other transformations; joining, diverging, or being stored with other data; and finally becoming output. This model of software design may sound simple, but it generates several interesting dividends. Among them are the following:

O *Absence of time in the data flow representation:* Since movement and transformation are the only characteristics represented by the data flow diagram, the concept of the passage of time along one or more data flow paths is not present (Fig. 7.4). The designer is free to concentrate on the clear establishment of what major or minor transformations must occur in order for the input data to be incrementally and correctly transformed into output.

O *Lack of a classical functional decomposition:* Top-down design has been described as showing only one path in a tree-like structure, because it assumes there is only one problem to be solved [12]. The use of the so-called data flow viewpoint reduces the effect of the designer's experience and biases on the results, and consequently retains the shape or structure of the system. Further on in the structured design process, these "natural aggregates"† of transformations and data flows play a vital role in the identification and organization of modules in the construction plan or physical design of the system.

---

*Its use has been actively promoted by YOURDON inc. through courses, textbooks, and publications in professional magazines. The use of structured design techniques is complemented by several texts [8, 9, 10, 11] and courses on the topic as well as on structured analysis.
†These are groups of processes, each of which is composed of interdependent transformations; they are usually grouped together physically on the structure chart.

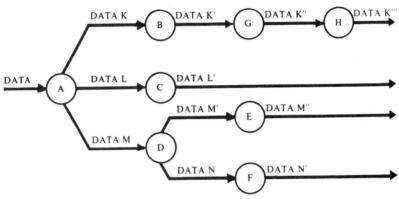

Figure 7.4. Example of a data flow diagram.

Although there exist several data dependencies in the above diagram, the *exact* order in which processes A through H will execute is not explicit. Time dependencies are not shown.

7.3.1.2 Abstract versus physical design rationale

One serious dilemma for a software designer is the chicken-and-egg problem of simultaneously trying to understand the design problem and to define a practical solution. It is a dilemma because, while he is composing design solutions to the problem, even at a high level, he may shift his focus to the details of implementation. This cycling between (abstract) high-level design issues and (physical) implementation issues increases the potential for mistakes to be made. Some key issue or subtle nuance regarding the problem may be overlooked, for example. To avoid this problem, structured design recommends a disciplined dichotomy between abstract or logical design issues and packaged or physical design. At first glance, this appears to be simply an outgrowth of the divide-and-conquer scheme of addressing problems. But there is more to this separation than that.

The designer first considers a logical solution to the problem posed in the requirements. This solution is devoid as much as possible of implementation considerations. Once he is satisfied that the abstract design is a complete and consistent solution to the problem posed by the requirements, he considers what changes should be made to the design in order to obtain one that would be prudent to *implement* in the current development environment.

This process is not unlike that followed by architects. They begin with an abstract or logical representation of the structure to be built (say, a single-family dwelling). This logical design is an artist's conception of the completed building. Although the proportions shown in the drawing are relatively close to what will eventually be built, this early design lacks three important characteristics:

☐ *Precision:* The *exact* dimensions of windows, doors, walls, and so on are not present. Although a master builder might be able to use the sketch to build a home that resembled it, the integrity of the relationships between dimensions might not be retained. In the case of software, it is not apparent whether or not these possible modules will actually become modules in the implemented version.

☐ *Detail:* Many significant features have been left out of the logical design. Basically, all of the essential functions are reflected (e.g., shelter from weather) but other important details (such as the exact path of main plumbing lines) are absent. The software analogy is that modules are all treated as black boxes. That is, we know *what* they do but not *how* they do it. At this point in the design, it is premature to add such details.

☐ *Practicality:* As attractive as the house may appear, the dimensions may violate one or more local building codes, and custom-made, possibly unavailable, items may be requested. Similarly, it may well be imprudent to build the abstract software model exactly as depicted. Operating environment, sizing, timing, and other factors must be considered in arriving at the final system model.

In spite of these apparent drawbacks, the definition of a logical design provides a relatively inexpensive way to establish whether the designer understands what the customer wants, whether it provides the customer with a means of communicating his questions and concerns to the designer, and whether it serves as an important starting point for the definition of the implementable design.

7.3.1.3 Design evaluation rationale

Perhaps the most unusual and valuable aspect of the structured design method is that it offers a set of non-mathematical criteria for evaluating a software design. The criteria can be applied regardless of whether the structured design method was used. Two classes of criteria are involved: system level (coupling) and module level (cohesion).

The system-level criterion, *coupling,* is a means of evaluating the relationship between modules* in a system. The concept of coupling describes the nature of the information transfer between modules. As modules are the basic building blocks of software systems, their relationships determine how easily the system may be maintained or enhanced: A high degree of independence of the modules that compose a system means that maintenance, modification, and expansion of any one module will not affect other modules. Conversely, the more interdependent and intertwined the modules, the greater the likelihood that the entire system, rather than a discrete portion, will have to undergo total change. Although the originators of this concept did not quantify the desirable system-level properties, they did categorize and rank several types of coupling, and provide a procedure for using them to evaluate design quality [7, 8]. Three categories of system-level design quality issues are described below:

☐ *Interface complexity:* The ideal is to have uncomplicated, easy-to-comprehend "clean" interfaces between modules. What is a clean interface? Low, more desirable coupling is possible if care is taken in the use of common environments (e.g., FORTRAN COMMON, PL/I INCLUDES, or common overlays). These environments can permit hidden or obscure dependencies to be created among modules utilizing the environment, often leading to unexpected and spectacular results when

---

*A module is defined as a lexically contiguous set of program statements that can be referred to by name.

seemingly insignificant changes are made. Avoiding common areas by employing communication through passed parameters, rather than by shared or global variables, is an effective way to combat this problem [7, 8]. For example, in FORTRAN, the case of labeled (versus unlabeled) COMMON reduces the undesirable side effects of complex interfaces.

☐   *Type of connection:* The way in which one module refers or connects to another affects the coupling level. The least desirable type of connection is to make use of knowledge of the internal details of the module being called, which may lead to undesirable side effects from seemingly harmless, local changes. The most desirable type is one in which the module is called by name.

☐   *Type of communication:* The simplest relationship that modules can have is to transmit data. However, some uses of this data can create undesirable side effects. For example, a common practice is to pass a set of flags or switches from one module to another, telling the subordinate module what to do. However, such switches are an indication that the called module is capable of performing more than one function or service for the calling module. Structured design recommends that such modules be split into two or more modules, so that each does one and only one task, thereby simplifying module connections.

An objection often posed to the principle of minimal coupling is that using passed parameters instead of common areas, and increasing the number of modules in order to simplify their relationships, are inefficient practices. However, the persistence of design errors, along with the increasing speed and size of today's hardware, and the extended life span required of major systems, makes this approach more cost-effective than attempting to maximize execution speed and minimize program length.

The three system-level criteria just described are summarized in Table 7.2.

Table 7.2
Relative Desirability of Module Coupling Factors

CHARACTERISTIC	RELATIVE DESIRABILITY		
	LOW	──────➤	HIGH
INTERFACE COMPLEXITY	UNCLEAR		SIMPLE
TYPE OF CONNECTION	INTERNALS OF MODULE		MODULE – BY NAME
TYPE OF COMMUNICATION	HYBRID	CONTROL	DATA

The evaluation criterion on the single-module level is referred to as *cohesion.* The level of cohesion exhibited by a module is an indication of its relative internal strength, in other words, of the functional connections between its processing elements.* Certainly, "strong" sounds better than "weak," but how do we measure or even rank the strength of a module? Seven ranked categories have been defined by Stevens et al. [7], from the most desirable (functional cohesion), to the least desirable (coincidental cohesion). In the case of functional cohesion, all elements (that is, calls, instructions, or groups of instructions) within the module contribute to the accomplishment of a single task, whether simple or complex. The elements that compose a coincidentally cohesive module, in contrast, contribute to the accomplishment of several unrelated tasks.

The basic scheme for determining the level of cohesion in a given module is to write a sentence that clearly and concisely states what the module does, and then analyze it for key words relating to time, sequence, compound or complex statements, lists, and so on. If all activities of a given module exhibit more than one type of cohesion, the strongest applies; if different subsets of activities have different cohesion levels, the weakest applies.

Perhaps the greatest benefit of these two types of design quality criteria — coupling and cohesion — lies in the fact that they enable the software designer to externalize the decisions he has made in deriving the design. The important thing, then, is not necessarily what level of coupling or cohesion is present, but rather that the software designer is able to justify to himself and others the decision to employ one level or another. Such criteria also have important fringe benefits, including enhanced communication to management regarding where to devote resources to improve system quality and reduce maintenance costs most effectively.

7.3.2 Approach

The basic strategy used in structured design is to identify the flow of data in the problem and to incorporate both detail and structure in an iterative fashion. A system specification that identifies inputs, desired outputs, and a description of the functional aspects of the system, should exist before design begins. The specification is used as a basis for the graphic depiction, called a data flow diagram, of the inherent data flows and data transformations (see Fig. 7.5). From the data flow diagrams, natural aggregates of these transformations and data flows are identified.

Following the structured design procedure (Fig. 7.6), this step eventually leads to the definition and depiction of modules and their relationship to one another and to various system elements, in a form called a structure chart (Fig. 7.7 — see also Chapter 4, Fig. 4.6). At this point, the system specification is re-examined, errors or omissions remedied, and the process selectively cycled through again (Fig. 7.8).

---

*An element can be an instruction, a group of instructions, or a call to invoke another module.

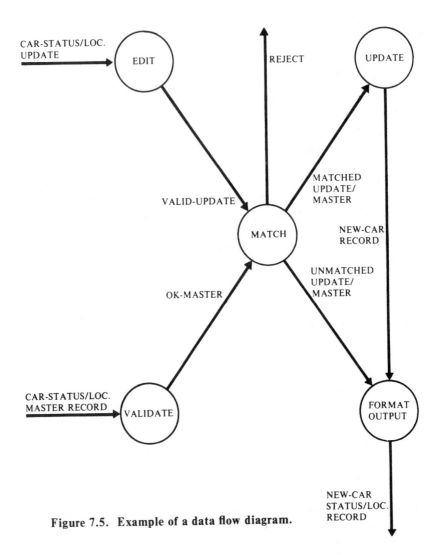

Figure 7.5. Example of a data flow diagram.

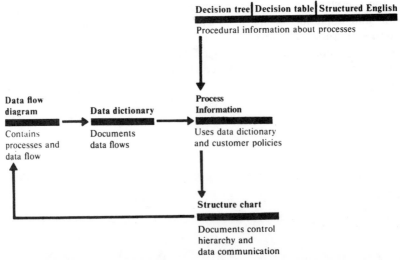

Figure 7.6. Overview of the structured design method.

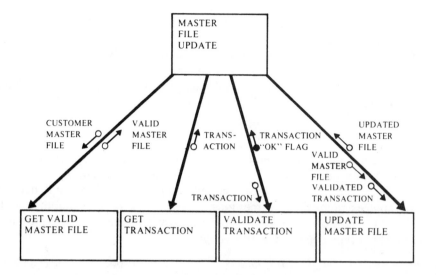

Figure 7.7. Example of a structure chart.

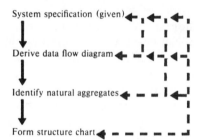

Figure 7.8. General flow of the structured design method.

7.3.3 Discussion

Structured design has gained wide popularity for two primary reasons. One is that it allows the software designer to express his perception of the design problem in terms he can identify with: data flows and transformations. The notation with which he expresses these flows is simple, easy to use, and understandable by management, customer, and implementer.

The other primary reason for this method's popularity is that it provides the designer with a means of evaluating his (and others') design, serving as a sort of benchmark against which to measure his success or progress. In this regard, the method is unique. In fact, if this method consisted of nothing more than the design evaluation concepts of coupling and cohesion, structured design would still be a significant contribution to the software field. These concepts may be fundamental principles of software development; they can be applied to any software design developed by any technique. Furthermore, they can (and should) be applied to existing software.

However, there are many other aspects of software design that this method leaves unaddressed. For example, the process of converting the design and module specification into pseudocode or a programming language is not dealt with explicitly. Second, even though excellent guidance is provided on how to organize and define modules, their internal workings are not as carefully attended to. Third, data flows and transformations are not easily identified with any degree of certainty. That is, different designers will view a given software design problem differently and consequently form different "pictures" of the data flows and transformations involved.

Finally, structured design has much to offer that is unique, tried, and tested. Although it does not address certain key software design issues, it is, in the main, a useful adjunct to the software designer's repertoire.

7.4 Summary

These three software design methods — SADT, SAMM, and structured design — have much in common beyond their data flow orientation. The use of hierarchies and of only syntactically different notational schemes tends to mask several deep-rooted conceptual differences among these methods. At the risk of oversimplifying, let us briefly focus on the areas of contention within this group of methods and present them in the order in which they appeared in this chapter:

Structured analysis and design technique. SADT aims to provide easily applied concepts and appropriate notation with which to express them. One of its more obvious differences from SAMM and structured design is that SADT notation is rich and relatively complex. The distinction between control data and mere input data is not one with which the user or customer feels comfortable. Experience with this method has shown that a SADT diagram can often be misinterpreted by someone who is conversant with the method but is not the author of the diagram. Depending on the author's use of the rich syntax, this misinterpretation can be serious.

The philosophical view is to let the analyst/designer express whatever he wishes and to have the internal and external inconsistencies and errors removed during the review cycle [13]. This is just the opposite of the force-fit sort of approach of structured design, and it may have a distinct advantage in situations that do not fit the patterns required by that type of approach. In large design efforts, such informality may be a hindrance, but both the notational richness and the almost laissez-faire expression philosophy are dealt with by the method's disciplined, well-structured review cycle and obligatory role-playing. Although there may be some organizational or management implications, the price of change may be worth it.

The matter of design quality is not well defined as it is in structured design, and the implication is that the wisdom of the local reviewing gurus will be reflected in their comments and the resulting designs. This is very different from the coupling and cohesion tests of structured design, but does take advantage of a human's ability to give an opinion or analysis that is more intuitive than based on anything definable.

Systematic activity modeling method. The fact that customers have had considerable influence on the development of SAMM is attested to by the simplicity of both its notation and conceptual basis. Also apparent is the influence of the developmental environment, and of its early applications involving manufacturing. The importance in manufacturing of knowing whether a part had been through some inspection processing is obviously different from the implications of knowing about looping in software. Although there are no stated quality-evaluation criteria in SAMM, the consistency and traceability concerns contribute to a design that has some desirable qualities.

Structured design. Although structured design's goals are similar to those of SADT, the means of attaining them are different. The emphasis in structured design is on providing the designer with an easy-to-use set of concepts and an almost casual primary notational scheme in the form of the data flow diagram. Used in conjunction with other tools (such as the data dictionary, structure charts, pseudocode, and data structure diagrams), it provides the primary building material upon which the system design is based. Through the use of peer-group reviews [9, 14] and the designer's own discipline and attention to detail, emphasis is placed on consistency, both inside a data flow diagram and in its relationship to other notational tools.

Within structured design's notational framework, virtually anything the analyst/designer wishes can be expressed in a consistent, coherent manner. When this is not possible, the difficulty is resolved by means of further interviews, reviews, or other schemes before proceeding to refine the design.

The distinction that is made between data and control information may be difficult for customers to comprehend. However, the heaviest customer involvement is during the initial development of the data flow diagram, which does not consider control information. This partial blessing is also a partial curse in that the data feedback so much a part of real-time application is somewhat awkward to depict; it definitely is not as naturally depicted as in SAMM, for example. Most important, structured design offers a set of measures of software design quality that provide invaluable feedback on the overall system design quality, as well as some implicit knowledge of how easy the system will be to maintain.

A pitfall of data flow-oriented methods

A problem common to all three of these methods is that of incorporating procedures from the old system into the one being designed. The issue is not one of whether old or new is good or bad, but rather one of predisposition. Does modeling based on the information flow in the current system predispose the software designer to structure the design in such a way as to retain many of the current procedures? The elimination of this difficulty is not an easy task, nor is it something that can be ignored or circumvented by assumptions. All too often, an automated system is just a computerized version of the manual system it replaced, with the full potential for automation untouched. This danger is particularly great with data flow-oriented methods. The process of eliminating these implementation-dependent features is referred to as logicalization, and its purpose is to remove the implementation-oriented information (the "how") and to retain only the essence of the problem (the "what"). All three methods allude to the need to avoid this pitfall, but do not provide concrete techniques for the purpose. Considerably more refinement and maturation of ideas along these lines is necessary before this ceases to be a major issue.

This set of data flow-oriented methods represents an excellent example of how the same fundamental concept can be utilized by different people and organizations with varying results. The differences reflect variations in experience and professional judgment. Negative remarks about any and all methods should not be interpreted as favoring one method over another; instead, they should be viewed as a relative way of presenting the former half of a cost/benefit trade. Since the respective authors of the methods have written numerous articles about their potential benefits, it is only prudent to consider the relative costs and risks associated with each method. All are useful, but the designer must be the final judge of which is best in a specific circumstance. A summary of comparison factors is presented in Table 7.3, followed by descriptions of the factors.

Table 7.3
Comparison of the Data Flow-Oriented Methods

	SOFTWARE DESIGN METHOD		
CHARACTERISTIC	**STRUCTURED DESIGN**	**STRUCTURED ANALYSIS AND DESIGN TECHNIQUE**	**SYSTEMATIC ACTIVITY MODELING METHOD**
CURRENT SYSTEM MODELING	YES	YES	YES
SYSTEM SPECIFICATION	YES	YES	YES
SYSTEM ARCHITECTURE	YES	SOMEWHAT	SOMEWHAT
LOGICAL DESIGN	YES	YES	YES
PHYSICAL DESIGN	YES	POTENTIALLY	POTENTIALLY
AVAILABILITY OF TUTORIAL MATERIALS	HIGH	LOW	LOW
AVAILABILITY OF TRAINING COURSES	PUBLICLY	BY ARRANGEMENT	BY ARRANGEMENT
ADAPTABILITY TO CURRENT MANAGEMENT APPROACH	HIGH	LOW	MODERATE
EASE OF USE (HIGH = EASY TO USE)	HIGH	LOW	MODERATE
LEARNING EFFECTIVENESS	HIGH	LOW	MODERATE
COMMUNICATION WITH CUSTOMERS	HIGH	LOW	HIGH
HIERARCHICAL IN NATURE	YES	YES	YES
PROLIFERATION LEVEL	HIGH	MODERATE	LOW
PROVISION OF OBJECTIVE EVALUATION CRITERIA	YES	NO	CONSISTENCY ONLY
BASIS OF METHOD	CONCEPTUAL	CONCEPTUAL/ PROCEDURAL	CONCEPTUAL/ PROCEDURAL
DEGREE OF TECHNICAL ISSUE COVERAGE	4 OUT OF 4	3 OUT OF 4	3 OUT OF 4
SUPPORT BY AN AUTOMATED TOOL	NO	YES	YES
SUPPORT BY QUALIFIED CONSULTANTS	YES	YES	BY ARRANGEMENT
MOST PORTABLE FEATURE (IF ANY)	COUPLING AND COHESION	DATA/CONTROL MODELING	LEVEL-BY-LEVEL CONSISTENCY

Characteristics of Data Flow-Oriented Methods

Current system modeling the ability of the method to provide users with a way to model an existing system, which may include manual tasks, physical objects, and geographic locations as well as the more classical functional needs and processes

System specification	the extent to which the method provides the necessary semantic and conceptual framework to permit the statement of requirements for an entire system, not just the software
System architecture	the ability of the method to allow flexibility in laying out the overall interface between the major system elements
Logical design	whether the method includes a clear, explicit recognition that an abstract, conceptual solution must be formulated and refined prior to the introduction of implementation issues
Physical design	whether the method explicitly addresses implementation issues apart from conceptualization of the logical design solution
Availability of tutorial materials	the degree to which articles, refereed papers, and instructional texts are available to a reader
Availability of training courses	the degree to which public courses are available (specially given courses at a customer's site are not considered in this category)
Adaptability to current management approach	the degree to which a pre-existing management or non-management hierarchy or organization will be affected by a design method's introduction of new job titles, procedures, and products
Ease of use	the ease with which a designer can effectively use the method; reduced by unique requirements such as templates and pre-printed forms
Learning effectiveness	the absence of subtleties in the method that might confuse a novice; intended to alert designers to the amount of care they must exert in order to avoid unforeseen difficulties
Communication with customers	the degree to which the method provides open communication between customer and designer (for example, through understandable diagramming techniques)
Hierarchical in nature	the extent to which the method provides a convenient scheme for controlling complexity via the organization of the design (and system) into ordered chunks that can be examined separately from the rest of the system

Proliferation level   the degree to which a method has spread as an indicator of its relative effectiveness; must be interpreted in conjunction with other factors

Provision of objective evaluation criteria   whether the method has a measure of design that would yield approximately the same result if used by two different (unbiased) designers

Basis of method   whether the method is based on some rationale, prescribed set of rules, or a combination of both; a method with a conceptual basis is more flexible for new applications than is a prescriptive, tactical one

Degree of technical issue coverage   the relative importance of any one or several of the four technical issue classes present in any software design effort: data structure, data flow, control structure, and control flow

Support by an automated tool   whether the method is supported by a computer-aided scheme to make changes, identify inconsistencies, and do clerical tasks, thereby enhancing the designer's effectiveness

Support by qualified consultants   the availability of experienced advisers to reduce the instances of misuse and of unsatisfactory results

Most portable feature   that part of the method, if any, that could be used totally apart from the original method (for example, using the coupling and cohesion characteristics for evaluation with some method other than structured design)

REFERENCES: Chapter 7

1. D.T. Ross and J.W. Brackett, "An Approach to Structured Analysis," *Computer Decisions,* Vol. 8, No. 9 (September 1976), pp. 40-44.

2. S. Hori, *CAM-I Long Range Planning Final Report for 1972,* Illinois Institute of Technology Research Institute (Chicago: December 1972).

3. *An Introduction to SADT® Structured Analysis and Design Technique,* SofTech Inc., Document No. 9022-78R (Waltham, Mass.: November 1976).

4. *SAMM (Systematic Activity Modeling Method) Primer,* Boeing Computer Services Co., Document No. BCS-10167 (Seattle: October 1978).

5. G.A. Miller, "The Magical Number Seven, Plus or Minus Two: Some Limits on Our Capacity for Processing Information," *Psychological Review,* Vol. 63 (1956), pp. 81-97.

6. *Functional Requirements for an Interactive Graphics Capability for SAMM Users,* Boeing Computer Services Co., preliminary draft (Seattle: March 1978).

7. W.P. Stevens, G.J. Myers, and L.L. Constantine, "Structured Design," *IBM Systems Journal,* Vol. 13, No. 2 (May 1974), pp. 115-39. [Reprinted in *Classics in Software Engineering,* ed. E.N. Yourdon (New York: YOURDON Press, 1979), pp. 207-30.]

8. E. Yourdon and L.L. Constantine, *Structured Design: Fundamentals of a Discipline of Computer Program and Systems Design,* 2nd ed. (New York: YOURDON Press, 1978).

9. M. Page-Jones, *The Practical Guide to Structured Systems Design* (New York: YOURDON Press, 1980).

10. T. DeMarco, *Structured Analysis and System Specification* (New York: YOURDON Press, 1978).

11. V. Weinberg, *Structured Analysis* (New York: YOURDON Press, 1978).

12. G. Goos, "Hierarchies," *An Advanced Course in Software Engineering,* ed. F.L. Bauer (New York: Springer-Verlag, 1973), pp. 29-46.

13. *Program Performance Specification for IDEF Support Tools (Build 1),* SofTech Inc., Document No. 1050-1 (Waltham, Mass.: October 1976).

14. E. Yourdon, *Managing the Structured Techniques,* 2nd ed. (New York: YOURDON Press, 1979).

CHAPTER 8
Data Structure-Oriented Methods

The ability to address and solve
poorly structured problems
is critical to success
in software design.
— L.P.

Software design methods attempt to enhance or complement the designer's abilities by providing some scheme or procedure such that reliance on whim, experience, and hearsay will be reduced. The data flow-oriented methods described in Chapter 7 advocated the identification and observation of the information that flows through the system; the structure and other characteristics of the resultant flow network were used as the basis for design. Data structure-oriented approaches take a similar view of data, but advocate observing data at rest. The emphasis is on identifying and observing logical relationships between discernible data elements, for these relationships form the basis of the program itself.

Data structure approaches claim that, given the same set of information, two experienced software designers would come up with the same design. The basic scenario is simple: The software designer first identifies the data needed by the program to do its job, then organizes it according to its natural hierarchy, and finally produces a program by following a translation procedure. Of the three approaches examined in this chapter — Jackson's method, Warnier's logical construction of programs, and structured systems development (a derivative of Warnier's method) — the first two were developed, apparently independently, in Europe. All three share a fundamental basis but employ different graphic techniques, and each treats the problem of translation of the data hierarchy in its own way. Although there are conceptual similarities, the degree to which the software designer is guided from data structure identification to code is quite different.

8.1 Jackson's method

The basic approach and style of Jackson's method* make it highly attractive to those working with commercial software design applications, such as in finance, inven-

*Michael Jackson, a software design consultant in England, developed this method and documented it in textbook form [1].

tory, banking, or insurance. The effectiveness of this approach in these application areas is evidenced by the zeal of many of its devotees (see Section 8.1.3) and the rate at which its popularity has grown.

8.1.1 Concept

Jackson's method views software as a mechanism that transforms input data into an output report via a set of coherent, synchronized operations. The problem for the designer is to determine what the operations and their sequence ought to be. Jackson attempts to overcome the lack of direction present in some top-down approaches by providing guidance to the designer to restrict possible system structures. The basic structure of the system is determined by the structure of the data it processes. According to Jackson, the software designer's problem is that of matching the structure of the input, output, and program. It is thus assumed that using input and output structures as a guide to program structure will result in a well-structured program. Apparent in this approach is the ease with which problems involving serial file structures can be solved. But the most important (and, possibly, dangerous) assumption underlying this method is that the software designer knows what the inherent data structure is or knows how to identify it. However, Jackson's method does not tell the designer *how* to structure data.

There have been a number of claims made regarding the use of Jackson's method, including that the quality of the results is not a function of the designer's experience or imagination; that each step in the software design process can be verified; that the method is easy to learn and to use; that two software designers working independently, and given the same problem, would obtain the same solution using this method; and that software designs obtained with this method may be implemented easily and practically. All of these claimed benefits may seem a bit optimistic. However, with a better understanding of the method, the reader will discover that this method can pay these dividends, given the proper circumstances.

8.1.2 Approach

The basic scenario for using this method is quite simple:

☐ Identify the structure of the input data and output report.

☐ Define a program structure based on these structures.

☐ Identify the discrete operations composing the program, and assign each to a component of the design.

The general flow of the Jackson methodology is shown in Fig. 8.1.

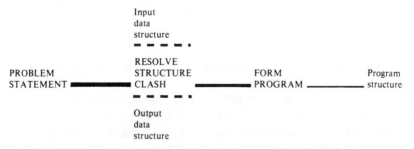

Figure 8.1. Jackson design methodology as a process flow.

There are two techniques encompassed by Jackson's methodology, including an analysis and requirements definition phase preceding design, but, as this book's subject is software design, only the design phase will be discussed here. The use of this technique is complemented by a specialized notation (see Section 5.7), which enables the software designer to depict iteration, selection, and sequence operations (Fig. 8.2). Individual operations can be combined to form hierarchies (Fig. 8.3).

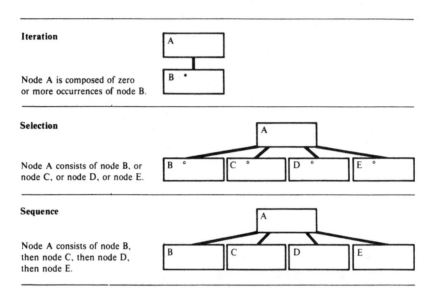

Figure 8.2. Notation used by the Jackson methodology.

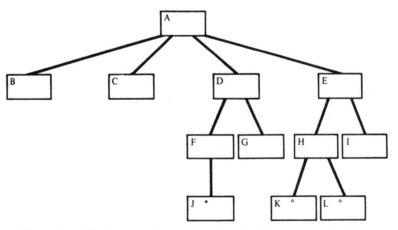

Figure 8.3. Depicting a hierarchy using the Jackson methodology.

Several types of problems encountered by the software designer are recognized and addressed by this method. Foremost among them is the *structure clash*, which refers to those instances where input and output data structures are markedly different, violating Jackson's requirement of a common program structure throughout all data structures. This and other problems are addressed in more detail in Jackson's book [1].

8.1.3 Discussion

As with other methods in this Part, we illustrate the use of the Jackson method by means of an example — in this case, a parts warehouse system: A parts supplier has an automated warehouse, in which a device controlled by a computer removes parts from the shelves. Within each warehouse, one of these robots collects parts from bins and puts them on a conveyor belt system that transports them to central dispatching, where the appropriate number of parts are distributed and the bins are returned to their assigned location.

In the early days of the system, reliability was high and preventive maintenance was done on weekends. However, business has improved so much that the system is in use 24 hours a day, 6 days a week. Breakdowns are more frequent and potentially disastrous in terms of production delays; there are now so many parts that it is no longer possible for people to rely on their own memories to find a part in one of the warehouses; and, due to problems with the computer, it is not feasible for all expediters to interactively inquire about parts locations at the same time. Consequently, management has decided that several hard-copy listings of part bin locations should be produced each day to serve as backup. Our job is to design the program to produce this report from the master file, using Jackson's method.*

The data needed to locate a part bin is the warehouse identification aisle number, aisle "slot" (position along the aisle), and shelf number or level in that position. To construct the report, we will use these pieces of data plus the quantity in the part bin. Using the notation adopted by Jackson's method, we can graphically display the structure of the input file (Fig. 8.4).

We now focus our attention on the output report. Other than the header and trailer, this report is just a list (ordered by part number) of the coordinates needed to locate a part manually. All information to locate a single part in a given warehouse appears on one line. A different line appears in the report for each part/warehouse combination. Using Jackson's graphic notation, we can display the structure of the output report (Fig. 8.5).

Next, we need to define a program structure that is compatible with both the input file structure and the output file structure. At this point, the fact that the use of this method has a minimal reliance on the designer's creativity becomes apparent. Using the guidelines provided, we can rather simply incorporate input and output structures to obtain an overall result. If we examine the input data structure and apply the guidelines, we find that iterations, such as warehouse group, are transformed into the processing of the body and an individual line in the program structure. Performing a similar transformation on the remaining elements gives us our overall program structure (Fig. 8.6).

---

*Since we are concerned with examining the use of this method, we will not address file access or organization, but merely attend to designing data structure.

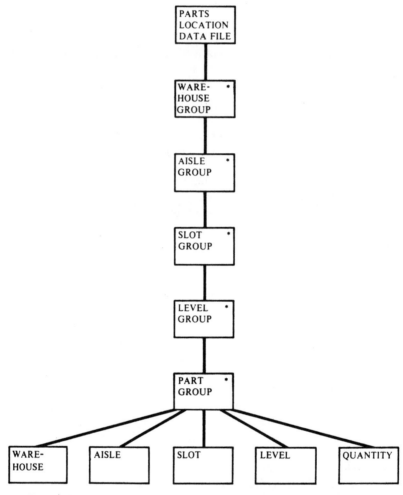

Figure 8.4. Input file structure example using Jackson's notation.

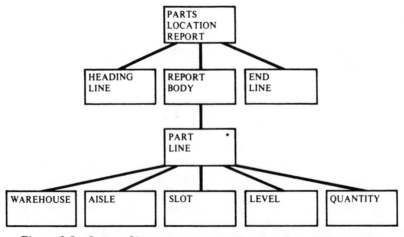

Figure 8.5. Output file structure example using Jackson's notation.

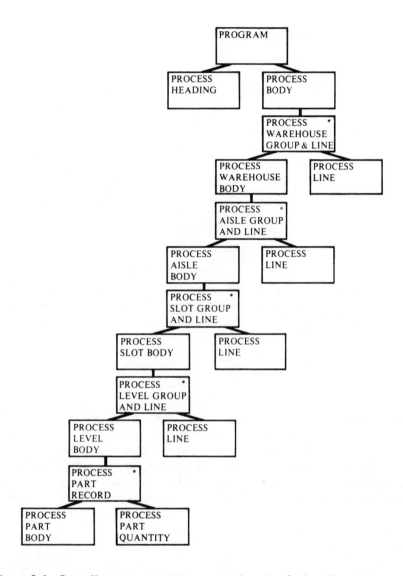

Figure 8.6. Overall program structure example using Jackson's notation.

Our next task is to translate the structure in Fig. 8.6 into METACODE, Jackson's version of pseudocode, which was developed to put diagrammed designs into codable form. The translation process is rather straightforward, although somewhat tedious; it is basically the repetition of algorithmic steps, outlined in Jackson's book [1]. Note that the lowest portion of the chart is the innermost part of the nesting of METACODE. As we move up the chart, we begin building program structure according to translation rules. These are apparent upon inspection and comparison of Figs. 8.6 and 8.7. The result of this translation for our example is presented in Fig. 8.7.

```
PPROGRAM seq
          process HEADING;
      PBODY    iter
          PWG&L    seq
              PWBODY iter
                  PAG&L    seq
                      PABODY iter
                          PSG&L    seq
                              PSBODY   iter
                                  PLG&L    seq
                                      PLBODY    iter
                                          PPARTR seq
                                              process PART BODY
                                              process PART QUANTITY
                                          PPARTR end
                                      PLBODY    end
                                          process LEVEL GROUP LINE
                                  PLG&L    end
                              PSBODY   end
                                  process SLOT GROUP LINE
                          PSG&L    end
                      PABODY end
                          process AISLE GROUP LINE
                  PAG&L    end
              PWBODY end
                  process WAREHOUSE GROUP LINE
          PWG&L    end
      PBODY    end
PPROGRAM end
```

Figure 8.7. METACODE description of example.

8.1.4 Comments regarding Jackson's method

The hypothesis that well-structured programs will result when input and output data structures are incorporated into a strategy for software design is plausible. It has an unmistakable air of intuitive truth about it, but it is an assumption, no more and no less. Although some recent work has been done to prove that this assumption is supportable in formal, mathematical terms [2], the causal link between it and well-structured programs is not hard and fast. This should not be interpreted as a fatal flaw in the method. On the contrary, those who use it are quite pleased with their results to date and consider the approach to be a real asset.

Another important aspect of this method is the delicate interplay between notions of data structure and program structure. In most business or commercial applications, the structure or organization of the input and the desired output are known in advance. The main issue facing the designer in such cases is not so much to define or discover the problem [3], but rather to identify the most prudent program structure that will accomplish a known task. This is very much a case of programming in the small — a single program as opposed to a system of programs [4] — or on a local level. To take this a step further, consider how effective this method would be if it were used to design software to control a new type of satellite — that is, in a situation in which the structure of the data is at first unknown and later is subject to a good deal of change.

Given a thoughtful selection of problems for its application, we can see the Jackson method is a powerful and successful software design approach.

8.2 Logical construction of programs

The logical construction of programs approach was developed by Jean-Dominique Warnier [5]. Warnier's mechanics, as this method is also known, is similar to Jackson's design methodology in that it assumes that data structure is the key to a successful software design effort. However, it provides users of the method with more detailed procedures on how to proceed from identifying data structure to formulating a design and writing pseudocode or code.

8.2.1 Concept

Conceptually, the approach assumes that the inherent structure of the input and output data is discernible, useful as a driving force in software design, and, when used as a design guide, will lead to a well-structured program.

8.2.2 Approach

The logical construction of programs approach employs four different design representation schemes, the first three of which are unique to this method: data organization diagram, logical sequence diagram, instruction list, and pseudocode (or code). The way in which these four schemes are used in succession during the design process is shown in Fig. 8.8.

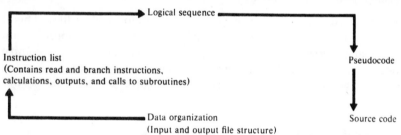

Figure 8.8. Evolution of code using Warnier's four representation schemes.

The procedure for obtaining a software design using the Warnier logical construction of programs method is relatively simple:

1. Identify all input data entities (their format is a secondary issue to that of their relationship to one another).

2. Organize the input data into a hierarchy.

3. Assign a description of each entity in the input file and note the number of occurrences (e.g., 1-employee file, n-employees; each employee record contains five entries: social security number, hire date, employee number, company address/location, and home address).

4. Perform the same process as in steps 1 through 3, but for output data.

5. Specify functional characteristics of the program by defining the type of instructions that will occur in the program in the following order: read instructions, branch (and related) instructions, computations, outputs, and calls to subroutines.

6.   Using a modified flowchart, display the logical sequence of instructions using special symbols to represent begin-process, end-process, branching, and nesting.

7.   Number each element of the logical sequence and expand it when possible, using combinations of the basic set of instructions listed above in step 6.

8.2.3 Discussion

We will examine the use of the method as applied to one of the classic commercial programming problems: We must write a program to report on salaries in our corporation, stating the total salaries paid in the corporation; the total in each company in the corporation; the total in each division; within each division, the total in each department; and within each department, the total in each group. We will use the active employee data file. Although some employees are technically inactive, this file lists employees currently on the payroll.

Referring to the seven-step procedure described in Section 8.2.2, we proceed as follows:

Step 1: *Identify all input data entities.*

Our input consists of the contents of the employee data file. This file contains one record per active employee. Each record contains employee name, employee social security number, date of hire, employee number, company location code, home address, and assignment code containing four parts (one each) to indicate the company, the division, the department, and the person's assigned group.

Step 2: *Organize the input data into a hierarchy.*

Several types of hierarchies are possible, ordered, for example, according to length of service with the corporation, or age. However, given our assignment, the most sensible one appears to be based on the assignment code values. Note that the corporation-company-division-department-group-employee relationship forms a hierarchy.

Step 3: *Assign a description of each input entity and note the number of occurrences.*

The results of this step are presented in Fig. 8.9a.

Step 4: *Perform steps 1, 2, and 3 on the output data.*

The results of these steps for the output data are presented in Fig. 8.9b.

(a)

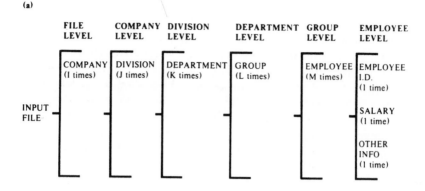

Figure 8.9a

(b)

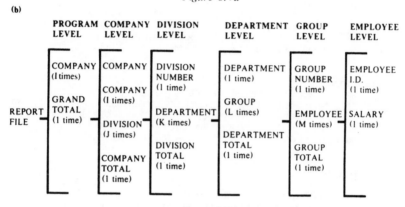

Figure 8.9b

Figure 8.9. The results of hierarchical organization and labeling of data entities.

Step 5: *Specify functional characteristics of the program by defining the types of instructions that will occur in the program.*

This step involves the identification of reads, branches, computations, and writes. Although a more detailed discussion of this step appears in Warnier's book [5], the basic scheme is to consider just what goes on at each level in the hierarchy. Are inputs needed? What will be output? How will we know when we are done at this level? What are the rules or processing details associated with the computation of our results? Supplying answers to these questions within Warnier's syntactic and semantic guidelines results in Fig. 8.10.

In Fig. 8.10, note the numbers that appear to the left of all instructions and to the right of some. The significance of these numbers is related to the hierarchy level and interdependence of the instruction. The input and output instructions have identifying numbers. The relative value and its corresponding implied sequencing are not important, but what is important is that each of these instructions has an identifier. The branch instructions carry two identifiers — one to the left and one to the right. The identifier on the left corresponds to that on the left of the calculation instruction associated with it.

In Fig 8.10, notice branch-instruction60, IF # EMPLOYEES PROCESSED = TO-TAL IN GROUP, is related to calculation60, ADD EMPLOYEE VALUES TO SUMMARY

VALUES FOR GROUP, and has the same primary identifier. They are related be-cause the calculation is summing employee salaries at the group level, while the branch is checking on whether all employees in a given group have been includ-ed. The number to the right side of the branch instructions refers to the pri-mary identifier of the read instruction, which should be branched to in the event the corresponding IF-test fails. If we have not finished processing all of the groups in a particular department, then we need to read in more group data. Hence, branch70 will continue to branch to read50 to get more data. However, if branch60 fails, the total employee data that has been read in has not been processed, so calculation60 will be re-executed and a test made again until branch60 is true.

READ INSTRUCTIONS:
10	READ INITIALIZATION RECORD
20	READ COMPANY DATA AT THE DIVISION LEVEL
30	READ DIVISION DATA AT THE DEPARTMENT LEVEL
40	READ DEPARTMENT DATA AT THE GROUP LEVEL
50	READ GROUP DATA AT THE EMPLOYEE LEVEL

BRANCHES:
60	IF # EMPLOYEES PROCESSED = TOTAL IN GROUP	60
70	IF # GROUPS PROCESSED = TOTAL # GROUPS	50
80	IF # DEPARTMENTS PROCESSED = TOTAL # DEPARTMENTS	40
90	IF # DIVISIONS PROCESSED = TOTAL # DIVISIONS	30
100	IF # COMPANIES PROCESSED = TOTAL # COMPANIES	20

CALCULATIONS:
60	ADD EMPLOYEE VALUES TO SUMMARY VALUES FOR GROUP
70	ADD GROUP VALUES TO SUMMARY FOR DEPARTMENT
80	ADD DEPARTMENT VALUES TO SUMMARY FOR DIVISION
90	ADD DIVISION VALUES TO SUMMARY FOR COMPANY
100	ADD COMPANY VALUES TO SUMMARY FOR CORPORATION

OUTPUTS:
70	PRINT GROUP AMOUNTS
80	PRINT DEPARTMENT AMOUNTS
90	PRINT DIVISION AMOUNTS
100	PRINT COMPANY AMOUNTS
110	PRINT CORPORATION AMOUNT

Figure 8.10. Example of a Warnier instruction list.

Step 6: *Using a modified flowchart, display the logical sequence of instructions.*

With the notation recommended in this step, each of the branching statements will take the general form shown in Fig. 8.11. Combining these, and noting the nesting that will occur as a result of the interdependencies among these processes, we have Fig. 8.12.

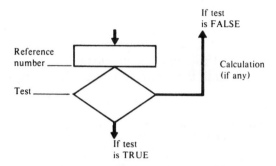

Figure 8.11. General form of branching statements in Warnier's approach.

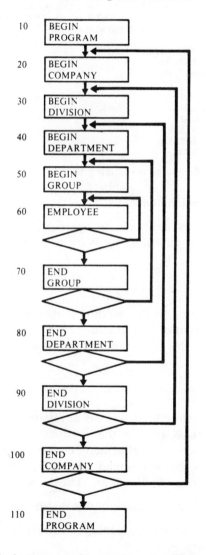

Figure 8.12. Logical sequence of example, using Warnier's mechanics.

Step 7: *Number each element of the logical sequence and expand it whenever possible.*

The "flowchart" developed in step 6 is simple enough to be converted to pseudocode, as shown in Fig. 8.13. However, direct conversion is not always possible; often, individual computation instructions need to be expanded into their own "flowcharts," until the entire system can be expressed in pseudocode.

```
INITIALIZE VARIABLES, CLEAR ARRAYS, ETC
FOR I = 1, UNTIL NO-OF-COMPANIES DO
     CORP-TOTAL = CORP-TOTAL + CO-TOTAL(I)
     FOR J = 1, UNTIL NO-OF-DIVISIONS DO
          CO-TOTAL(J) = CO-TOTAL(I) + DIV-TOTAL(J)
          FOR K = 1, UNTIL NO-OF-DEPARTMENTS DO
               DIV-TOTAL(J) = DIV-TOTAL(J) + DEPT-TOTAL(K)
               FOR L = 1, UNTIL NO-OF-GROUPS DO
                    DEPT-TOTAL(K) = DEPT-TOTAL(K) + GRP-TOTAL(L)
                    FOR M = 1, UNTIL NO-OF-EMPLOYEES DO
                         GRP-TOTAL(L) = GRP-TOTAL(L) +
                                             EMPLOYEE-SALARY(M)
                    ENDDO
               ENDDO
          ENDDO
     ENDDO
ENDDO
OUTPUT CORP-TOTAL
OUTPUT CO-TOTALS
OUTPUT DIV-TOTALS
OUTPUT DEPT-TOTALS
OUTPUT GRP-TOTALS
```

Figure 8.13. Pseudocode corresponding to the "flowchart" in Figure 8.12.

8.3 Structured systems development

Orr's structured systems development approach to software design [6] is based upon the approach originally published by Warnier as well as on some concepts from HIPO (see Section 3.2).

8.3.1 Concept

The basic concept utilized in this method is that well-structured programs are the result of accurate identification of the structure of the data involved, and production of the eventual code to reflect this structure. In this way, it is yet another refinement of the data-structure approach.

8.3.2 Approach

The approach used by structured systems development is more along the lines of a step-by-step sequential process than is the Warnier approach. The user is carefully guided through the definition and refinement of the design by following a series of seven steps. Users of this method should be familiar with the basis and notational scheme of the Warnier method (Section 8.2). The design steps are listed below:

☐ Express the problem in the form of a Warnier diagram.

☐ Identify system outputs, particularly the rate at which they occur and their inherent structure.

☐   Identify the logical database of the system.

☐   Form the system requirements into a basic system flow hierarchy.

☐   Establish whether the required data already exists.

☐   Identify real-world events that affect the database.

☐   Place logical updating actions into the basic system hierarchy.

The user of the method should view the design process as being repetitive, not simply a one-time event. However, the design cycle should only be repeated as many times as is necessary for each system output.

8.3.3 Discussion

Due to the similarity between this approach and Warnier's, an example will not be presented here. The reader may refer to the preceding section for an example.

The instructions provided to users of this method clearly demonstrate the problems associated with extending a method that has a local, small-problem vision beyond its original scope. For instance, the rules at each step and the means of identifying important aspects of the design problem or solution are not definitive. The steps tell us what must be done, but not how to do it. However, this approach does enable the user to create effective solutions for design problems that are complex but small, or that are well-interfaced local parts of a large system.

8.4 Summary

The data structure-oriented methods provide software designers with rapid and procedural means of obtaining well-structured modules and pseudocode. They rely on a property of the system that is not as likely to change as some others, such as company policy. However, these methods will not stand the designer in good stead when the data structure is unknown or undergoing definitional change, or when a user interface is being designed. Their primary value appears to be in the rapid definition of a single module or relatively small subsystem. Although some other method would have to be used to identify this overall system structure, these methods would be effective on a local basis within such a structure. A summary of their characteristics is presented in Table 8.1, using the terms defined below the table.

Table 8.1
Comparison of Data Structure-Oriented Methods

CHARACTERISTIC	SOFTWARE DESIGN METHOD		
	JACKSON'S METHOD	LOGICAL CONSTRUCTION OF PROGRAMS	STRUCTURED SYSTEMS DEVELOPMENT
CURRENT SYSTEM MODELING	NO	NO	NO
SYSTEM SPECIFICATION	NO	NO	NO
SYSTEM ARCHITECTURE	YES	YES	YES
LOGICAL DESIGN	SOMEWHAT	SOMEWHAT	SOMEWHAT
PHYSICAL DESIGN	YES	YES	YES
AVAILABILITY OF TUTORIAL MATERIALS	MODERATE	HIGH	HIGH
AVAILABILITY OF TRAINING COURSES	BY ARRANGEMENT	PUBLICLY	PUBLICLY
ADAPTABILITY TO CURRENT MANAGE-MENT APPROACH	HIGH	HIGH	HIGH
EASE OF USE (HIGH = EASY TO USE)	LOW	HIGH	HIGH
LEARNING EFFECTIVENESS	LOW	MODERATE	MODERATE
COMMUNICATION WITH CUSTOMERS	LOW	MODERATE	MODERATE
HIERARCHICAL IN NATURE	YES	YES	YES
PROLIFERATION LEVEL	MODERATE	MODERATE	MODERATE
PROVISION OF OBJECTIVE EVALUATION CRITERIA	SOMEWHAT	NO	NO
BASIS OF METHOD	CONCEPTUAL/ PROCEDURAL	CONCEPTUAL/ PROCEDURAL	CONCEPTUAL/ PROCEDURAL
DEGREE OF TECHNICAL ISSUE COVERAGE	3 OUT OF 4	3 OUT OF 4	3 OUT OF 4
SUPPORT BY AN AUTOMATED TOOL	NO	NO	NO
SUPPORT BY QUALIFIED CONSULTANTS	BY ARRANGEMENT	YES	YES
MOST PORTABLE FEATURE (IF ANY)	DATA STRUCTURE MODELING	DATA STRUCTURE MODELING	DATA STRUCTURE MODELING

Characteristics of Data Structure-Oriented Methods

Current system modeling   the ability of the method to provide users with a way to model an existing system, which may include manual tasks, physical objects, and geographic locations as well as the more classical functional needs and processes

System specification   the extent to which the method provides the necessary semantic and conceptual framework to permit the statement of requirements for an entire system, not just the software

System architecture   the ability of the method to allow flexibility in laying out the overall interface between the major system elements

Logical design   whether the method includes a clear, explicit recognition that an abstract, conceptual solution must be formulated and refined prior to the introduction of implementation issues

Physical design   whether the method explicitly addresses implementation issues apart from conceptualization of the logical design solution

Availability of tutorial materials   the degree to which articles, refereed papers, and instructional texts are available to a reader

Availability of training courses   the degree to which public courses are available (specially given courses at a customer's site are not considered in this category)

Adaptability to current management approach   the degree to which a pre-existing management or non-management hierarchy or organization will be affected by a design method's introduction of new job titles, procedures, and products

Ease of use   the ease with which a designer can effectively use the method; reduced by unique requirements such as templates and pre-printed forms

Learning effectiveness   the absence of subtleties in the method that might confuse a novice; intended to alert designers to the amount of care they must exert in order to avoid unforeseen difficulties

Communication with customers   the degree to which the method provides open communication between customer and designer (for example, through understandable diagramming techniques)

Hierarchical in nature   the extent to which the method provides a convenient scheme for controlling complexity via the organization of the design (and system) into ordered chunks that can be examined separately from the rest of the system

Proliferation level — the degree to which a method has spread as an indicator of its relative effectiveness; must be interpreted in conjunction with other factors

Provision of objective evaluation criteria — whether the method has a measure of design that would yield approximately the same result if used by two different (unbiased) designers

Basis of method — whether the method is based on some rationale, prescribed set of rules, or a combination of both; a method with a conceptual basis is more flexible for new applications than is a prescriptive, tactical one

Degree of technical issue coverage — the relative importance of any one or several of the four technical issue classes present in any software design effort: data structure, data flow, control structure, and control flow

Support by an automated tool — whether the method is supported by a computer-aided scheme to make changes, identify inconsistencies, and do clerical tasks, thereby enhancing the designer's effectiveness

Support by qualified consultants — the availability of experienced advisers to reduce the instances of misuse and of unsatisfactory results

Most portable feature — that part of the method, if any, that could be used totally apart from the original method (for example, using the coupling and cohesion characteristics for evaluation with some method other than structured design)

REFERENCES: Chapter 8

1. M.A. Jackson, *Principles of Program Design* (London: Academic Press, 1975).

2. M.W. Alford, "Towards Theoretical Foundations for the Michael Jackson Design Methodology," unpublished presentation at COMPSAC 79 (November 1979).

3. P. Freeman, "Toward Improved Review of Software Designs," *Proceedings of the 1975 National Computer Conference,* Vol. 44 (Montvale, N.J.: AFIPS Press, 1975), pp. 329-34.

4. F. DeRemer and H. Kron, "Programming-in-the-Large Versus Programming-in-the-Small," *Proceedings of the 1975 International Conference on Reliable Software* (New York: IEEE Computer Society, 1975), pp. 114-21.

5. J.-D. Warnier, *Logical Construction of Programs,* 3rd ed., trans. B. Flanagan (New York: Van Nostrand Reinhold, 1976).

6. K.T. Orr, *Structured Systems Development* (New York: YOURDON Press, 1977).

CHAPTER 9
Prescriptive Methods

Seek not to understand
that you may believe,
but believe
that you may understand.
—St. Augustine

Many software design efforts have resulted in the invention of some scheme or technique that has significantly enhanced project success. Some of these have been published; in fact, approaches designed for individual projects constitute the largest class of software design methods available. These methods are largely prescriptive, in that they dictate procedures the software designer must follow in order to ensure success. Unlike the other methods discussed earlier in Part III, prescriptive methods generally do not possess an underlying rationale. Instead, the emphasis is on a prescribed regimen. Some of the methods may mature with time and be expanded both in areas of application and number of users, but at this time each is used by a somewhat limited community.

Any of the seven prescriptive methods discussed in this chapter offers some features that may be useful to a software designer. However, most of these methods require lengthy study and research to be used as prescribed by their authors. Hence, the prescriptive methods will be presented in an even more abbreviated form than that of Chapters 7 and 8. This brevity will enable the reader to identify and utilize concepts readily transferred to his problem; resources for further research will be pointed out. Many of these methods possess characteristics that complement or enhance the use of other methods.

9.1 Chapin's approach

Chapin's method is used as an adjunct to the structured design method (Section 7.3). It focuses attention on the process and basis for decomposition of functions into subfunctions, a process referred to as *parsing* [1].

9.1.1 Concept

This method recognizes the value of structured design techniques [2], but views design as a two-part process: The first is the act of creating the design, while the second part is the critical evaluation (and probable refinement) of the design. Chapin's contention is that the software designer needs much more help in the composition or first part of this process. Hence, he has composed a set of guidelines to aid the software designer, particularly the designer using structured design, in the creation of a design. These guidelines, described in the next section, incorporate advice on what to do as well as why.

9.1.2 Approach

Chapin's approach embraces the concepts and notation associated with structured design (Section 7.3). It assumes that the initial or top-level set of functions in the design is readily established, and that the real problem in design is parsing these functions once they have been identified. Chapin's ten guidelines are briefly described below.

☐ *Decompose each function in such a way that its external characteristics (inputs and outputs) will be incorporated into the design.*

The designer should focus on those attributes external to the function: input and output. The result is the identification of potential subfunctions whose hierarchical relationships are not identified. These relationships are ascertained and the separation of potential subfunctions from useful or prudent ones is accomplished through the application of the other guidelines.

Stated another way, this guideline amounts to recommending that the structuring and organization of the design be somewhat forestalled until the designer has a fairly complete list of the subfunctions.

☐ *Decompose so as to linearize the control sequence of the subfunctions.*

The identified subfunctions should be demonstrably linear, meaning execution generally proceeds from left to right. Inputs to the sequence of functions come in at the left, and outputs of each subfunction act as the input to the next subfunction in the execution order.

☐ *Identify the decision-making or selective mechanisms and those subfunctions affected by them.*

The designer must now identify the subfunctions appropriate under a given set of data conditions, those appropriate under other conditions, and the superfluous or redundant subfunctions.

☐ *Decompose to support subfunctions that will be repeated.*

The designer must distinguish between data that changes during looping operations and data that does not. Also, attention is focused on what must take place before a group of repeated operations is initiated, and under what circumstances it will terminate.

☐ *Decompose so as to focus on coherent sets of inputs, transformations, and outputs.*

Follow this guideline to reduce the occurrence of redundant input or output sets; that is, instances of the same set of inputs (data item and value) being utilized by more than one subfunction resulting in different outputs. The converse is true of outputs.

☐   *Subordinate process functions to decision-making ones.*

Localize and structure decision-oriented parts of the design while clarifying the scope of effect of a specific branch or choice.

☐   *Postpone implementation decisions and collect them into identified subfunctions.*

Implementation decisions include data formats, use of functions supplied by the operating system, and constraints on timing and size.

☐   *Minimize data communications between functions.*

Follow this guideline to its logical conclusion to ensure low coupling and high cohesion.

☐   *Decompose each function so as to accomplish a single-entry, single-exit design.*

Use the concept of hierarchy in the design and simplify control flow.

☐   *Decompose functions into subfunctions such that the level of abstraction is uniform.*

Follow this guideline to ensure that, if a function is decomposed into several subfunctions, each of these would possess an equivalent level of abstraction with respect to its siblings at that level in the hierarchy (Fig. 9.1).

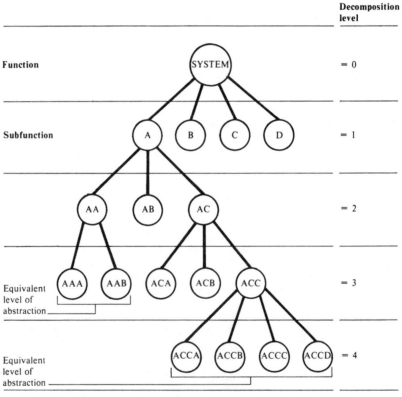

Figure 9.1. Decomposition for uniform abstraction levels.

9.2 Design by objectives

The approach of Design By Objectives (DBO) attempts to effectively address what may be the most crucial aspect of design: ensuring that the design solution reflects the customer's or user's true needs. Developed over a period of eleven years, the DBO method is actually a combination of several techniques that originated under a variety of circumstances [3, 4].

9.2.1 Concept

The primary intent of this collection of techniques is to match the user's real, measurable software needs to the design of a suitable system. The emphasis in DBO is on what is measurable, rather than what is desired. For example, if the customer wishes to have a system developed to improve customer service, this must be stated in a measurable way, in terms of an index or some such measure of customer service whose minimum value and desired value after installation have also been established. Design by objectives requires such measurable values to be an intrinsic part of the software design effort.

Many software design methods dwell almost exclusively on the identification of functional requirements. DBO bases the software system design on system quality and local decisions, as well as on functionality. It views the software system design process as one of identifying desirable system attributes and of basing all design decisions on the attainment of these attributes. This philosophy of DBO tends to externalize software design decision making, which increases traceability and consistency of features in the final product.

9.2.2 Approach

DBO incorporates several forms of objective criteria definition and attainment (Fig. 9.2). The basic strategy is to identify a means of attaining it. Each combination of objective and attainment mechanism and measure aids the designer and user to proceed incrementally and consistently from some problem and undefined ideas to a clearly defined solution that exhibits desirable properties.

Each tool utilized in DBO is described below:

☐ *Functional requirements* state what the system must do.

☐ *Attribute requirements* complement functional requirements in that they relate to the quality of the means of accomplishing the function (e.g., cost, accuracy, and reliability).

☐ *Function/attribute component table* is a matrix that effectively assigns specific functions and attributes to software, hardware, or human system components.

☐ *Technique/attribute handbook* is a catalog of the characteristics exhibited by systems when a particular technique is used.

☐ *Quality control* is a delineation of the degree to which planned levels of attributes are being reached.

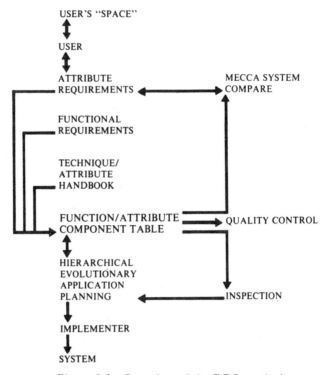

Figure 9.2. Overview of the DBO method.

☐ *Hierarchical evolutionary application planning* (HEAP) is basically a tool for continuous project planning and monitoring. It employs top-down decomposition of the project, continual refinement of the project plan during the course of the project, and the quantification of control parameters.

☐ *Inspection* is the use of project inspections [5], walkthroughs, and re-views to identify aspects in need of rework.

☐ *Multi-element component comparison and analysis* (MECCA) is an ap-proach for selection of system-level alternatives.

These graphic elements all take the same general form. An example of a top-level at-tribute specification (a statement of attribute requirements) is given in Fig. 9.3. A framework for the design specification expansion is presented in Fig. 9.4. The user of these and other diagrammatic forms within DBO is free to create column and row head-ings appropriate to a particular design effort.

The interplay of these various elements of DBO within the general scenario shown in Fig. 9.2 is what makes DBO function as a method.

ATTRIBUTE	DESCRIPTOR						
	MEASURABLE	UNITS	WORST CASE	BEST CASE	NORMAL	RELATIVE IMPORTANCE
MAINTAINABILITY	YES	TIME TO REPAIR	60 MIN.	—	15 MIN.	1
PORTABILITY	YES	NUMBER OF MINIS OR MAINFRAMES WITH < 1 MAN-WEEK OF WORK	2	—	3	10
EXTENSIBILITY	YES	NUMBER OF HUMAN RESOURCE HRS. TO ADD FEATURE (EXCLUDING FEATURE DEVELOPMENT)	40	—	8	3
DEVELOPMENT COST	YES	NUMBER OF HUMAN RESOURCE HRS. + SUPPORT COST × DOLLAR CONVERSION	ESTIMATED + 100%	ESTIMATED	—	3
RELIABILITY	YES	mean time between failure	7 DAYS	—	30 DAYS	1

Figure 9.3. Top-level attribute specification.

DESIGN DECISION REFERENCE CODE	BACKGROUND			
	DESCRIPTION	PRIMARY AND SECONDARY JUSTIFICATION	DEVELOPMENT TIME/ SUPPORT	COST
1A roblem fol	"LOGON" AND "HELP"	1. xample an 2. in used be	40 LABOR HRS. 2 HRS. COMPUTER TIME	~$2K
1B olve to de	ust progr	1. will it 2. alysis, com	g an if or actors these	tand better t
1C lowing the	posite of use	egree is rang	esistance ski	n and pressu
1D igned be				
⋮				

Figure 9.4. Design specification expansion.

Note: Nonsense type is used to represent actual variables supplied by the user of the method.

9.2.3 Discussion

DBO might be referred to as *matrix-driven design* in that decisions, evaluations, goals, progress toward goals, and system hierarchy are all documented and employed in matrix form. This form enables the software designer to rapidly identify portions of the system that are poorly defined by the user or that are viewed as unclear by the designer. It also forces decisions and quantification, and reduces the possibility of hidden or non-externalized design decisions.

DBO can be used in conjunction with some other software design method to overcome its failure to specifically address the construction of an implementable model of the code. This lack is not as serious as the lack of specific guidance on design composition. DBO serves as a valuable analysis tool, but its value as a design tool is limited to an adjunct or secondary role with some more specific primary method. However, as we've described, the method does provide several possible means to improve the effectiveness of many of the other software design methods discussed in this book, for although the same set of matrices may not be used, a subset of one or more specific to the problem could be.

9.3 Problem analysis diagram

Problem Analysis Diagram (PAD) utilizes the basic concepts of top-down design and iterative stepwise refinement. In use at Hitachi Laboratories in Japan since 1973, it has provided notable improvement in programmer productivity [6]. PAD provides a generalized procedure designed to utilize the most desirable features of the Warnier diagram, Pascal, Ferstl charts, and some of their supporting concepts.

9.3.1 Concept

PAD is intended as an improvement or extension of Warnier's diagrammatic approach (see Section 8.2). However, it does not utilize the same conceptual basis. PAD's objectives are to extend the control structures available in Warnier diagrams, facilitate direct translation into code, and enhance the readability and flexibility of the diagramming scheme. PAD also enables the designer to portray graphically the occurrence of parallel processes and some real-time characteristics.

9.3.2 Approach

Similarly to other prescriptive software design methods, PAD provides a sequence of steps for the software designer to follow in designing a system. These steps are listed below:

1. Beginning with a vague notion of what the program or system is to do, identify the sequence in which each portion of this loosely defined procedure is to occur.

2. Identify those portions of the procedure that will be repeated, together with the initiating and terminating conditions for repetition.

3. Identify the conditions under which each portion of the procedure will be executed.

4. If parallel processing is required, identify which portions will be run in parallel.

5. Repeat steps 1 through 4 until the procedure is thoroughly specified and refinement is complete.

Each of the above is documented using PAD notation (see Section 6.11). This process is depicted graphically in Fig. 9.5.

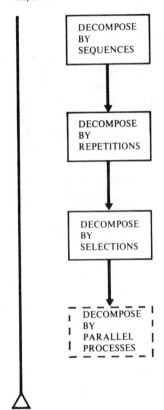

Figure 9.5. Process flow of the PAD approach.

9.3.3 Discussion

This approach places heavy emphasis on the use of diagrams as a means of not only documenting software designs, but also enhancing and complementing the software designer's abilities. Its procedural nature does enable the software designer to come up with some sort of design quickly and to enhance it over time. Its graphic and procedural emphasis on the use of basic constructs (sequence, repetition, and selection) can aid in the refinement of designs into quality programs. However, PAD does not provide quality assessments, nor does it take a system-level viewpoint. It can also be used during development as a means of defining individual predicate tests to exercise all branches [6]. According to research performed at Hitachi, its effectiveness for the design of individual programs has been demonstrated.

9.4 Higher order software

The Higher Order Software (HOS) methodology was originally developed for aerospace applications. It is viewed by its proponents as an effective means of formally defining large, complex systems so as to make them reliable [7]. The methodology has been refined and its application extended into other types of problems, including computer-aided manufacturing.

9.4.1 Concept

HOS utilizes three complementary conceptual tools: axioms for structuring processes, a representation scheme, and a language, AXES [8], for describing processing transformations and data. We will limit our discussion to the axioms and the representation scheme, as the programming language level is too detailed for this book. The axioms each refer to actions or responsibility of a single module of interest. A given module is governed by the following axiomatic premises: The module controls the invocation of functions that are its *immediate* subordinates; is responsible only for entities in its own output space; can refuse to accept invalid elements of its own, and only its own, input set; and controls the ordering of each tree for its *immediate* subordinates.

The axioms are directed at issues of consistency, correctness, and attention to detail in the definition of interfaces. The basic effect of applying this set of axioms is precise interface definition and ease of maintenance.

The representation scheme of HOS consists of three different complementary means of expressing an algorithm: control maps, structured design diagrams (see Section 6.8), and pseudocode or source code. Control maps, expressed in mathematical terms, capture the functional nature of the algorithm, and reflect the influence of the axioms. The structured design diagram is a GOTO-less design representation scheme. The equivalence between control maps and structured design diagrams is shown below in Fig. 9.6.

a) **Control Map Representation of Logic**

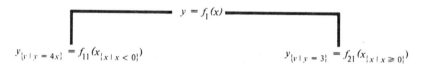

$$y = f_1(x)$$

$$y_{\{v\,|\,y\,=\,4x\}} = f_{11}(x_{\{x\,|\,x\,<\,0\}}) \qquad\qquad y_{\{v\,|\,y\,=\,3\}} = f_{21}(x_{\{x\,|\,x\,\geqslant\,0\}})$$

b) **Equivalent Structured Design Diagram**

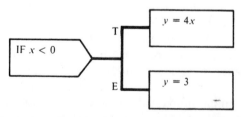

IF $x < 0$
T : $y = 4x$
E : $y = 3$

Figure 9.6. Equivalence between control maps and structured design diagrams.

9.4.2 Approach

The procedural flow of HOS is shown below in Fig. 9.7. Notice the incorporation of automated aids and the role of the axioms described above.

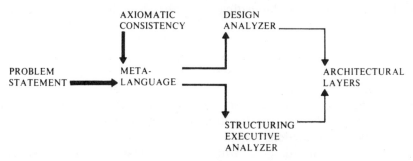

Figure 9.7. Procedural flow of HOS.

9.4.3 Discussion

The basic premises of HOS have much in common with other methods. For example, the effect of some of the axioms will be to define modules that are functional, highly independent, and able to be replaced by equivalent functions due to simple interfaces. The goal of assuring axiomatic consistency is laudable, particularly since there is an automated tool to help us do this. However, the mathematical formalism needed to use this method effectively, combined with the realities of changing requirements and design concepts, makes HOS a difficult method to use. Still, in applications such as single, critical executive programs, where errors of certain types are intolerable, the effort required to use this method may be well justified.

9.5 Information hiding

The approach of information hiding was proposed by Parnas [9] in response to the need for additional guidance to the software designer.* Appearing in 1972, it represented a logical next step in the evolution of software design following the advent of modular programming. Parnas' method presents design heuristics that enhance the designer's ability to compose designs having desirable qualities, such as module independence and minimal ripple or secondary effects from changes. It has been classified as a prescriptive method, since it does not use the same sort of conceptual basis as many others do. However, its goals and results have much in common with structured design [2].

9.5.1 Concept

The primary intent of information hiding is to provide the designer with a means of composing modular systems having more desirable qualities than those produced using flowchart-oriented approaches. Three systems criteria are foremost in this approach: changeability, comprehensibility, and the possibility for independent or parallel development of different parts of the system.

---

*The information hiding approach has prompted a development of a related technique known as data abstraction, and the publication of several articles on its applications [10].

The method's primary goal is attained through the achievement of the actual definition of modularity. The technique is to "hide" information about each module from the module that interfaces with it. That is, no module can make use of the means to calculate or access information that was employed by another module.

This hiding is akin to eliminating the least desirable types of coupling (see Chapter 7), and treating each module as a black box, as is done in structured design.* The difference between Parnas' approach and the flowchart-oriented approach is showing what needs to be done as opposed to showing how it must be done. For example, we could picture a program as a flowchart, and overlay each process in it with crosshatching and shading for every instance in which knowledge of the data structure of another process was used. The flowchart might look like Fig. 9.8. Note that the resulting modules would not be very useful in another application, since they may contain unique combinations of functions or share data structures. Changes in requirements, operating environment, and/or data structure would result in widespread undesirable effects or "rippling." An alternative decomposition may or may not result in more modules, but the modules present would be simple (having a single function), reusable, and easier to test, integrate, and maintain. Information hiding is the classic example of the effective difference between procedure-oriented thinking in software design versus function-oriented thinking.

Procedural thinking employs internal or implicit knowledge of what must be done and externalizes how it will be done, while a conceptual approach internalizes the how and externalizes the what. An alternative view of these issues is to ask, "Which is more likely to change during development and later, during maintenance — the basic functions performed by the system, or the ordering or arrangement of these functions?" Experience indicates that the basic functions stay approximately the same, while the arrangement undergoes considerable change. Hence, Parnas' approach will reduce maintenance problems.

9.5.2 Approach

Information hiding does not provide a step-by-step procedure by which to decompose a system into modules, but it does provide some general guidelines to help the designer during design:

☐ Hide a design decision in each module in the system from the other modules in the system.

☐ Avoid the sharing of data, data structures, accessing mechanisms, and/or the modification of data between modules.

☐ Consider the instructions by which a module can be called part of the module, so that its author is responsible for the calls to it and is aware of any potential misuse or other interface difficulties.

☐ Utilize control block modules to hide control block formats, such as those used in operating system queues.

---

*A black box is a functional entity that provides a service, but those requesting and receiving the service are unaware of how it is being accomplished.

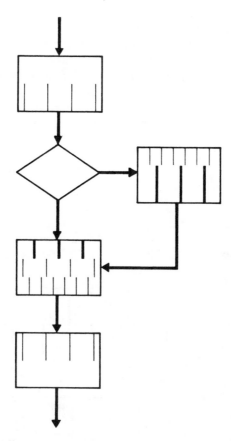

Figure 9.8. Replication or sharing of functions and data structures.

☐ Hide knowledge of specialized meanings and organizations of data, tags, and so on, in a module.

☐ Hide the order in which certain data elements will be processed within a module.

The use of this method is not as straightforward as many of the others, since it does not offer procedural, tutorial guidance. The basic scheme for using it would be to obtain a hierarchical decomposition in some fashion, apply the guidelines provided, refine accordingly, and begin again. Designs obtained utilizing this method will have properties similar to those obtained using structured design [2]. Specifically, the resulting hierarchy will be such that the upper portions will possess sequencing and decision information, while the lower portions will do the actual processing and have a high degree of reusability (Fig. 9.9). The result of applying this approach and extending it to an actual application are best described by Heninger et al. [11, 12].

9.5.3 Discussion

Information hiding has much to offer the software designer in terms of its insightful heuristics and the quality of the resulting systems. Unfortunately, its description, though widely available, is not of a nuts-and-bolts nature such that novice and expert alike are guided from problem to acceptable solution. This is regrettable since this method addresses real issues such as how to design for ease of change. Perhaps too little attention is paid to the means by which decomposition is initially derived. It appears to be assumed that the designer will somehow come up with this with certain guidelines in mind. However, the localization of knowledge about other parts and features of the system seems to be an almost common requirement of good software design. Information hiding provides yet another means of attaining this goal. It is a primary candidate for use in a complementary role with any of several other software design methods and notation schemes.

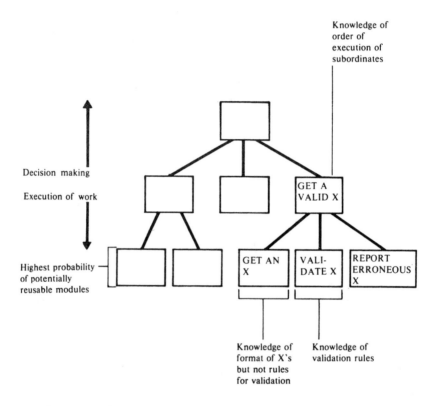

Figure 9.9. Incidence of functional modules.

9.6 META stepwise refinement

META stepwise refinement, published by Ledgard [13], externalizes what effective software designers already do: It combines the top-down concepts of Mills [14], Wirth [15], stepwise refinement, and level structuring [16].

9.6.1 Concept

META stepwise refinement consists of three concepts: disciplined (or structured) programming, problem solving by iteration, and return on investment or cost-effectiveness. How this combination of concepts contributes to the overall theme of this method will be made clearer in the next section. Each concept in this approach is described on the next page.

○ *Disciplined programming* refers both to the process of decomposing the solution space in order to identify alternative solutions, and to the breaking down of a given solution into its constituent attributes. It is not decomposition in the classic sense of the word, as discussed below.

○ *Problem solving by iteration* refers to both the process of stepwise refinement in which the design problem is solved iteratively and to the addition of detail with each iteration.

○ *Return on investment or cost-effectiveness* sharply focuses on the time and energy necessary to apply the other two concepts. In this case, further refinement is done only on the most promising of the alternative solutions, making for a more prudent, cost-effective expenditure of resources.

Finally, the META refinement discipline is directed at postponing detailed design decisions until the appropriate amount and kind of information is available.

9.6.2 Approach

This technique presumes the existence of an exact, stable problem definition. Starting at the highest level of abstraction, the designer first composes a simple statement of the solution to the problem. Next, several solutions are generated, all containing the same level of detail, but each being more detailed than the initial solution. Each set of equivalent solutions constitutes a level of refinement. The designer selects the best of these solutions at that level, which is now treated in the same manner as the initial solution; that is, several equivalent solutions of more detail are generated, and so forth. The process ends when a level of refinement is reached that can be directly implemented in the intended programming language (Fig. 9.10).

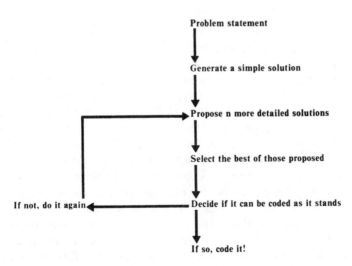

Figure 9.10. META stepwise refinement as an iterative process.

9.6.3 Discussion

As I have mentioned, META stepwise refinement amounts to the externalization of the type of mental process many designers engage in. Experienced software designers will interject detail into the design only in a controlled and calculated manner. They tend to avoid great leaps into detailed issues, but rather to dwell on the big picture and approach the detailed picture carefully. During this process they try to identify several alternative approaches and to select the best from among these. Hence, the META method merely formalizes what many designers are already doing.

Left unaddressed are some serious and troublesome issues. One issue is how can truly different alternative designs be composed. Basically, a person has a certain viewpoint and experience set, which are difficult to change. Hence, it is unlikely that one individual will identify fundamentally different designs from which a best design could be chosen. Perhaps this problem could be resolved by utilizing a programming team, or by employing different methods to compose the designs.

But another more troubling problem remains: This method depends heavily on the software designer's ability to discern the best design from among several alternatives, but no guidelines or selection criteria are provided. One possible way in which this method might be made more effective would be to utilize a design team to obtain multiple solutions, employ the evaluation criteria of another method (such as coupling and cohesion from structured design), and use this method as an overall scenario for planning and project control.

9.7 Program design language

Program Design Language (PDL) is a formalization of the use of pseudocode (see Section 6.1). PDL [17] is based on an application of the concept of iterative refinement, employs a top-down design philosophy, and is supported by an automated aid.

9.7.1 Concept

As with other top-down approaches, the main idea in PDL is to start with a simple statement of the design and to refine it by successively adding more and more detail. But the goals of this method go beyond top-down design as an end in itself. A primary objective of this method is to be user-friendly; that is, to be lucid, and comfortable for people to use. An underlying assumption of PDL is that if people (specifically designer and, possibly, customer) understand the design, they will be less likely to overlook some error or inconsistency in it. So, the approach that resulted from this view utilizes a slightly modified version of the English language. After all, it is people, not machines, who must comprehend and communicate the design.

The English-like statement of the PDL-generated design also gives the software designer the flexibility to state the design in such a way that it can be selectively refined as information becomes available. The designer can refine one portion of the system while leaving another in a very high-level state. (This capability is a characteristic of other top-down design methods.) As the requirements for this less-refined portion become better known or more stabilized, the designer can focus attention on it. When the refinement is "complete" (as described in Section 9.7.2), coding may begin.

9.7.2 Approach

The problem with many software design methods is that they recommend that the design be refined, but they are not very specific on what must be present in the design in order for coding to begin. In PDL, however, the design must exhibit a specific set of traits: definition of all system-level and module-level interfaces; identification of and response to all error conditions; identification of all modules and their means of invocation; and definition of all control blocks, global data, and processing algorithms composing the modules.

The basic idea of the preceding list is to be certain that no loose ends exist when coding begins. The overall procedure of PDL is shown in Fig. 9.11.

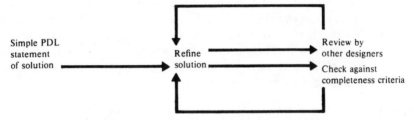

Simple PDL
statement
of solution

Refine
solution

Review by
other designers

Check against
completeness criteria

Figure 9.11. Overview of refinement process in PDL.

The basic construct syntax or semantics is that of pseudocode (see Section 6.1), but is presented in abbreviated form in Fig. 9.12. Note that the constructs (sequence, iteration, and selection) suggested by Böhm and Jacopini [18] constitute the basic set. Depending on the circumstances, users of this method may find it useful to extend this set. The SORT algorithm (from Section 6.1) is expressed in PDL form in Fig. 9.13.

The IF-construct

```
IF ____
  .
  .
  .
ENDIF
```

Forms of the DO-construct

```
DOWHILE or DOUNTIL or DOFOR
  .
  .
  .
ENDDO
```

Figure 9.12. Constructs other than sequence used in PDL.

```
EXCHSORT (TABLENAME, TABLESIZE)
     DO UNTIL NO ITEMS EXCHANGED
          DO FOR EACH PAIR OF ITEMS IN TABLE (e.g., 1-2, 2-3, 3-4, . . .)
               IF FIRST IN PAIR > SECOND ITEM IN PAIR
                    EXCHANGE THESE ITEMS
               ENDIF
          ENDDO
     ENDDO
```

Figure 9.13. The EXCHANGE SORT expressed in PDL.

9.7.3 Discussion

PDL is extremely effective at accomplishing its primary goal: communication between designers to refine the design in a cost-effective manner. Other goals include the ease with which modification and updating can be accomplished, since a text editor, word processor, or custom-built translator can be utilized. However, PDL's use of a means of communication that is so much like code can lead to some software design and development difficulties when used on systems containing several modules. Most maintenance and development problems are a result of structural, not procedural, improprieties, and users of PDL are vulnerable to this type of error. It does not explicitly address structural issues, only procedural ones.

In addition, the similarity of this medium of expression to code can quickly lead the poorly disciplined designer into coding from the outset rather than design. PDL possesses no objective criteria with which to evaluate the quality of a design. However, the use of this method on individual modules, whose role in an overall hierarchical structure has been established with some other method, is a proved means to cost-effective design of high-quality modules.

9.8 Summary

The seven prescriptive software design methods discussed in this chapter provide an interesting diversity in viewpoint and approach. They range in scope from an adjunct approach to another software design method (Chapin's approach) to a form- or table-driven design (DBO) in which everything is measurable. In the sense that they are mostly program- or module-oriented, the prescriptive methods are all correct and incorrect. For the most part, they fail to address squarely those issues that have most often been the downfall of a system design — architectural issues.

However, most of these methods (as well as other prescriptive ones not discussed here) provide those using other, non-prescriptive methods with a useful ally. Most contain heuristics that are highly portable among different types of systems and different software design methods. Perhaps their greatest utility is their use in conjunction with other methods. The characteristics of these methods are summarized in Table 9.1, and the descriptions of the characteristics are presented below.

Characteristics of the Prescriptive Methods

Current system modeling   the ability of the method to provide users with a way to model an existing system, which may include manual tasks, physical objects, and geographic locations as well as the more classical functional needs and processes

System specification   the extent to which the method provides the necessary semantic and conceptual framework to permit the statement of requirements for an entire system, not just the software

System architecture   the ability of the method to allow flexibility in laying out the overall interface between the major system elements

Table 9.1
Comparison of the Prescriptive Methods

CHARACTERISTIC	CHAPIN'S APPROACH	DESIGN BY OBJECTIVES	DESIGN BY PAD	HIGHER ORDER SOFTWARE	INFORMATION HIDING	META STEPWISE REFINEMENT	PROGRAM DESIGN LANGUAGE
CURRENT SYSTEM MODELING	NO	YES	YES	NO	NO	NO	YES
SYSTEM SPECIFICATION	NO	YES	NO	POT	NO	NO	NO
SYSTEM ARCHITECTURE	NO	NO	NO	NO	YES	NO	NO
LOGICAL DESIGN	NO	NO	NO	NO	YES	NO	NO
PHYSICAL DESIGN	YES	POT	YES	YES	YES	YES	YES
AVAILABILITY OF TUTORIAL MATERIALS	HI	HI	LOW	HI	MOD	LOW	MOD
AVAILABILITY OF TRAINING COURSES	ARR	ARR	–	ARR	–	–	ARR
ADAPTABILITY TO CURRENT MANAGEMENT APPROACH	HI	MOD	HI	MOD	HI	HI	HI
EASE OF USE (HIGH = EASY TO USE)	MOD	LOW	HI	LOW	MOD	MOD	HI
LEARNING EFFECTIVENESS	HI	MOD	HI	LOW	MOD	HI	HI
COMMUNICATION WITH CUSTOMERS	MOD	HI	HI	LOW	MOD	–	HI
HIERARCHICAL IN NATURE	YES	SOM	YES	YES	YES	YES	YES
PROLIFERATION LEVEL	LOW	LOW	LOW	LOW	MOD	–	MOD-HI
PROVISION OF OBJECTIVE EVALUATION CRITERIA	STR	YES	SOM	SOM	YES	–	–
BASIS OF METHOD	HEU	CON/HEU	HEU	MAT	CON	CON	CON
DEGREE OF TECHNICAL ISSUE COVERAGE	2 OUT OF 4	2 OUT OF 4	3 OUT OF 4	2 OUT OF 4	3 OUT OF 4	–	2 OUT OF 4
SUPPORT BY AN AUTOMATED TOOL	NO	NO	NO	YES	NO	NO	YES
SUPPORT BY QUALIFIED CONSULTANTS	ARR	ARR	NO	ARR	ARR	NO	ARR
MOST PORTABLE FEATURE (IF ANY)	DEC HEU	CON	NOT	AXI	CON	CON	PSE

KEY

MAT = mathematics	SOM = somewhat	CON = conceptual
STR = structured design	MOD = moderate	AXI = axioms
PSE = pseudocode	HI = high	DEC = decomposition
POT = potential	NOT = notation	
ARR = by arrangement	HEU = heuristic	

Logical design — whether the method includes a clear, explicit recognition that an abstract, conceptual solution must be formulated and refined prior to the introduction of implementation issues

Physical design — whether the method explicitly addresses implementation issues apart from conceptualization of the logical design solution.

Availability of tutorial materials	the degree to which articles, refereed papers, and instructional texts are available to a reader
Availability of training courses	the degree to which public courses are available (specially given courses at a customer's site are not considered in this category)
Adaptability to current management approach	the degree to which a pre-existing management or non-management hierarchy or organization will be affected by a design method's introduction of new job titles, procedures, and products
Ease of use	the ease with which a designer can effectively use the method; reduced by unique requirements such as templates and pre-printed forms
Learning effectiveness	the absence of subtleties in the method that might confuse a novice; intended to alert designers to the amount of care they must exert in order to avoid unforeseen difficulties
Communication with customers	the degree to which the method provides open communication between customer and designer (for example, through understandable diagramming techniques)
Hierarchical in nature	the extent to which the method provides a convenient scheme for controlling complexity via the organization of the design (and system) into ordered chunks that can be examined separately from the rest of the system
Proliferation level	the degree to which a method has spread as an indicator of its relative effectiveness; must be interpreted in conjunction with other factors
Provision of objective evaluation criteria	whether the method has a measure of design that would yield approximately the same result if used by two different (unbiased) designers
Basis of method	whether the method is based on some rationale, prescribed set of rules, or a combination of both; a method with a conceptual basis is more flexible for new applications than is a prescriptive, tactical one
Degree of technical issue coverage	the relative importance of any one or several of the four technical issue classes present in any software design effort: data structure, data flow, control structure, and control flow
Support by an automated tool	whether the method is supported by a computer-aided scheme to make changes, identify inconsistencies, and do clerical tasks, thereby enhancing the designer's effectiveness

Support by qualified consultants	the availability of experienced advisers to reduce the instances of misuse and of unsatisfactory results
Most portable feature	that part of the method, if any, that could be used totally apart from the original method (for example, using the coupling and cohesion characteristics for evaluation with some method other than structured design)

REFERENCES: Chapter 9

1. N. Chapin, "Function Parsing in Structured Design," *Infotech State of the Art Report on Structured Analysis and Design*, Vol. 2 (Maidenhead, Berkshire, England: Infotech Information Ltd., 1978), pp. 25-43.

2. E. Yourdon and L.L. Constantine, *Structured Design: Fundamentals of a Discipline of Computer Program and Systems Design*, 2nd ed. (New York: YOURDON Press, 1978).

3. T. Gilb, "Design by Objectives: A Structured Systems Architecture Approach," *Infotech State of the Art Reports* (Maidenhead, Berkshire, England: Infotech Information Ltd., 1980).

4. _____, "Structured Design Methods for Maintainability," *Infotech State of the Art Report on Structured Software Development*, Vol. 2, ed. L.A. Belady (Maidenhead, Berkshire, England: Infotech Information Ltd., 1979), pp. 85-98.

5. H. Remus, *Directions for the Application of Structured Methodologies*, IBM Corp., Publication TR 03.050 (San Jose, Calif.: IBM Santa Teresa Labs, 1978).

6. Y. Futamura, T. Kawai, H. Horikoshi, and M. Tsutsumi, "Development of Computer Programs by PAD (Problem Analysis Diagram)," *Proceedings of the Fifth International Software Engineering Conference* (New York: IEEE Computer Society, 1981), pp. 325-32.

7. M. Hamilton and S. Zeldin, "Higher Order Software — A Methodology for Defining Software," *IEEE Transactions on Software Engineering*, Vol. SE-2, No. 1 (March 1976), pp. 9-31.

8. _____, "The Relationship Between Design and Verification," *The Journal of Systems and Software*, Vol. 1, No. 1 (January 1979), pp. 29-56.

9. D.L. Parnas, "On the Criteria to Be Used in Decomposing Systems into Modules," *Communications of the ACM*, Vol. 5, No. 2 (December 1972), pp. 1053-58. [Reprinted in *Classics in Software Engineering*, ed. E.N. Yourdon (New York: YOURDON Press, 1979), pp. 141-50.]

10. R. Ford, *A Survey of the Development and Implementation of Data Abstraction*, Department of Computer Science Technical Report 79-3 (Pittsburgh: University of Pittsburgh, July 1979).

11. K.L. Heninger, "Specifying Software Requirements for Complex Systems: New Techniques and Their Application," *IEEE Transactions on Software Engineering*, Vol. SE-6, No. 1 (January 1980), pp. 2-13.

12. _____, R.A. Parker, and D.L. Parnas, "Abstract Interfaces for Embedded Software: Design Techniques and Their Application," *Proceedings of the Fifth International Conference on Software Engineering* (New York: IEEE Computer Society, 1981), pp. 195-204.

13. H.F. Ledgard, "The Case for Structured Programming," *BIT*, Vol. 13 (1973), pp. 45-47.

14. H.D. Mills, "Top-Down Programming in Large Systems," *Debugging Techniques in Large Systems*, ed. R. Rustin (Englewood Cliffs, N.J.: Prentice-Hall, 1971), pp. 41-55.

15. N. Wirth, "Program Development by Stepwise Refinement," *Communications of the ACM*, Vol. 14, No. 4 (April 1971), pp. 221-27.

16. O.J. Dahl, E.W. Dijkstra, and C.A.R. Hoare, *Structured Programming* (London: Academic Press, 1972).

17. S.H. Caine and E.K. Gordon, "PDL — A Tool for Software Design," *Proceedings of the 1975 National Computer Conference*, Vol. 44 (Montvale, N.J.: AFIPS Press, 1975), pp. 271-76.

18. C. Böhm and G. Jacopini, "Flow Diagrams, Turing Machines and Languages with Only Two Formation Rules," *Communications of the ACM*, Vol. 9, No. 5 (May 1966), pp. 366-71. [Reprinted in *Classics in Software Engineering*, ed. E.N. Yourdon (New York: YOURDON Press, 1979), pp. 13-25.]

PART IV

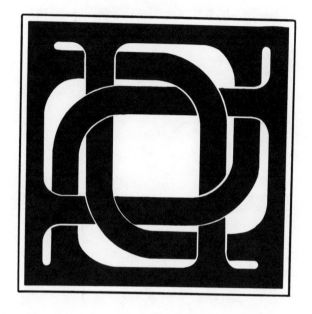

Software Design Engineering

PART IV
Software Design Engineering

*When the map
and the terrain disagree,
trust the terrain.*
—aphorism of the Swiss army

We began this book with a discussion of software engineering in general, and focused on software design in particular; then we began to study the methods and techniques used to enhance the software designer's abilities. Throughout these discussions, a recurrent theme has been that the nature of a particular design problem may not always be such that the method or technique we happen to be using will be effective. This does not mean that such methods and techniques are useless — quite the contrary. If they had little practical value, they would not have been selected for this book. Rather, their ineffectiveness is a symptom of a higher-level problem.

This higher-level problem is analogous to a collision between reality and the idealized concepts upon which methods and techniques are founded. A software design method or technique is based on its author's perception of reality. If you as a designer share a common viewpoint and environment with a method's author, then the method will be effective. But this correspondence is rarely the case.

The collision between real-world problems and theoretical approaches to their solutions is not unique to software; all engineering fields experience it. To understand how other disciplines resolve this problem, think of this sports analogy: Successful coaches possess at least one common characteristic — the ability to build a strategy for offense and defense that takes advantage of the skills of the available players. This approach is usually tempered, but not driven, by the coach's philosophy of play. Similarly, successful software designers are able to compose effective approaches to software design that focus on the most important issues of a particular design effort. This collection of approaches constitutes a methodology composed for a specific problem. A methodology may be influenced by a particular viewpoint, and it may not be altogether new: It is usually a modification of one or more methods and techniques orchestrated into a coherent theme. Some of these composed or contrived methodologies have stabilized and have been so consistently successful that they have become one of the methods described in a previous chapter.

These methods constitute an interesting phenomenon. Often the type of system being designed is similar to others designed previously, or is of the same general nature

195

(e.g., business and accounting packages), so that the same method can be used over and over with a high degree of success. An easy trap to fall into, however, is to conclude from such success that *the* software design method has been found.

Another contributing factor involved in such dangerous thinking is the role a software design method may play. It may provide some much-needed generalized procedure on how to design; and as people are very uncomfortable about doing a job such as design without knowing *how* to do it, any method that provides a proceduralized scheme is likely to be well received. This need for procedure tends to limit one's vision somewhat, and may lead to an idealized view of the method's effectiveness. For example, an article published a few years ago commented both pro and con on several software design methods.* The article elicited several letters from ardent fans of one method or another, claiming that if method X had truly been understood, the negative comments would not have been made. However, the fact remains that it may be impossible for a method that is effective in designing a bill of materials package to be equally successful at designing flight control software for NASA's Space Shuttle. These two problems share some intrinsic properties, but differ in critical ways.

In other fields of engineering, the collision between reality and theory is accepted as a fact of life. In software engineering, by contrast, many feel that if their favorite approach does not provide an adequate solution, then, perhaps, the problem needs to be restated so as to match the solution. Surprisingly, this attitude of changing the terrain to suit the map has been successfully employed by more than one high-technology systems and software house. In this case, the customer is pressured into believing that regardless of what he said he wanted, what he really wanted was . . .

Firms and individuals who proceed in this manner rely heavily on an aura of state-of-the-art expertise, supported by their reputation and typically by one or more brilliant key individuals. Fortunately, such firms are few; but many individuals exhibit the same sort of behavior pattern. They labor under the misconception that technology is a secret, and choose to overlook the fact that it is a system: a set of techniques, procedures, and practices that mutually support each other and provide at least the potential for responding to the customer's problems. Fortunately, there is growing skepticism regarding the magic supposedly possessed by specific methods and techniques, and an increasing use of their basic concepts as a starting point for the definition of unique methodologies.

This section addresses two classes of topics that relate to the practice of software design. The first class, discussed in Chapter 10, contributes to an approach for defining a software design methodology based on the characteristics of the problem environment. The emphasis is on a generalized approach that can be adapted by the reader to a specific design problem environment. Chapter 11 describes some of the major problem areas with which the software designer must contend. Many of these issues must be addressed anew with each software design effort and within the larger view of software engineering. My intent is to provide reassurance to the reader that experiencing these problems does not necessarily mean that the designer is doing something wrong; all software designers have to face up to such issues. These issues constitute areas for further research and refinement in the effort to make software design a true engineering discipline.

---

*L.J. Peters and L.L. Tripp, "Comparing Software Design Methodologies," *Datamation*, Vol. 21, No. 11 (November 1977), pp. 89-94.

CHAPTER 10
Developing a Software Design Methodology

*Diversity in software design approach
is the most cost-effective means
of controlling diverse problems.* *
                              —L.P.

A lot of useful software has been built using one or more of the methods and techniques presented earlier. But a lot of useful software has also resulted from software technology that is definitely not state-of-the-art but perhaps of a home-grown variety. How can we explain this? A complete explanation may not be possible, but at least a partial one is. Discussions conducted with software development groups in various companies have revealed that a lot of what goes into a software project comes from people's minds and experience, rather than out of books. To what can we attribute software design success — methods or people?

Maybe the question should be modified to include a third possibility: the overall collection of management techniques, interpersonal relationships, and ad hoc method development that is associated with any project. In sum, this third factor is the environment within which the software design effort is actually carried out. An important aspect of this environment is its response to the varied and special character of the design effort it undertakes. This response depends upon an ability to choose, match, and cross-check methods, techniques, personnel, and opinions.

This chapter will present a framework for creating a methodology to meet the demands of a specific software design problem. This framework is intended to be of use to all readers, but should not be viewed as the last word on the subject. It is the result of externalizing and organizing my own experience and that of my clients and colleagues. Hence, the process has been somewhat idealized and organized into distinct steps. It should be viewed as an indication of what can be done and as a guide for creating a system of methods and techniques for the reader's own environment. Examples of some composed methods are also provided.

---

*See Ashby's Law of Requisite Variety in W.R. Ashby, *Introduction to Cybernetics* (New York: John Wiley & Sons, 1961).

10.1 Overview of the process

None of the software design methods examined for this text came about as a result of a scientific experiment. They were not derived from mathematical equations or formal propositions. Instead, they resulted when software designers extricated themselves from "sticky wickets" by inventing something. The invention may have been a diagramming scheme or a design approach, but it was an experiment. The successful experiments were refined and used again in other efforts. Those that seemed to have wide application became some of the methods and techniques in this book.

Today, many software designers would prefer to use one method or another and let it go at that. But sometimes the tried-and-true method does not work. What then? Let's start at the beginning. The primary issue is, Why use any method at all? Some possible reasons include: "We always use it." "The boss said to use it." "It is new." "We read an article about it." "We went to a class on it." "The customer likes it." Or, "Nothing else has worked." These and others have been put forward as viable justifications during consulting sessions. Although they all have some validity, few indicate that a conscious, calculated decision was made, and none reveal the basis for the decision.

In order to define (or design) a methodology* that will be effective in a given software design situation, there must exist an effective match between the overall character of the problem and the features of the solution approach. This sounds simple enough, but it requires classifying problems and solution approaches in revealing ways, and considering personnel and customer factors. An example of matching methods to changing problems is found in the logging industry: Years ago, selected cutting was used as a means of obtaining trees to be sent to the sawmill, meaning that only the best, most mature trees were selected, felled, and carefully removed so as not to damage other trees. Rapid increase in demand for wood products forced the adoption of a "clear cutting" policy (cutting down all trees in a specific area), which, in turn, forced the incorporation of more mechanized means of moving logs to sawmills and the adoption of new re-planting techniques.

The software industry faces a similar challenge. The demand for more maintainable systems of ever-increasing complexity has forced the adoption of concepts from other fields, as well as the creation of some new ones specific to software. These new concepts include the use of team programming; informal and formal reviews; greater attention to planning; and an increased emphasis on designing for maintainability. The demand for higher quality, more maintainable systems has been increased by the advent of minicomputers. Developers of software using such systems often work independently, frequently creating untransportable, unmaintainable systems.

The process by which a methodology may be formulated to address a specific set of problems is shown in Fig. 10.1. As stated earlier, this process is the result of externalizing and organizing my own experiences in this area and those of many colleagues and clients. In 1976, I conducted a study of the relative effectiveness of software design methods. About a dozen designers in several firms were asked to relate their experiences with the method they used, and to send an example of part of their design so that a real, non-textbook application could be examined. They all had identical responses! Although the survey was limited, the similarity of the designers' responses

---

*A methodology is a collection of principles and techniques designed for a particular problem or system.

was uncanny. They all related that the particular method had improved the design process compared with their previous procedure (which was, for the most part, made up as they went along or not well defined); and they all were reluctant to provide any documentation of a design they had done.

The former response was to be expected — using some sort of method is likely to be better than using none at all. But the latter response was a bit puzzling. Some of the firms were re-contacted and the designers persistently queried as to why they had declined to provide real examples. In response, they indicated that the method was not employed exactly as they had learned, for they had to modify it to overcome a difficulty encountered in their project. The customizing process reported by survey respondents is expressed in a flow diagram in Fig. 10.1. Not all of the factors were considered in every case; the figure is a composite of these processes and data flows.

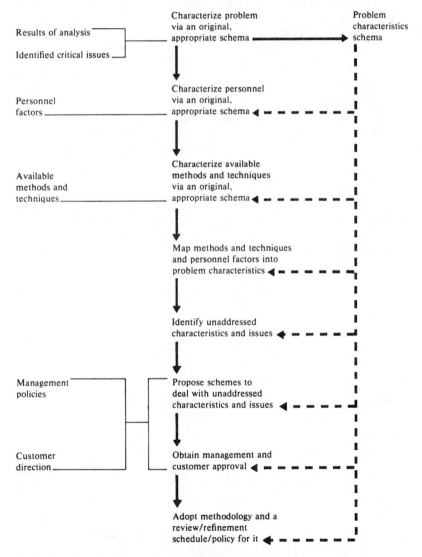

Figure 10.1. Overview of the methodology development process.

Our chief purpose in customizing is to ensure that the pertinent questions are answered by a prudent and conscious selection of technological tools to use. Stated another way, this amounts to matching the tools or solution approach to the problem.

10.2 Framework for developing a software design methodology

After several years' experience in designing software, many software engineers realize that, although each software design effort is unique, there are striking similarities between many of them. Carefully laid out, sets of these similarities may form a systematic framework for classifying software design efforts into primary and secondary categories. Without much effort, one could list different types of systems very quickly, including

information-based systems	electronic switching systems
procedure-oriented systems	scientific engineering systems
interactive graphics systems	batch systems
business-oriented information systems	real-time systems
numerical control systems	data entry systems

But, as in the case of top-down design, we need to determine whether this is a very useful partitioning for our purpose. Obviously, this list is not perfect. But it is an attempt to classify systems. Many alternative lists are possible and useful. Before we look more closely at the problem of decomposition, let us first examine the software designer's four generic concerns: relative importance of system qualities; changeability of features; constraints changeability; and customer concurrences.

☐ *The relative importance of system qualities:* Although several different sets of software qualities have been proposed [1, 2], five common ones are described in Table 10.1. The problem for the software designer is that these qualities are not mutually compatible. For example, a concern for efficiency may encourage the use of system support modules that are not available in other systems. Using such features helps efficiency but hurts portability. Similar oppositions exist between other pairs of qualities.

Software design is an almost continual process of making decisions. Having a ranking system of values ensures that these decisions will reflect a realistic actualization of the customer's wishes. The customer is the prime source for composing such a relative ranking scheme. Certainly, the software designer can give advice regarding the prudence and implications of placing portability, for example, at the top of the list. But he must be aware of the fact that there are tradeoffs and limits to what can be done. Such a value set, resulting from ideal ranking considerations combined with expected tradeoffs, stabilizes much of what is unstable about designing software.

☐ *The features or functions most and least likely to change, and in what way:* In Part I, the concept of prototyping was discussed, with an admonition to prototype only those portions of a system that are most likely to be in the final system — its skeleton. Knowing that one portion or another of a system is likely to undergo rethinking or disappear altogether enables the designer to put valuable human resources where they will do the most good. The project management implications are also significant, in that project planning is keyed to the classification of functional characteristics as specified by the customer with the advice and consent of the designer.

☐ *The constraints or limits most and least likely to change, and in what way:* The effects of limits, such as the maximum number of inquiries or transactions or the composition of customer files, are similar to those of system features, but more subtle. Basically, these tend to ripple from, say, the database to the graphics interface and on.- Such limits play a key role in establishing an effective design envelope for the system.

☐ *The degree to which the customer understands and concurs with the design:* Perhaps the most disturbing aspect of software design is how well the customer comprehends the design. The designer knows what is in the design, but does the customer? How can the designer be certain that the customer has a good sense of what the system will be like when it is delivered? Does the customer comprehend the impact of the directions he has given the design group? Much of the resolution of these and related questions can be accomplished at design reviews with the customer. If the customer asks pertinent questions, or has an advisory group doing so, these concerns are diminished. But, in the absence of an alert customer and/or an advisory group, a demonstrably effective way of communicating software designs to customers is needed.

Table 10.1
Some Basic Software Properties

PROPERTY	DESCRIPTION
Maintainability	the degree to which a program or system can be cost-effectively made to perform its functions in a possibly changing operating environment
Efficiency	the degree to which the implementation of the program or system corresponds to the most cost-effective computing resource utilization
Extensibility	the degree to which the program or system accommodates cost-effective change in order to address a new requirement or a modified requirement
Reliability	the degree to which the program or system operates in a user-acceptable manner when used in the environment for which it was designed

The key to discerning problem characteristics is the reconciliation of these and any other concerns of the software design group with the characteristics of a particular problem. Although each software design project is unique, all software design problems have some things in common. What makes a particular software design effort unique is the degree to which some characteristic (such as database issues) eclipses the rest of the issues, and the specific ways in which issues manifest themselves. For example, if a credit card company with tens of millions of active and inactive customers wished to have an on-line query capability designed, a set of methods and techniques that did not explicitly address database interface issues would not be as effective as one that did. Intuitively, the processing details of the actual functional capabilities are minor in comparison with database implications in this case. But most software design projects do not present themselves quite so clearly. The key is to identify what issues are critical and proceed from there.

One way of relating several diverse factors such as we have listed is to utilize a technique called morphological analysis [3], which has been used to organize an apparently chaotic mass of facts [4, 5]. Morphological analysis uses a matrix of elements selected to represent a larger class of issues. If there are *n* classes of issues, they form an *n*-dimensional space. The classes of issues with which we will be concerned in defining a software design methodology are the following:

○ *Human interface:* Several different classes of people will be viewing, designing, defining, refining, and reviewing the software critically. The success of the design effort depends on how effectively the methodology externalizes issues with which each group in the human interface is concerned. The groups that compose the human interface category are customer, user (not always the same as the customer), designer, analyst (responsible for specification), and implementer (responsible for code, checkout, and installation).

○ *Technical elements:* In all software designs, there are five basic classes of technical concerns: control structure, control flow, data structure, data flow, and system architecture (which coordinates the other four).

○ *Representation:* Throughout the design effort, communication among the project participants is a key to success. Although different participants have different concerns, their collective concerns may be organized into three groups: conceptualization (composing the design), implementation (externalizing packaging and operating environment issues), and realization (relating to the individual what the completed system will be like).

These three classes form a three-dimensional space within which the concerns of the software designer, including the four generic concerns mentioned above, can be organized in order to support methodology development. The factors are listed in Table 10.2 and are shown as a three-dimensional morphological box in Fig. 10.2.

The factors depicted in Fig. 10.2 represent a sample set and are not necessarily ideal in all cases. There are many other factors that one may wish to include, such as development cost, schedule, program size, and execution time. But these factors have not been shown to have a causal effect in bringing about an abstract design. That is, they do not come to the forefront during the software engineering of the logical, abstract design needed prior to the production of a blueprint of the planned system. The blueprint has a one-to-one correspondence with the system as it will be built. The conventional wisdom on this subject is to design the ideal system, then to adjust this ideal design as necessary in order for it to meet performance, cost, and scheduling requirements, thus assuring that as much of the idealized system as possible has been retained in the resulting system. Thus, the factors in Fig. 10.2 portray the fundamental structure of the software design methodology. The reader may wish to modify or embellish this model for his own use; it will be used here to demonstrate the design methodology development process.

10.2.1 Relational spaces

The three-dimensional space depicted in Fig. 10.2 contains three planes formed by unique combinations of the individual axes. Some of the intersections of the steps (or fine structure) on each axis will be of no use, while others will form an important part of our model. Each of the planes, together with fine-structure intersections, will be described below.

Table 10.2
Issues and Issue Categories

CATEGORY	INCLUDED ISSUES OR FINE STRUCTURE
HUMAN INTERFACE	CUSTOMER
	USER
	IMPLEMENTER
	DESIGNER
	ANALYST
TECHNICAL ELEMENTS	CONTROL STRUCTURE
	CONTROL FLOW
	DATA STRUCTURE
	DATA FLOW
	SYSTEM ARCHITECTURE
REPRESENTATION	CONCEPTUALIZATION
	IMPLEMENTATION
	REALIZATION

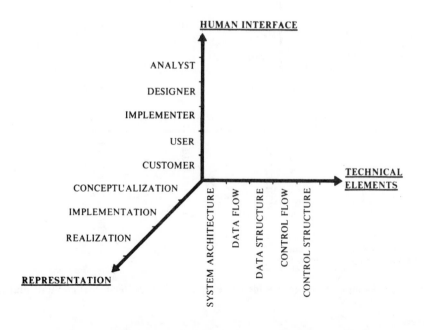

Figure 10.2. Working morphology for methodology composition.

10.2.1.1 Human interface/technical element plane

The human interface/technical element plane contains what is probably the most common set of issues that software designers face on an immediate, day-to-day basis. In many cases, however, the software designer is not consciously aware of these issues, but only of their symptoms. More external concern is exhibited regarding technical matters than human interface ones. This plane can be depicted as a matrix, which in turn can be used to resolve classes of issues associated with this plane. Other classes of issues may be important to some readers, but for purposes of discussion we will limit ourselves to two: human priorities and technical issues.

Human priorities refer to the relative importance placed on technical issues by each type of human interface. Technical issues refer to the relative importance of the technical issues to the system at hand. The relative priorities will generally vary not so much from one generic sort of system to another, but rather from one system with its set of environmental and political restrictions to another. For example, some systems that must deal with large databases would require placing great technical importance on data structure, while the design of an executive for an electronic switching system would require heavy technical emphasis on control flow and control structure. In both cases, the technical concern would be matched by the designer and implementer, but not necessarily by the customer. Combining the human interface and technical element priorities yields a range of values or a composite score. Composite priorities for this plane are shown in Fig. 10.3.

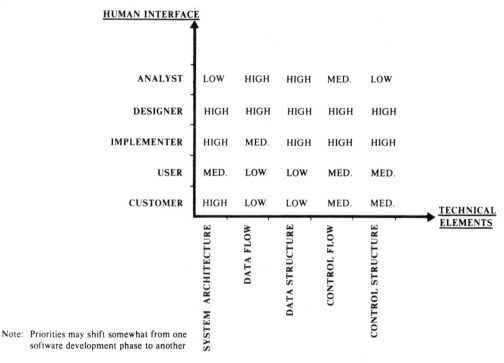

Figure 10.3. Composite priorities for the human interface/technical element plane.

10.2.1.2 *Human interface / representation plane*

The human interface/representation plane relates the three classes of information — conceptualization, implementation, and realization — that are transmitted among various roles or people. Again, composite priorities are portrayed for the general case (Fig. 10.4). These will be referred to again when we consider the technical elements/-representation plane. Note the divergence of importance of information communication among our five classes of human interfaces.

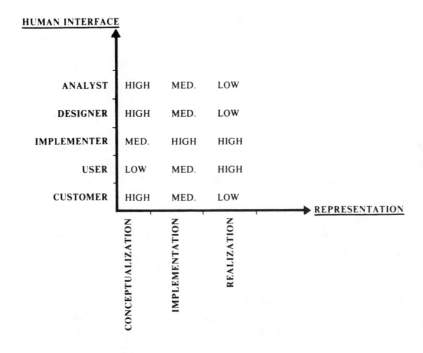

Figure 10.4. Composite priorities for the human interface/representation plane.

10.2.1.3 *Technical elements / representation plane*

The technical elements/representation plane highlights the issues presented in Part II without the factor of a human recipient for the representation. Hence, rather than corresponding priorities, each intersection of representation and technical element indicates the relative number of representation schemes effectively addressing these issues (Fig. 10.5).

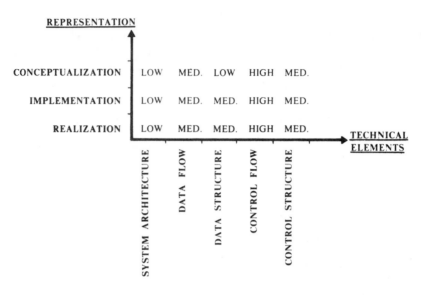

Figure 10.5. Correspondences between technical elements and representation schemes.

10.3 Developing a software design methodology

The term *software design methodology* has been widely used and misused in software engineering literature. As described earlier, it refers to a collection of techniques, methods, and common practice directed at the problem of designing software. In reviewing the summaries of software design representation schemes and software design methods presented in Parts II and III, the reader will have noted that each of these design tools has some features that make it more effective at solving certain design problems than others. This fact implies that many (perhaps most) real-world software design problems require the use of some modification or combination of established software design methods or techniques. The sections that follow present optional viewpoints for selecting techniques.

10.3.1 Microscopic view

On the immediate problem level, individual techniques or methods can be selected on the basis of their ability to adequately address specific, single-issue problems. For example, the representation of the control flow of a software system is a problem on the microscopic scale; it can be considered and resolved on a localized basis, de-coupled from other software design problems. This can also be done for other issues such as selecting the method or the life cycle model to be employed. However, this amounts to a tactical response to each type of problem as it occurs, rather than a strategic plan that coordinates all such decisions.

10.3.2 Macroscopic view

A strategic approach to the composition of a software design methodology involves the use of microscopic-view solutions identified and coordinated at the system level. Most large systems do not lend themselves to program-oriented views but to system-oriented ones. A system view would clearly identify the need for different methods and techniques, the likely candidates based on their compatibility and effectiveness, and the types of factors to be addressed ad hoc. Where do these ad hoc solutions come from? Perhaps from experience with many projects or a trial-and-error approach to one project; but the need for such invention can be greatly reduced by trying to select and engineer a software design methodology for a project.

10.4 Case studies

In software design, as in other fields, the best teacher is experience. Often, a designer's experience may provide insights to other designers when they find themselves in a similar situation. For this reason, specific examples of situations in which a combination of methods or techniques was employed will be cited. However, these will be presented in an abstracted, somewhat idealized form, often with more than one project melded into one, and with project identity and participants concealed. The intent of the case studies is to describe what can be done and to provide some useful ideas for future reference.

10.4.1 Case 1: a manufacturing engineering aid

☐ Task: to design and develop software for operation in batch mode to execute many engineering calculations

☐ Problem description: the engineering formulae to require a great deal of iteration

☐ Participants: manufacturing engineers; software analysts and designers

☐ Special considerations:

　○ previous software for this manager proved unreliable and difficult to maintain

　○ the engineering group to be given maintenance responsibility after development is completed

　○ the engineering manager to be able to track the status of the system at all times during the project

　○ documentation to be thorough, and cost-effective to maintain

☐ Approach:

　○ software development and engineering personnel to be one development team and to share responsibilities; that is, each software person to work with one engineer in a co-author role

　○ all analysis, design, and development to be performed using top-down modern programming practices and each deliverable (e.g., analysis documents) to be signed off by both the responsible engineer and the software counterpart

　○ analysis to be performed using a data flow-oriented approach simpler than SADT [6], but more rigorous than data flow diagrams [7]; the SAMM [8] approach selected

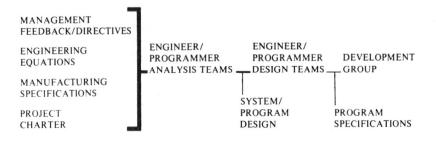

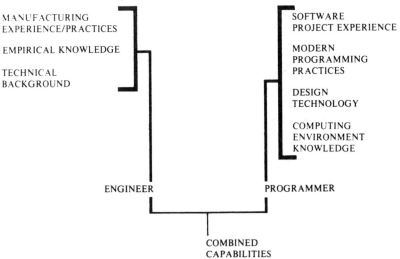

Figure 10.6. Information flow in Case 1.

O the overall information flow shown in Fig. 10.6 to be employed

O peer-group reviews to be utilized in addition to management/technical milestone reviews

O an automated means of linking the code and design to be employed in such a way as to ensure that they remain coherent; the information flow for the implementation of this aspect shown in Fig. 10.7

a) PHASE 1 — IDENTIFY/ORGANIZE/DOCUMENT
WHAT MUST BE DONE

PROCESS   **LISTING OF RESULTS**

Structured specification in pseudocode
(including equations) for each future
module (review — ↓ — refine)

Put into card image file as FORTRAN comments

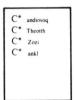

b) PHASE 2 — IDENTIFY/ORGANIZE/DOCUMENT
HOW SPECIFICATION WILL BE ACCOMPLISHED

PROCESS   **LISTING OF RESULTS**

Describe implementation of specification in
terms of pseudocode (review — ↓ — refine)

Put into card image file as different FORTRAN
comments

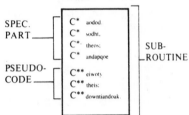

c) PHASE 3 — IMPLEMENT PSEUDOCODE IN FORTRAN
AND PLACE RESULTS IN AN ADJACENT LOCATION

PROCESS   **PROGRAM LISTING**

In FORTRAN, implement the pseudocode
(review — ↓ — revise)

Insert into appropriate files

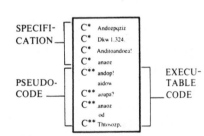

Figure 10.7. Phases in the program development process.

Note: Nonsense type is used to represent actual variables supplied by the user of the method.

○ necessary automated aids to be built as a parallel effort since no appropriate package marketed at time of project (Fig. 10.8)

□ Results: feedback overwhelmingly positive, particularly in the following areas:

○ customers able to see how the project was organized and executed, and able to participate in every facet

○ schedules maintained at major milestones, in spite of some minor milestone slippages due to the use of a "design/develop-to-cost" philosophy (that is, given a fixed resource, the problem was solved in a way that did not exceed it)

○ system maintenance by the engineers an achievable goal

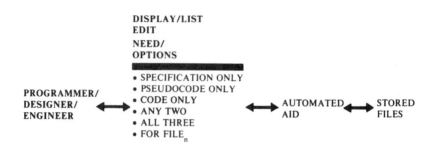

Figure 10.8. Development team interface with automated tool.

☐ Lessons learned:

○ customer participation strongly aids customer acceptance of a system or changes in schedule; the system becomes the customers' and not the developers'

○ phasing and utilizing incremental steps from analysis through pseudocode can work if (and, perhaps, only if) a practical means of incorporating changes to the requirements, design, and code is employed; doing business in a manual fashion is not practical in most projects

○ incorporating pseudocode (as comments) into the deliverable system saves programming resources; when the maintenance programmer is making a change to the code, the design documentation is also being accessed*

10.4.2 Case 2: A software design aid

☐ Task: to define, design, and develop an interactive graphics system to support the use of a software design technique

☐ Problem description: funding and flow time for this effort were incredibly short of the mark; the most conservative estimate was that the effort only had one-third of the resources needed, while others were one-sixth or less

☐ Participants: an outside customer who did not have a great deal of software experience; a software development team made up primarily of new graduates who had even less experience than the customer

☐ Special considerations:

○ since successful performance on this contract could lead to considerably more business from this customer, the pressure to do well was strong

---

*A variation on this approach involves the use of a more elaborate interface processor, which provides aggregate statistics on the number of changes made to a particular subsystem over a given reporting period, and other measures important to the project manager.

- the customer owned some database management and graphics interface software that could be used in this system; but this software was not particularly well written, and was not documented

- one individual who had used the customer's software could aid in its application to this problem

☐ Approach:

- the view of design as a discovery process to be employed; analysis and specification efforts to be incorporated into the logical design effort (a radical approach); a functional requirements document to serve all three purposes, containing a view of the system's interaction with a user as well as its internal logical structure, and to be walked through with the customer; and upon approval, this would become the baseline requirements/design document

- the results of the first step to be refined, packaged, and detailed to give a physical design, for specifying the construction of the system

- in order to ensure delivery of an appropriate system, a prototype version to be built and delivered early in the contract; to consist of the basic functional elements (such as the pre-existing software), some stubbed routines, and the proposed screen format; this enables us to identify and resolve any problems due to moving the system from our computer to the customer's, to give the development staff some confidence, and to get preliminary feedback from the customer

- the chief programmer team form of organization to be employed, but an alternative (for example, a democratic or egoless structure) to be substituted in case of difficulties, as we did not have sufficient resources to experiment patiently

- a "design/develop-to-cost" philosophy to be used, in which the price or resource level allocated to each subsystem determines how elaborate it is*

- in order to ensure high software quality, coupling and cohesion concepts from structured design [9] to be employed as evaluation criteria

- since specifications were to be developed in concert with the user/customer, a concise set of measurable functional specifications essential for design, acceptance testing, and implementation; a user's manual and test plan to be started at the beginning of the project

☐ Results: system delivered within budget, but delivery date postponed due to changes requested by customer after the change deadline

---

*An analogy here is to the difference between an economy sub-compact and a luxury car. From a transportation standpoint, they are functionally identical, but in overall design the sub-compact is less elaborate.

☐   Lessons learned:

    ○   prototyping, when used in a disciplined manner, works; it allows both customer and contractor to experience what the system is like before it is too late to make changes

    ○   chief programmer teams do not always work; they may have been successful elsewhere, but my experience on this and other projects has been otherwise, as most team members prefer "glamorous" work to "grunt" work; we substituted a "build-team" approach, wherein team members are on an equal footing, each responsible for a portion of the system, architectural decisions are made as a group, and a spokesperson is elected when needed; following this method, change decisions took longer to make, but their implementation was extremely rapid and relatively problem-free

    ○   a design-to-cost approach can work effectively when used in a disciplined manner; in this case, the number and size of the documents that would ordinarily be delivered were reduced, but not their quality

    ○   it is best to do the hard or treacherous parts of system design and implementation first and the easy parts last; our early prototyping revealed that operating system differences between facilities required approximately three person-weeks of effort; had this problem cropped up during delivery, short cuts might have harmed contractor credibility

    ○   utilizing text-processing systems for project documentation pays off, as changes are easy to make and the configuration control is enhanced; it is possible to correct known documentation problems at the last minute without unacceptable delays

10.5 Other software design practices

In addition to the definition and use of a customized software design methodology within the context of a software development life cycle, other design practices are necessary to ensure success. Four primary areas of concern are software design standards, reviews, test plan definition, and user's guide development, each of which must be considered in the design process. A brief discussion of each topic follows, with references to more detailed treatments.

10.5.1 Software design standards

The software design methods discussed in Part III addressed the problem of composing software designs. They provided guidelines, notational schemes, and specific practices aimed at the narrow issues facing software designers, while ignoring many of the larger issues. Software design standards form one such issue, as they affect the way in which the design organization interfaces with the customer and with other development organizations.

The concept of standards has a long history, beginning with craftsmen of various kinds who needed standard forms and measures so as to make products easier to duplicate. Similarly, standard drafting and labeling practices in engineering aid the understanding of drawings and make it easy to find a desired dimension or value. In software design, standards have been largely resisted, ignored, circumvented, and considered a bother. Government agencies have attempted to remedy this situation by imposing several types of standards on the contractors who develop software for them, but they are often not able to comprehend the delivered software design document even though it complies with the standards. Perhaps we should address the question of standards by determining the information set required in order for someone to understand the software design, and treat as a separate issue the means by which this set of information is provided.

The basic questions that one needs to resolve in order to merely understand a software design include, What does it do? How does it do it? Why is it being done that way and not some other? What alternatives, if any, were considered and rejected? for what reasons?

Part I stressed the need for externalization of the software designer's thinking. In the development of software design standards, that need becomes apparent once again. Standards are a necessity in projects involving more than one small design development team. The way in which they are met can differ from project to project, but the basic information issues stay the same. Note that any one of several combinations of software design representation schemes could be used to depict design information, and any one of several software design methods or combinations of methods could be used to compose the designs.

10.5.2 Software design reviews

The practice of having code and designs reviewed by people other than the authors has gained wide acceptance in the software industry. This practice was aided greatly by Weinberg's efforts [10] and further popularized by Yourdon [11]. Reviews are needed because the author of any work is usually the least likely person to spot its deficiencies, particularly in the case of personal, creative products like software designs and code.

Types of reviews range from informal peer reviews to formal, contractually required ones at which the customer/user will be present. Paradoxically, it is often true that the more informal the review, the higher its technical content. Any type of review often causes us to incidentally identify errors or shortcomings in our design or code when we attempt to explain it to someone else.

Much has been written about the conduct of reviews [12]. An abbreviated list of some common guidelines for conducting reviews follows.

- The project plan should include regularly scheduled reviews for each group on moderate-sized parts of the design area for which the group is responsible.

- At every review, formal or otherwise, someone should document "action items" (agreements about changes, or who will check certain information, for example) and accompanying estimated completion dates; such notes should be retained by the program librarian or project documentation specialist, to prevent unkept promises.

- Reviewees should remember that a successful review will identify at least one problem or area of improvement in the design — which should *not* be interpreted as a personal attack.

☐ Reviewers should keep personal feelings out of their review comments or disqualify themselves.

☐ Issues of personal style should not be raised; the main issue for all is the state or quality of the design as it stands.

☐ Nit-picking should be avoided, as it usually indicates lack of under-standing; if a reviewer dislikes or likes something about the design, he should say so but be prepared to explain why.

☐ Physical design issues should not be discussed until the logical design has been satisfactorily refined.

☐ A reviewee should remember that the purpose of a review is to obtain a consensus, not to win everyone over to his viewpoint.

10.5.3 Test plan definition

Software system designs cannot be tested until they are implemented. They can be reviewed, refined, and evaluated, but not tested. Therefore, the tests to be per-formed are often based upon examinations of the completed code. The software is test-ed to see that it does what it does, not to see whether it does what it was intended to do. One way to ensure that the software will be tested in the latter way is to design and organize its intended functions into a top-down testing strategy. In this method, the test cases are defined during design. These cases are generic in nature and do not in-volve real data. For example, a statement like "a non-alpha character input to the vali-date module (module x)" captures the nature of the test that is needed without stating how the test will be done or getting into the module's implementation details; this statement represents a test specification or functional test requirement. Since the designer considers how and when the system will work, module by module and subsys-tem by subsystem, he is better able to identify shortcomings in the design and address them before the expense of implementation is incurred [13, 14].

10.5.4 User's guide development

The discussions of the nature of design in Part I described the plight of the designer with respect to time: He must deal with the present, but mentally project him-self into the future, to assess the ramifications of decisions and issue resolution on the eventual system. This skipping back and forth in time is prone to error; because "men-tal time travel" does not require much discipline or precision, one can engage in it ha-phazardly and overlook some important factor.

A mechanism is needed to enable the designer to view time with precision, exam-ine the results so as to resolve some issues, and identify others that are too detailed to be addressed until later in the project. An effective way to resolve such issues is to be-gin developing the user's manual during design. Discipline and management control are required to prevent premature resolution of implementation issues and an atmo-sphere of "code it first." The preliminary version of the user's manual also enables the customer to see what the system might be like to use, and so reduces the possibility of a mismatch between what the customer expects the system to be and what it actually is. Combined with the disciplined use of prototypes, early development of the user's guide can greatly aid the designer.

10.6 Summary

The software engineering methods and techniques produced to date are responses to needs perceived by their authors. Many of these are widely applicable in principle but may require some modification in specific applications. Often, such modifications lead to still other modifications, resulting in a unique software design approach. What we are dealing with is a paradoxical situation: The more effectively an approach addresses one set of software design problems, the less likely it is to be effective at solving some other set — however slight the difference.

The key to success for the software designer is to recognize and respond to the need for diversity in his approach; that is, to respond to different situations in different ways rather than oversimplifying the differences in order to encourage the use of a single fixed software design approach. All of the methods and techniques discussed in this book attempt to establish and address *the* software problem by oversimplifying to some extent.

A cost-effective means of reducing the oversimplification is to incorporate complementary features in addition to custom-tailored ones. Surrounding all of this extemporaneous composition and invention is an informal procedure — a meta-method — from which methodologies can be developed. It is likely that the future developments in software design will include the introduction of a more formal meta-method, providing an invaluable means of responding to diversity.

EXERCISES: Chapter 10

1. Review the software life cycle models presented in Part I, and select three.

    a. For each, identify a set of factors that will determine whether the project will succeed.

    b. Identify a set of factors common to all three.

    c. Evaluate these factors for your last three projects. Can you see why they were successful or unsuccessful?

2. How is your organization now structured (e.g., as a chief programmer team) for analysis, design, and development? Is it the same for all three phases? for all projects? How would you change it, and why?

3. Given that the primary functions of management are planning, scheduling, and controlling, describe how organizational structure, life cycle model, type of project, and personnel characteristics can affect project success.

4. What constitutes a complete software design in your present organization or in your last software design project? What quality evaluation criteria were applied in ranking design quality? How would/did standards in both of these areas help or hurt the design effort?

REFERENCES: Chapter 10

1. B. Boehm et al., "Characteristics of Software Quality," *TRW Series on Software Technology* (New York: North-Holland Publishers, 1978).

2. L.J. Peters, "Design Practices to Effect Quality Software," *Software Quality Management,* eds. J.D. Cooper and M.J. Fisher (New York: Petrocelli/Charter, 1979).

3. F. Zwicky, "The Morphological Approach to Discovery, Invention, Research, and Construction," *New Methods of Thought and Procedure,* eds. F. Zwicky and A.G. Wilson (New York: Springer-Verlag, 1967).

4. A.D. Hall, III, "Three Dimensional Morphology of Systems Engineering," *IEEE Transactions on Systems, Science, and Cybernetics,* Vol. SSC-5, No. 2 (April 1969), pp. 156-60.

5. L.J. Peters and L.L. Tripp, "A Model of Software Engineering," *Proceedings of the Third International Conference on Software Engineering* (New York: IEEE Computer Society, 1978), pp. 63-70.

6. *An Introduction to SADT® Structured Analysis and Design Technique,* SofTech Inc., Document No. 9022-78R (Waltham, Mass.: November 1976).

7. T. DeMarco, *Structured Analysis and System Specification* (New York: YOURDON Press, 1978).

8. S.S. Lamb, V.G. Leck, L.J. Peters, and G.L. Smith, "SAMM: A Modeling Tool for Requirements and Design Specification," *Proceedings of COMPSAC 78* (New York: IEEE Computer Society, 1978), pp. 48-53.

9. E. Yourdon and L.L. Constantine, *Structured Design: Fundamentals of a Discipline of Computer Program and Systems Design,* 2nd ed. (New York: YOURDON Press, 1978).

10. G.M. Weinberg, *The Psychology of Computer Programming* (New York: Van Nostrand Reinhold, 1971).

11. E. Yourdon, *Managing the Structured Techniques,* 2nd ed. (New York: YOURDON Press, 1979).

12. _____, *Structured Walkthroughs* (New York: YOURDON Press, 1978).

13. R.W. Jensen and C.C. Tonies, *Software Engineering* (Englewood Cliffs, N.J.: Prentice-Hall, 1979).

14. W.C. Hetzel, ed., *Program Test Methods* (Englewood Cliffs, N.J.: Prentice-Hall, 1973).

CHAPTER 11
Issues in Software Design

People — not methods —
create software designs.
—L.P.

Design is a personal, problem-solving activity whose success depends upon the systematic application of reason, empirical knowledge, and intuition. The software designer is challenged in many ways. Some of the most troubling of these challenges are associated with fundamental conceptual views and not with detailed technical problems. These troublesome aspects are macroscopic, and almost metaphysical in nature, rather than microscopic. Many of them are presented in this chapter as a means of putting software design technology in perspective and not as an indictment of it.

The intent of this chapter is twofold: First, after reviewing the sampling of software design technology presented earlier in this book, the reader is ready to examine the environment within which such technology will be applied. Second, the success or failure of a software design effort is often more dependent upon the ability of the design team to come to grips with macroscopic issues than with technical details. Failure to deal with these issues adequately can result in delivery of a design that is technically superior but that does not solve the customer's problem.

The issues causing much of the debate surrounding software design can be loosely organized into three major classes. One class contains issues that are a consequence of the actual practice of software design. They are technical issues, such as the issue of software design documentation, in which what is practical, not what is theoretically possible, takes the forefront of the discussion. The second major class of issues is conceptual in nature and is related to the more esoteric aspects of software design, such as the need for and types of education in software design. The third class of issues relates to the economics of software design, including problems associated with the specification of software designs, the measurement of their quality, and the portability of designs.

This chapter presents many of the high-level issues facing software design today, issues that are most controversial at this time. (Certainly, this list will have to be updated in the future.) Much of what is said may contradict the conventional wisdom of one corner of software design and engineering or another. The reader is encouraged to view these discussions objectively, particularly with respect to questions related to non-trivial systems. The objective here is to stimulate further discussion of the topics in other forums, and to provide an impetus for further study and understanding of the nature of software design.

11.1 Practical issues in software design

The most obvious area of concern in software design comprises questions of software design practice. All of the software engineer's activities are contingent on the resolution of technical issues, including software design documentation; the role of automated aids; the role of prototypes; the relationship between executable code design and database design; and the relationship between design and analysis.

11.1.1 Software design documentation

The speculation that goes on about many existing programs and software designs uncannily parallels the speculations about the ruins at Stonehenge, except that while the mystery of Stonehenge centers on its purpose, very often the purpose of an obscurely written program is the only known element. The syntactical description of a program looms up out of the foggy printout, offering little hint as to why it took that particular form. Much energy can be expended trying to figure out this puzzle.

This situation exists on a broad scale throughout the data processing industry for a number of reasons. Because of its historical reputation as being outmoded, software design documentation is usually treated as outdated information. To avoid this fate, software designs must be documented in such a way as to be credible and updatable throughout the life of the system. The primary reason for the limited success of software design documentation is that the focus of attention is still on the code. In spite of the availability of dozens of software design composition and representation schemes, text processors, and automated software design aids, software designs are still discarded and allowed to fall into disarray.

Compare this to the situation that exists in other engineering fields, such as aircraft manufacturing, where the emphasis is on maintainability. A *system* of documentation schemes, reviews, control boards, release nomenclature, and document controls is created to guarantee that the product is maintainable. This is true whether the product is one of a kind or mass produced. Can you imagine trying to modify a Formula I race car to overcome some new stresses by merely inspecting the car and not referring to the blueprints (design) and supporting engineering computations?

How might we resolve the issue of maintaining sufficient documentation? Today's high labor costs and the increasing complexity and importance of the systems being attempted are forcing us to resolve design documentation problems. In the twenty or so years since firms began to cope with major software development and utilization, many data processing professionals have seen a succession of systems that have been built, been outgrown, and become unmaintainable only to be replaced by another system that goes through the same cycle.

The use of a defined software design methodology that includes documentation standards is definitely increasing. Also spreading is the acceptance of the fact that the design of any reasonably large software system cannot be cost-effectively kept up to date through manual means: Some degree of automation is necessary. The greater the use of automation, the higher the probability that system design documents will be kept up to date.

Examples of automated aids include text processors, specialized comment cards in programs, data dictionary packages, automated drafting tools, and interactive graphics packages. The basic classes of information that should be kept in the design package are listed below.

Design rationale	Data flow
Critical issues/design objectives	Logical design
Operating environment	Physical design
Assumptions	Design quality evaluation
Test plan/generic test cases	System architecture
Data structure	User's manual
Control structure	Specification/design element
Control flow	cross-reference

Some of the information listed is not normally considered to be an intrinsic part of the design. It is, however, an essential part of the legacy that the initial design team can bequeath to its successors.

11.1.2 The role of automated aids in software design

Anyone who has spent much time building or using an automated aid has had to come to grips with the question of just how much of software design can be automated. Design consists of problem solving, which involves local, automatable thinking and actions as well as intuitive insights — an intuitive flash [1]. In discussions about the degree to which such insights are automatable, I cite an incident involving an architectural firm that hired a recent graduate in architecture. His first assignment was to spend whatever amount of time it took to automate the estimating procedure used by the firm's estimator. The firm was well known for its highly competitive bids, but the estimator was past retirement age and wished to retire eventually. After about six months, the junior architect gave up. He had identified and automated much of what the estimator was doing, but other aspects of the estimating task remained elusive. These were based on the estimator's judgment, for lack of a better term, and this judgment did not lend itself to automation. Use of a decision table or other explicit scheme revealed frequent occurrences of "maybe" and "sometimes," which required intuitive human judgment.

The point of the story is that human beings are unique in their problem-solving ability. Facing a new type of problem, they are able to bring much of their total problem-solving experience to bear on it. So what does all of this have to do with the issue of automated software design aids? Just this: Many tools being developed or proposed are intended to be software design systems in the sense that given a specification, the tool will design the system. Is this really possible? That is for the reader to decide. But it should be intuitively obvious that we should automate that which is automatable and offers the highest return on our investment. Drudgery tasks like data dictionary updating, configuration control, diagramming, and text editing are easily and profitably automated with off-the-shelf packages. But what about specification consistency checking or design quality evaluation? What should and should not be automated is still a subject of much heated debate and is definitely an open issue in software design.

11.1.3 The role of prototypes

In Part I, the concept of prototyping was briefly discussed. The use of prototypes as a design tool still remains something of a radical or experimental practice. The radical label is applied partly because much of what is written about the software development life cycle tends to portray software development as a logical, predictable progression from problem statement to problem resolution [2]. The classic waterfall chart (see Section 2.4.1) is viewed as the way in which systems should be built. But what about user satisfaction? Has the designer done an adequate job if an elegant design results in an impressively structured, implemented system with which the user is dissatisfied? Definitely not! So how can we ensure that the system meets the user's needs? Besides working with the user to understand his problems and viewing them as abstractions, the designer must address the down-to-earth realities of the system.

In software engineering, designers are in the business of designing custom-built, one-of-a-kind systems. The issues in software design differ from those in many other engineering fields in that mass production is not a problem. Instead, it is important that we realistically portray system features as they will interface with the user/customer. For example, during design and review of an interactive graphics system, the user may not fully comprehend the implications of the proposed command structure and screen format. When the system is delivered, he may find that the command list would be easier to use if the most frequently used commands were presented together and were accessible with some sort of shorthand command, rather than the standard one. When do we want to know about this — during design or after the initial delivery? The answer is obvious; but the use of a skeleton or prototype system to prevent last-minute dissatisfaction presents a challenge in discipline and control.

In other engineering fields, people are formally trained in the use and value of mock-ups and prototype models. In those cases, it is understood from the start that the model is not the same as the delivered system and, perhaps more importantly, the design engineers involved in the mock-up development and design will not do the actual system construction. But in software, the gap between system definition and design activity has been bridged by the use of the same teams of people from analysis through implementation. This practice has resulted in many systems that were built first and designed (if ever) later; hence, the admonition from many in this industry that coding must not begin prior to the completion of the specification and design. To resolve this difference of opinion, consider the building of a prototype primarily as a means of obtaining a better design since it provides valuable feedback regarding the user/customer's actualized needs.

11.1.4 Separation of executable code design from database design

The importance of the design of databases to the overall system design is roughly at the point where software design was fifteen years ago — something done only as a prerequisite to getting the system running. Many people view software design as being limited to the design of executable code, with database as something of an afterthought. This book reflects that state of affairs in software design technology today in the amount of space devoted to each of these topics. For example, the software design methods discussed in Part III dealt exclusively with the design of the executable code in the system. But many systems that have been in use a few years, and some recently developed ones, are beginning to show what can happen when this dichotomy between database and software design is maintained. The executable software and database are coming to be viewed as merely separate elements in an information system, elements that must be considered together with regard to their hierarchical role and interfaces, but considered separately with respect to the details of their operation. This shift should bring us to a systems view of software design in less time than the current view took to develop.

11.1.5 Separation of analysis and design

Some in the software field believe that an adequate, complete, and consistent set of requirements must be available and frozen before design can begin. An underlying assumption of most of the software design methods available today, this belief stems from a misunderstanding of how engineering is actually conducted. In spite of the availability in other engineering disciplines of a large body of empirical knowledge and mathematical relationships, there is still a good deal of interplay between the design of a system and its specification. Many unaddressed requirements are discovered during design. But in software, many designers feel that requirements — all requirements — can and must be defined prior to the beginning of the design effort [3]. This position may be due primarily to a lack of understanding of engineering practice, but it may also stem from the nature of software design itself. It differs from much of engineering in that the realm within which the result of our efforts will operate defies comprehension. Hence, since we are dealing with logic, we should be able to complete our requirements definition prior to beginning design. The only problem with this view is that software designers and customers are not all logically perfect thinkers.

11.2 Conceptual issues in software design

The practice of software design is merely a reflection of the philosophy of the designer as an individual and of the industry as a whole. There are probably as many views as there are design issues. The following remarks describe two issues that the author views as being of primary importance: education and economics.

11.2.1 Educating software designers

Over the last twenty years, the need for software professionals has continually increased. People from a wide range of backgrounds have been drawn into the software profession for different reasons. We have all worked with designers and programmers who have no formal (either college or professional seminar) training in the use of computers. What they have learned has been picked up in the trenches for the most part, and through personal contact with other programmers. Typically missing in the background of many software designers is some concise survey of what heuristics are available and when they are of the most use. With the possible exception of a handful of university courses that survey software design methods and techniques, little of typical university training meets the software designer's needs. Computer science course work tends to emphasize mathematical modeling of algorithms, construction of compilers, and use of the latest and greatest programming language. This is not necessarily the best way to train people to solve unstructured or poorly stated problems, which are the very problems that cause us the most difficulty as an industry.

This situation is not unique to software design or software engineering, for it exists in systems engineering as well [4]. What is unique is the somewhat immature state-of-the-art of software design as evidenced by the availability of single-subject professional education classes. These tend to aid practicing software designers by bridging the gap between what is theoretically explainable and what is real.

The problem goes deeper than education. The educational issues are aggravated by the very culture in which we live. The implication that we are all entitled to immediate gratification exaggerates the effects of an educational system which, from grade school on, establishes and reinforces the view that success is the ability to find the right answer, and that all other answers must be wrong. Hence, we are predisposed to seeking *the* right answer as quickly as possible. Where do we learn that in design no answer is right or wrong, but many are possible? Where do we learn to identify alternatives, form a basis for selection, and evaluate our results?

What is a reasonable course of action for the industry? Perhaps a cooperative effort between universities and professional training organizations directed at the full spectrum of the software designer's needs. At the university level, such design courses are difficult to teach and grade because they are inexact and rely heavily on case studies and projects. Moreover, the number of survey texts is quite limited. But similar problems have existed and been dealt with in the field of business administration.

Because most software designers and engineers have little or no formal training in either their field in particular or engineering in general, their view of engineering is somewhat utopian. As evidence, consider the proliferation of articles that express alarm at the inadequacies and inaccuracies of cost and schedule estimation, project planning and controls, software testing methods, and so on. In software, we are dealing with what are essentially one-of-a-kind products. Whenever such endeavors have been undertaken in other fields, cost and schedule accuracy have been spectacularly unpredictable, regardless of whether they were moving ahead the state-of-the-art (take, for example, the cases of the New Orleans Superdome, the Boeing 747, and most custom-built homes). Those who possess an engineering background recognize that the design-to-cost or develop-to-cost approach is the most prudent way to address such problems.

How can such empirical knowledge be made available at the university level? The use of case studies would help, as would the classroom exercise of solving such poorly stated problems as will be encountered in the real world. But courses of this type require much more work than is necessary for more deterministic treatments of a subject. Effective instruction in software design and similar disciplines may necessitate upgrading of instructors' salaries and resources. This would encourage improvements and perhaps entice those with industry experience to participate.

There is a definite need for formal and professional training. The pre-professional student is in need of a pragmatic basis with which to practice this profession.

11.2.2 The economics of software design

In Part I, statistics were cited to indicate that software design errors are more costly to repair, more persistent, and more numerous than other types of errors. Although such figures have been available for several years, they are not, perhaps, widely known. If they were, we might not have as many unresolved economics issues. These issues will be discussed within the contexts of qualitative and quantitative evaluation, specification technology, and design portability.

11.2.2.1 Qualitative software design evaluation

Few of the software design methods discussed in Part III included measures of software design quality. These utilized qualitative standards and models useful in design reviews for objectivity (see Section 7.3). Each of the other methods in Part III seemed to imply that its practitioners would obtain a successful design if all the prescribed guidelines were followed as dictated. The implication is that if the design were implemented and found to be faulty, then the designer obviously did not follow the method carefully.

But how can we objectively establish the quality of a design prior to implementation? In other technological fields, such as architecture, electrical engineering, and aerospace engineering, the issue of design quality is addressed in three coordinate ways. One approach is the use of mathematical models of the system to locate any error that violates conservation of energy or some other principle of physics. This type of check is included in standard engineering practice, which refers to the body of empirical principles and rules forming the framework within which design decisions can be made. Examples of such rules include building codes and safety factors, which have resulted from many years of positive and negative experiences. For example, the 1971 earthquake in the Los Angeles area damaged or destroyed newly constructed, reinforced concrete pilings. The physics of such structures is not well understood due to the lack of uniformity of aggregate and other materials, making mathematical modeling unwieldy. Examination of the damage revealed the need to change construction practice and standards in ways that could not have been identified a priori. This is similar to the situation in software engineering, in which the understanding and mathematical modeling of systems can be so difficult. Do we ever perform a post-mortem on a project or system that failed?

Other fields have gone a step beyond mathematical modeling and standards; they have employed the use of prototypes as a means of evaluating designs. Prototypes are used during the design of systems that will be mass produced, as well as those that will be made only once. The prototype provides an economical means to bridge the gap between what is conceptually possible (the map) and what actually is (the terrain).

In software design, we have only recently begun to consider some of these design evaluation practices seriously. In many quarters, the adoption of software design standards has been stoutly resisted. Sometimes, resistance stems from opposition to infringement of artistic rights and sometimes from a counterproposal that is deemed more efficient. But nothing is free — custom, non-standardized design and systems are more expensive to build and maintain than mass-produced ones — although, perhaps, a lot more fun to build. In the area of modeling, the field of software design has possibly matured the most. Several dozen published and unpublished software design representation schemes provide designers with ample opportunity to view a system in orthogonal ways. However, most software designers have their favorite ways to proceed and are not enthusiastic about trying new ones. Prototyping, for example, in its avowed, open use in software design is the newest evaluation technique. It is still being met with considerable resistance, much of which may be due to restrictions imposed by management.

Progress in the area of qualitative software design evaluation will be the greatest when the tradeoffs among standards, models, and prototypes are considered together as a system, rather than separately. A system view will underline both the necessity and the economic advantages of standardizing as much as we can about software design.

11.2.2.2 Quantitative software design evaluation

A second form of software design evaluation is quantitative in nature. In this regard, the analogy with other branches of engineering is fairly strong. Outside software engineering, the quality of a design in quantitative terms has little to do with the solution of equations, but a great deal to do with the relative ease with which a design can be implemented and maintained and with the cost of each activity. It is in estimating costs for implementation and maintenance that the lack of standards and empirical studies in software design causes problems.

Currently, the primary concern in software design is with the technical quality of the design — with such issues as correctness, completeness, coupling, and cohesion — and not with economic factors. This is due in large part to a lack of reliable, experience-oriented data. Although intuition indicates that "quality" designs will be less expensive to build and maintain, supporting data is sorely needed.

Resolution of the quantitative aspect of software design evaluation may not be possible without a shift in perception by software designers from viewing software engineering as an artistic cottage industry to regarding it as a true engineering profession.*

11.2.2.3 Specification technology

One area in which economics and the desire for a better software product have combined to produce some positive results is in software specification, the basic notion being that the better the statement of what is desired, the higher the probability that the design and product will fulfill these needs. This notion is not new, but many different approaches have been used to accomplish such goals. The major thrusts in this direction include the following approaches:

O   formalized (mathematical) statement of requirements

O   automated, interactive problem definition and consistency analysis

O   use of graphic modeling techniques, which lend themselves to translation into software designs

Many of the schemes proposed for specifying systems concentrate on technical issues and ignore communication; that is, the customer and user of the system need to understand what is being specified so as to judge whether it meets perceived needs. A technologically superior specification, nearly ideal design, and elegant implementation are useless to the customer if they solve the wrong problem.

11.2.2.4 Portability of software designs

The most potentially reusable portions of any system are the individual subsystem, or module, designs. However, little of this potential is being realized. Much of current software design practice is analogous to what would occur in the building industry if it were necessary to define a new set of lumber dimensions for each new house designed. Perhaps the artist in many software designers causes each software design effort to be approached as a new adventure in creativity. Maybe the problem arises because computer manufacturer policy has made portability of non-trivial code impractical

---

*Work has already begun with respect to coding (see Section 6.8 on GREENPRINT [5]), and may eventually be extended to design.

if not impossible. Possibly it is dissatisfaction with all existing software designs, since they all contain some imperfection. For whatever reason, software designs are rarely re-used.

As we learn more about software design and the basic steps needed to produce a system or module design, it becomes more likely that some set of software designs will be used over and over again. Granted, the design may be modified slightly due to some idiosyncracy associated with a particular system, but the basic design will remain.

11.3 Summary

Software design is still in its childhood. Much like the larger field of software engineering, it is experiencing some growing pains. One of the most serious of these is the emergence of at least two major "subcultures" within software engineering. One subculture views the issues in software development as being unique, bearing little or no resemblance to other fields of engineering, and believes that software designers are not engineers. Ideal models, mathematics, and a purely top-down problem solution are the order of the day. The other subculture views software development as simply another type of engineering. The types of problems being addressed are not just similar, but identical to those faced by all engineers — past, present, and to come. This group has positive feelings about what works, what is real, and what is prudent, and somewhat negative ones about what is "theoretically possible." They are faced with building systems to solve users' problems in computing environments, and with software design tools and programming languages, which, although often imperfect and cumbersome, constitute the only tools available.

It is unfortunate that there is not much cooperation between these two subcultures. The truly difficult problems in software engineering design would be made considerably easier and more cost-effective to solve if research of the right type were available. For example, a great deal of material has been published recently regarding the development of new programming languages — a challenging but deterministic type of problem. Developing new languages is useful, of course, but how does this return compare with the investment of time and expertise? Consider this: The few studies in software design [6] indicate that the most persistent, numerous, and costly errors in software systems can be attributed to deficiencies in the specification and design — *not* to language or implementation problems! It is time for software engineers to consider whether research and technology development efforts are being expended where they will do the most good.

REFERENCES: Chapter 11

1. W.R. Spillers, ed., *Basic Questions of Design Theory* (New York: American Elsevier, 1974).

2. B.W. Boehm, "Software Engineering," *IEEE Transactions on Computers,* Vol. C-25, No. 12 (December 1976), pp. 1226-41. [Reprinted in *Classics in Software Engineering,* ed. E.N. Yourdon (New York: YOURDON Press, 1979), pp. 325-61.]

3. National Bureau of Standards Workshop on Software Requirements Standards (Gaithersburg, Md.: March 1978).

4. A.D. Hall, III, "Three Dimensional Morphology of Systems Engineering," *IEEE Transactions on Systems, Science, and Cybernetics,* Vol. SSC-5, No. 2 (April 1969), pp. 156-60.

5. L.A. Belady, C.J. Evangelisti, and L.R. Power, "GREENPRINT: A Graphic Representation of Structured Programs," *IBM Systems Journal,* Vol. 19, No. 4 (1980), pp. 542-53.

6. B.W. Boehm, R.L. McClean, and D.B. Urfrig, "Some Experience with Automated Aids to the Design of Large-Scale Reliable Software," *IEEE Transactions on Software Engineering,* Vol. SE-1, No. 1 (March 1975), pp. 125-33.

Epilogue

Writing a book is a lot like designing a system; one only finishes because time, money, and/or patience have run out. There is much, much more to be said about what design is and how it manifests itself when the product is software. But this book is intended to be a concise compendium of software design methods and techniques, with references to more detailed works describing each. As such, it presents what is currently available in software design technology.

I have attempted to present these techniques in a reasonably objective way, but some prejudices have no doubt been apparent to the reader. One prejudice in particular is that I view software design not as a deterministic process but as one that could be conducted ad infinitum. As a result, I have presented design as a somewhat artistic practice, rather than a well-defined step-by-step procedure. Proponents of the procedural view, on the other hand, feel that the software designer must be given a specific means of obtaining software designs. Such proponents have defined and promoted many software design methodologies. My experience has been that methodologies need to be modified when used on a real software design problem, with nearly every software design problem requiring a somewhat different modification of the methodology. For this reason, I have presented a very open structure within which to design software, and have provided the reader with a collection of tools with which to compose a software design, and some insight regarding their use. After all, it is the software designer who best knows the characteristics of a particular problem. Software design is an unstructured problem-solving activity and has been presented here with only as much structuring as is necessary for communication. The ability to address and solve poorly structured problems is critical to success in software design.

Even a brief perusal of this text will have revealed the tremendous diversity of many elements of software design technology, as well as the need for further development and refinement of techniques to address the critical issues in software design. I hope that this book will be followed by many texts treating this subject in survey or compendium form. Readers are invited to communicate new techniques, modifications of old ones, and experiences with new combinations of methods and techniques to me through the publisher, as material for future editions. With sufficient sharing of ideas and experiences, a body of empirical knowledge will be assembled and will contribute to a major modification of our view of software engineering and design: the discovery that software engineering and design are a system of methods and techniques — *not* a secret.

Subject Index

Author Index